올클
수능
어법
완성

올클 수능 어법 완성

지은이 NE능률 영어교육연구소 민판규 황선용
연구원 김지현 이정아 김은정
영문 교열 Patrick Ferraro August Niederhaus
표지·내지 디자인 닷츠
맥편집 김재민

43 SINCE1980 rd
Let's grow together
NE능률이
미래를
창조합니다.
건강한 배움의 고객가치를 제공하겠다는 꿈을 실현하기 위해
40년이 넘는 시간 동안 열심히 달려왔습니다.
앞으로도 끊임없는 연구와 노력을 통해
당연한 것을 멈추지 않고
고객, 기업, 직원 모두가 함께 성장하는 NE능률이 되겠습니다.
NE 능률

Preface

지금 이 시간에도 많은 분들이 수능이나 학교 내신에서 영어 점수를 향상시키기 위해 많은 노력을 하고 계실 것이라 생각됩니다. 특히, 어법 유형은 문항 수가 적은 데 반해 난이도와 배점이 높아 대비하는 데 어려움을 느끼시는 분들이 많을 것입니다.

여러분의 이런 고민을 덜어드리고자, NE능률에서 새로운 어법 시리즈를 내놓게 되었습니다.

〈올클(All Clear) 수능 어법〉 시리즈는 수능에 꼭 나오는 핵심 어법 포인트만 모아 정리한 시리즈로, 수능 어법을 처음 공부하는 분들을 위한 〈start〉편과 실전 수능을 대비할 수 있도록 수능 난이도로 구성된 〈완성〉편 두 권으로 구성되어 있습니다.

〈올클 수능 어법〉 시리즈는 수능 출제 빈도가 높은 주요 어법 포인트를 빠짐없이 다루었으며, 수능, 모의평가, 학력평가에 나온 기출 문장들을 최대한 활용하여 실전 난이도로 구성되었고, 어법 포인트를 집중적으로 훈련할 수 있도록 충분한 양의 문제를 수록하였습니다.

특히 〈완성〉편은 수능, 모의평가, 학력평가 기출 어법문제를 분석하여 자주 나오는 포인트를 세분화하였고, 각 출제 포인트별 공략법과 주의하여 학습해야 할 요소를 대표 기출 예문과 함께 제시하였습니다. 또한 챕터별로 실전 기출 문제를 배치하여 앞서 학습한 포인트별 공략법을 적용해볼 수 있도록 구성하였습니다.

〈start〉 편으로 어법에 관해 어느 정도의 기본과 실전 감각을 쌓았다면, 실전 수능과 유사한 난이도로 구성된 〈완성〉편으로 수능 어법을 완벽하게 준비할 수 있을 것입니다.

〈올클 수능 어법〉 시리즈를 통해 수능 어법을 완벽하게 대비하고, 여러분의 꿈에도 한 걸음 더 가까이 다가갈 수 있기를 기원합니다.

Structure & Features

핵심 어법 POINT

POINT 01 ★★★★

평가원 및 교육청 어법 기출 문제에 자주 출제되는 필수 어법 포인트와 기출 예문들을 제시하였습니다. 각 어법 포인트 아래 별표로 출제 빈도를 표시하여, 해당 포인트의 중요도를 나타내었습니다. 〈대표 예문〉에서 핵심 어법 포인트와 공략법을 학습하고, 아래 〈기출 예문 PLUS〉의 추가 예문들을 통해 해당 포인트의 공략법을 완벽하게 자신의 것으로 소화할 수 있도록 구성하였습니다.

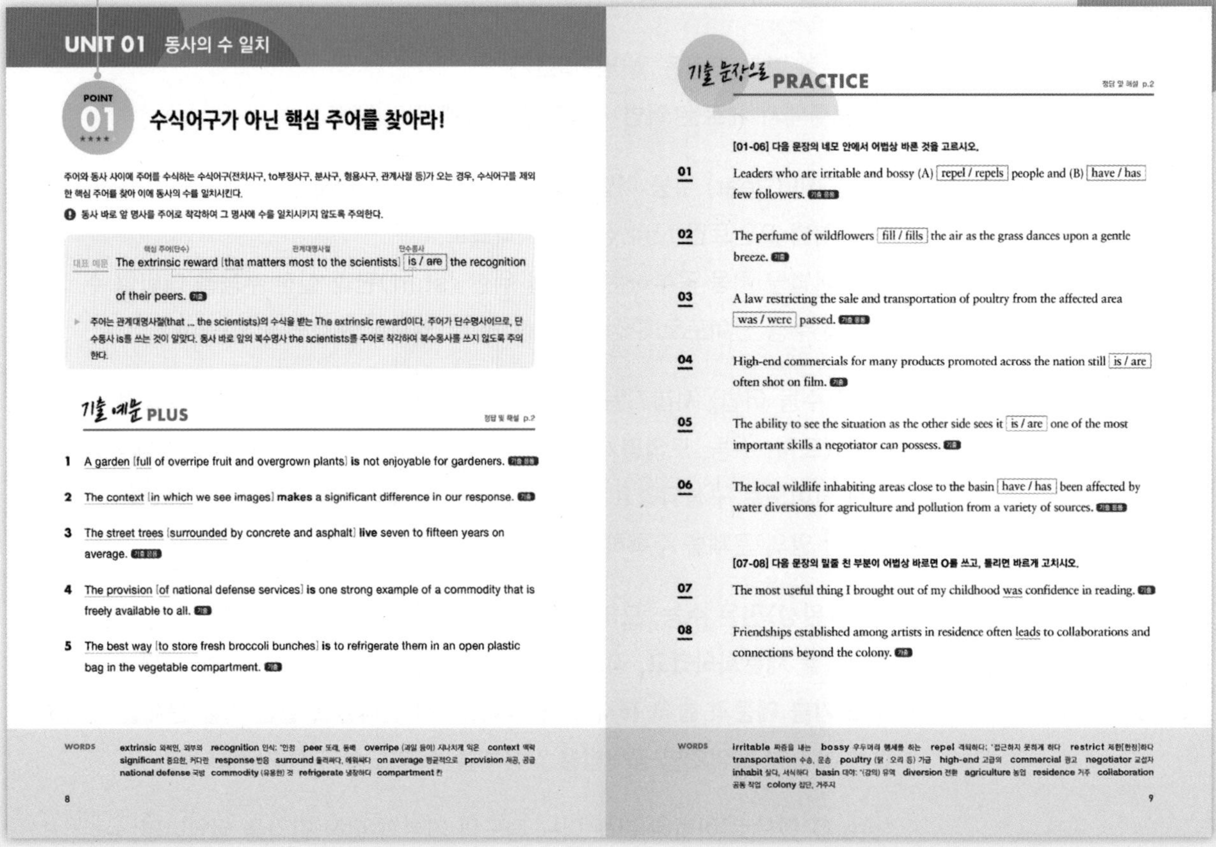
UNIT 01 동사의 수 일치

POINT 01 ★★★★ 수식어구가 아닌 핵심 주어를 찾아라!

주어와 동사 사이에 주어를 수식하는 수식어구(전치사구, to부정사구, 분사구, 형용사구, 관계사절 등)가 오는 경우, 수식어구를 제외한 핵심 주어를 찾아 이에 동사의 수를 일치시킨다.

동사 바로 앞 명사를 주어로 착각하여 그 명사에 수를 일치시키지 않도록 주의한다.

대표 예문 The extrinsic reward [that matters most to the scientists] is / are the recognition of their peers. 기출
(핵심 주어(단수) / 관계대명사절 / 단수동사)

▶ 주어는 관계대명사절(that ... the scientists)의 수식을 받는 The extrinsic reward이다. 주어가 단수명사이므로, 단수동사 is를 쓰는 것이 알맞다. 동사 바로 앞의 복수명사 the scientists를 주어로 착각하여 복수동사를 쓰지 않도록 주의한다.

기출 예문 PLUS — 정답 및 해설 p.2

1 A garden [full of overripe fruit and overgrown plants] is not enjoyable for gardeners. 기출 응용

2 The context [in which we see images] makes a significant difference in our response. 기출

3 The street trees [surrounded by concrete and asphalt] live seven to fifteen years on average. 기출 응용

4 The provision [of national defense services] is one strong example of a commodity that is freely available to all. 기출

5 The best way [to store fresh broccoli bunches] is to refrigerate them in an open plastic bag in the vegetable compartment. 기출

WORDS extrinsic 외적인, 외부의 recognition 인식; *인정 peer 또래, 동배 overripe (과일 등이) 지나치게 익은 context 맥락 significant 중요한, 커다란 response 반응 surround 둘러싸다, 에워싸다 on average 평균적으로 provision 제공, 공급 national defense 국방 commodity (유용한) 것 refrigerate 냉장하다 compartment 칸

8

기출 문장으로 PRACTICE — 정답 및 해설 p.2

[01-06] 다음 문장의 네모 안에서 어법상 바른 것을 고르시오.

01 Leaders who are irritable and bossy (A) repel / repels people and (B) have / has few followers. 기출 응용

02 The perfume of wildflowers fill / fills the air as the grass dances upon a gentle breeze. 기출

03 A law restricting the sale and transportation of poultry from the affected area was / were passed. 기출 응용

04 High-end commercials for many products promoted across the nation still is / are often shot on film. 기출

05 The ability to see the situation as the other side sees it is / are one of the most important skills a negotiator can possess. 기출

06 The local wildlife inhabiting areas close to the basin have / has been affected by water diversions for agriculture and pollution from a variety of sources. 기출 응용

[07-08] 다음 문장의 밑줄 친 부분이 어법상 바르면 O를 쓰고, 틀리면 바르게 고치시오.

07 The most useful thing I brought out of my childhood was confidence in reading. 기출

08 Friendships established among artists in residence often leads to collaborations and connections beyond the colony. 기출

WORDS irritable 짜증을 내는 bossy 우두머리 행세를 하는 repel 격퇴하다; *접근하지 못하게 하다 restrict 제한[한정]하다 transportation 수송, 운송 poultry (닭·오리 등) 가금 high-end 고급의 commercial 광고 negotiator 교섭자 inhabit 살다, 서식하다 basin 대야; *(강의) 유역 diversion 전환 agriculture 농업 residence 거주 collaboration 공동 작업 colony 집단, 거주지

9

기출 문장으로 PRACTICE

앞에서 학습한 어법 포인트와 공략법을 연습해 볼 수 있도록 실전 기출 문장에서 발췌한 문제들을 제시하였습니다. 포인트의 중요도에 따라 문제 수를 조정하였고, 최대 16문제까지 배치하여 충분한 연습을 해볼 수 있도록 구성하였습니다.

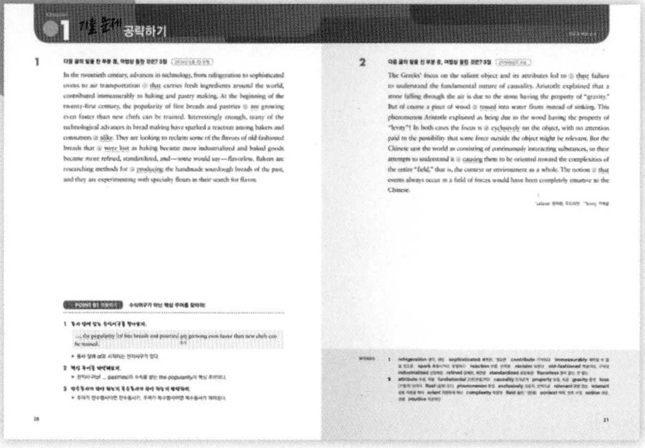

기출 문제 공략하기

한 Chapter의 마무리 단계로, 기출 어법 문제를 배치하였습니다. 앞서 기출 문장으로 연습했던 어법 포인트를 지문에 적용해보면서 실전 문제 풀이 감각을 길러볼 수 있습니다. 〈POINT 적용하기〉에서 출제 포인트를 다시 한 번 짚어주고, 문제를 성공적으로 공략할 방법을 안내하였습니다.

Actual TEST

지금까지 학습한 모든 어법 포인트를 총체적으로 점검할 수 있도록 최신 수능 출제 경향 및 난이도를 반영한 5회분 모의고사를 배치하였습니다. 한 문제 한 문제 차분히 풀어나가면서 실전 수능에 완벽하게 대비할 수 있습니다.

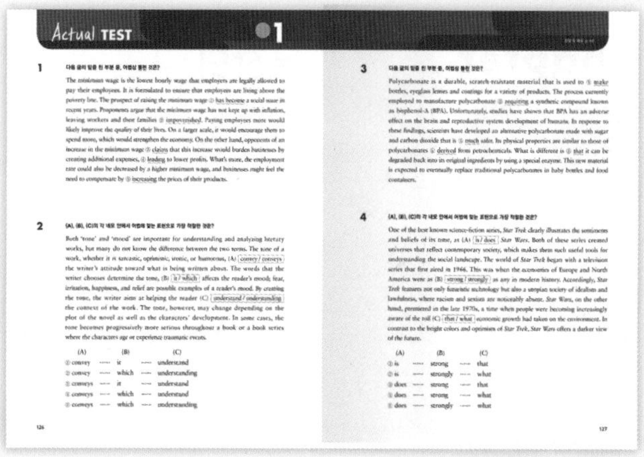

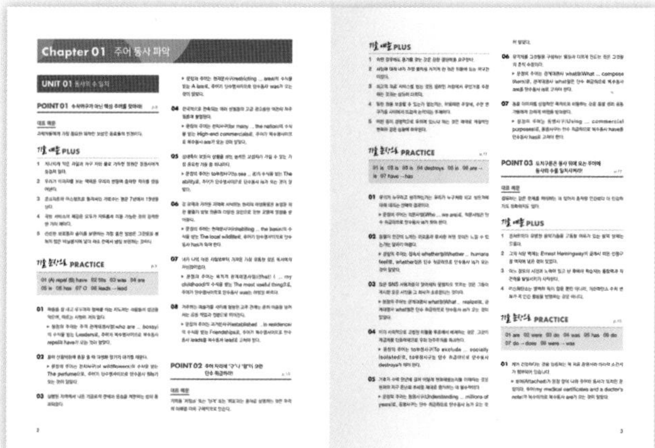

상세하고 정확한 정답 및 해설

모든 문장 및 지문의 정확한 해석과 각 문제의 상세한 해설을 수록하였습니다. 문장 해석이나 문제 풀이에 막힘이 있을 때 참고하면 이 책을 공부하는 내내 친절한 가이드가 되어줄 것입니다.

Contents

Chapter 06

동사 I

Chapter 07

동사 II

Chapter 08

형용사와 부사

Chapter 09

대명사

Chapter 10

Actual TEST

Chapter 01

주어 동사 파악

UNIT 01
동사의 수 일치

UNIT 02
동사 vs. 준동사

POINT 01 ★★★★ 수식어구가 아닌 핵심 주어를 찾아라!

주어와 동사 사이에 주어를 수식하는 수식어구(전치사구, to부정사구, 분사구, 형용사구, 관계사절 등)가 오는 경우, 수식어구를 제외한 핵심 주어를 찾아 이에 동사의 수를 일치시킨다.

❗ 동사 바로 앞 명사를 주어로 착각하여 그 명사에 수를 일치시키지 않도록 주의한다.

대표 예문 The extrinsic reward(핵심 주어(단수)) [that matters most to the scientists](관계대명사절) is / are(단수동사) the recognition of their peers. 기출

▶ 주어는 관계대명사절(that ... the scientists)의 수식을 받는 The extrinsic reward이다. 주어가 단수명사이므로, 단수동사 is를 쓰는 것이 알맞다. 동사 바로 앞의 복수명사 the scientists를 주어로 착각하여 복수동사를 쓰지 않도록 주의한다.

기출 예문 PLUS

정답 및 해설 p.2

1 A garden [full of overripe fruit and overgrown plants] **is** not enjoyable for gardeners. 기출 응용

2 The context [in which we see images] **makes** a significant difference in our response. 기출

3 The street trees [surrounded by concrete and asphalt] **live** seven to fifteen years on average. 기출 응용

4 The provision [of national defense services] **is** one strong example of a commodity that is freely available to all. 기출

5 The best way [to store fresh broccoli bunches] **is** to refrigerate them in an open plastic bag in the vegetable compartment. 기출

WORDS extrinsic 외적인, 외부의 recognition 인식; *인정 peer 또래, 동배 overripe (과일 등이) 지나치게 익은 context 맥락 significant 중요한, 커다란 response 반응 surround 둘러싸다, 에워싸다 on average 평균적으로 provision 제공, 공급 national defense 국방 commodity (유용한) 것 refrigerate 냉장하다 compartment 칸

기출 문장으로 PRACTICE

[01-06] 다음 문장의 네모 안에서 어법상 바른 것을 고르시오.

01 Leaders who are irritable and bossy (A) [repel / repels] people and (B) [have / has] few followers. 기출 응용

02 The perfume of wildflowers [fill / fills] the air as the grass dances upon a gentle breeze. 기출

03 A law restricting the sale and transportation of poultry from the affected area [was / were] passed. 기출 응용

04 High-end commercials for many products promoted across the nation still [is / are] often shot on film. 기출

05 The ability to see the situation as the other side sees it [is / are] one of the most important skills a negotiator can possess. 기출

06 The local wildlife inhabiting areas close to the basin [have / has] been affected by water diversions for agriculture and pollution from a variety of sources. 기출 응용

[07-08] 다음 문장의 밑줄 친 부분이 어법상 바르면 O를 쓰고, 틀리면 바르게 고치시오.

07 The most useful thing I brought out of my childhood <u>was</u> confidence in reading. 기출

08 Friendships established among artists in residence often <u>leads</u> to collaborations and connections beyond the colony. 기출

WORDS irritable 짜증을 내는 bossy 우두머리 행세를 하는 repel 격퇴하다; *접근하지 못하게 하다 restrict 제한[한정]하다 transportation 수송, 운송 poultry (닭 · 오리 등) 가금 high-end 고급의 commercial 광고 negotiator 교섭자 inhabit 살다, 서식하다 basin 대야; *(강의) 유역 diversion 전환 agriculture 농업 residence 거주 collaboration 공동 작업 colony 집단, 거주지

POINT 02 ★★★★★

주어 자리에 "구"나 "절"이 오면 단수 취급하라!

to부정사구, 동명사구와 같은 명사구나, 관계대명사 what절, 접속사 whether절, 의문사절과 같은 명사절은 주어로 쓰일 수 있는데, 이 경우 단수 취급하므로 단수동사가 와야 한다.

❗ 구 또는 절 안에 쓰인 명사를 주어로 착각하여 이에 동사의 수를 일치시키지 않도록 주의한다.

대표 예문 [**Describing** memory in terms of 'stores' or 'levels' or 'loops'] ~~make~~ / makes our understanding more concrete. 기출

(동명사구 주어(단수) — 단수동사)

▶ Describing이 이끄는 동명사구가 주어인데, 동명사구는 단수 취급하므로 단수동사 makes를 쓰는 것이 알맞다. 동명사구 안의 복수명사(stores, levels, loops)를 주어로 착각하여 복수동사를 쓰지 않도록 주의한다.

기출 예문 PLUS

정답 및 해설 p.3

1 [To be courageous under all circumstances] **requires** strong determination. 기출

2 [What interested me the most about the new house] **was** the stable in the backyard. 기출

3 [Getting first-rate health care] **is** quite different from ordering something from an online bookstore. 기출

4 [Whether or not we can catch up on sleep — on the weekend, say —] **is** a hotly debated topic among sleep researchers. 기출

5 [Which species is competitively superior] sometimes **depends** on conditions such as seasonal variation. 기출

WORDS concrete 콘크리트로 된; *구체적인 courageous 용감한 circumstance 환경, 상황 determination 결심, 결단력 stable 마구간 first-rate 일류의, 최고의 catch up on (뒤떨어진 일을) 만회하다 competitively 경쟁적으로 superior 우수한, 우월한

정답 및 해설 p.3

[01-05] 다음 문장의 네모 안에서 어법상 바른 것을 고르시오.

01 Who we believe we are [is / are] a result of the choices we make about who we want to be like. 기출

02 Whether an animal can feel anything resembling the loneliness humans feel [is / are] hard to say. 기출

03 What many social networking site users may not realize [is / are] that the company owns every photo they have posted. 기출 응용

04 To exclude those from voting who are already socially isolated [destroy / destroys] our democracy, as it creates a caste system. 기출

05 Understanding how the climate has changed over millions of years [is / are] vital to properly assessing current global warming trends. 기출 응용

[06-07] 다음 문장의 밑줄 친 부분이 어법상 바르면 O를 쓰고, 틀리면 바르게 고치시오.

06 What makes organisms different from the materials that compose them <u>are</u> their level of organization. 기출

07 Using animal images for commercial purposes <u>have</u> been strongly criticized by animal rights activists. 기출 응용

WORDS **resemble** 닮다, 비슷하다 **post** 발송하다; *게시하다 **exclude** 제외[배제]하다 **voting** 투표, 선거 **isolate** 격리하다, 고립시키다 **democracy** 민주주의 **caste system** 계급 제도 **vital** 필수적인 **assess** (특성 등을) 재다, 가늠하다 **organism** 유기체 **compose** 구성하다 **commercial** 상업의 **criticize** 비판[비난]하다

POINT 03 ★★★★★

도치구문에서는 동사 뒤에 오는 주어에 동사의 수를 일치시켜라!

강조하려는 어구가 문장의 첫머리에 올 때, 주어와 동사의 순서가 바뀌는 도치가 일어날 수 있다. 이때, 동사의 수는 동사 뒤에 오는 주어에 일치시킨다.

도치구문

문장 첫머리에 오는 강조어(구)	도치구문 형태
1 **부정어구:** no, not, never, few, little, hardly, rarely, only(의미상 부정어) 2 **보어:** 형용사나 분사 3 **장소나 방향을 나타내는 부사구**	1 **일반동사가 쓰인 문장:** 「do[does/did]+주어+동사원형」, 「have[has/had]+주어+p.p.」 2 **be동사/조동사가 쓰인 문장:** be동사/조동사가 주어 앞으로 나감

대표 예문 Rarely (부정어) is / ~~are~~ (단수동사) a computer (주어(단수)) more sensitive and accurate than a human in dealing with the same matter. 기출 응용

▶ 부정어 Rarely가 문장의 첫머리에 나와 주어와 동사가 도치된 문장이다. 동사 뒤에 오는 주어 a computer가 단수명사이므로 단수동사 is가 와야 한다.

기출 예문 PLUS

정답 및 해설 p.3

1 Rare **is** the musical organization that can afford to hire famous musicians for every concert. 기출

2 On the wall of his dining room **were** framed quotations from the writings of Ernest Hemingway. 기출 응용

3 Only after some time and struggle **does** the student begin to develop insights and intuitions. 기출

4 Not only **is** carbon dioxide plainly not poisonous, but changes in carbon dioxide levels don't necessarily mirror human activity. 기출

WORDS **sensitive** 민감한 **accurate** 정확한 **deal with** ~을 처리하다 **rare** 드문, 보기 힘든 **framed** 액자에 넣은 **quotation** 인용구[문] **struggle** 고투, 노력 **insight** 통찰력 **intuition** 직관력 **plainly** 분명히 **poisonous** 유독한 **mirror** 반영하다

기출 문장으로 PRACTICE

정답 및 해설 p.3

[01-06] 다음 문장의 네모 안에서 어법상 바른 것을 고르시오.

01 Attached [is / are] my medical certificates and a doctor's note verifying that I am in good health.

02 In the distance below [was / were] the escaped prisoners able to see the wavering beam of a flashlight. 기출 응용

03 So hopeless [do / does] tens of thousands of Syrians feel that they attempt to flee their country and become refugees.

04 No longer [was / were] being young criminals their only option in life; instead, they had a variety of other opportunities. 기출 응용

05 Only in the last few decades [has / have] food become so plentiful and easy to obtain as to cause fat-related health problems. 기출

06 They talk about focusing on the process and following the process. Rarely [do / does] they talk about scoring a goal or a point. 기출

[07-08] 다음 문장의 밑줄 친 부분이 어법상 바르면 O를 쓰고, 틀리면 바르게 고치시오.

07 Not only <u>do</u> the number of migrating birds vary by month, but it also varies by species.

08 Next to the dolls <u>were</u> a small box made of ivory, containing tiny combs and a silver mirror. 기출 응용

WORDS **attached** 첨부된 **certificate** 증서, 증명서 **verify** 입증[확인]하다 **wavering** 흔들리는, 펄럭이는 **escaped** 탈출한 **flee** 달아나다, 도망하다 **refugee** 난민, 망명자 **decade** 10년 **plentiful** 풍부한 **related** (~에) 관련된 **migrate** 이동하다 **vary** 서로 다르다 **ivory** 상아

POINT 04 ★★★★★

「부분표현+of+명사」는 명사에 동사의 수를 일치시켜라!

「부분표현+of+명사」가 주어 자리에 올 경우, 동사는 of 뒤에 오는 명사에 수를 일치시킨다.

all / most / half / some / the majority / the rest / 분수 등	+	of + **단수명사** + **단수동사**
		of + **복수명사** + **복수동사**

❗ 「one[each] of+명사」가 주어 자리에 올 경우, 단수인 one[each]이 주어이므로 뒤에 단수동사가 와야 한다.

주어(부분표현+of+단수명사) 동사(단수)

대표 예문 Some of the water [~~come~~ / comes] from underground sources and some from rain. 기출

▶ 주어 자리에 「Some of+명사」가 쓰였으므로, of 뒤에 오는 명사에 동사의 수를 일치시켜야 한다. the water는 단수명사이므로 단수동사 comes가 오는 것이 알맞다.

기출 예문 PLUS

정답 및 해설 p.4

1 Lastly, most of the tensions and quarrels [between children] **are** natural. 기출

2 One of the common problems [of sensitive people] **is** an excess of delta brainwaves. 기출

3 All of us **use** the cultural knowledge we acquire as members of our own society to organize our behavior. 기출

4 Two thirds of the total U.S. primary energy production **comes** from natural gas, coal, and petroleum. 기출 응용

5 In most wilderness areas, the majority of groups [visiting the area] **are** small — usually between two and four people. 기출

WORDS **source** 원천; *수원 **tension** 긴장, 갈등 **quarrel** 언쟁, 다툼 **excess** 지나침, 과잉 **brainwave** 뇌파 **acquire** 습득하다 **primary** 주된, 주요한 **coal** 석탄 **petroleum** 석유 **wilderness** 황야, 황무지

기출 문장으로 PRACTICE

정답 및 해설 p.4

[01-06] 다음 문장의 네모 안에서 어법상 바른 것을 고르시오.

01 He went to Oxford, where some of the best scientists in England [was / were] working at the time. 기출

02 One of the most difficult things many successful people do [is / are] to challenge their own beliefs. 기출

03 In the United States, most of the advertising during the run-up to Christmas [tend / tends] to be aimed at children. 기출 응용

04 The decision is viewed as an undesirable one, but the majority of residents [say / says] they have to accept it. 기출 응용

05 Almost all of the community members [follow / follows] the guidelines for what is "appropriate" for their roles. 기출 응용

06 Around half of posts on social networking sites [is / are] "me" focused, which means they are related to what people are doing now. 기출 응용

[07-08] 다음 문장의 밑줄 친 부분이 어법상 바르면 O를 쓰고, 틀리면 바르게 고치시오.

07 Each of our decisions <u>are</u> a determination about the nature of "the good life." 기출

08 The rest of the bird's body <u>seem</u> to have been covered in much shorter feathers, which would have kept out the cold. 기출

WORDS **challenge** 이의를 제기하다 **run-up** 준비 (기간) **be aimed at** ~을 겨냥하다 **undesirable** 원하지 않는, 바람직하지 않은 **resident** 거주자, 주민 **accept** 받아들이다 **appropriate** 적절한 **determination** 결정 **nature** 자연; *본질

POINT 05 ★★★★★

동사(v) 자리인지 준동사(to-v / v-ing) 자리인지 구분하라!

모든 문장이나 절은 주어와 동사가 반드시 필요하다. 동사는 '~다'의 의미로 주어의 동작이나 상태를 서술하는데, to부정사, 동명사 등의 준동사는 명사, 형용사, 부사 역할을 하므로 동사 자리에 올 수 없다.

문장의 동사 vs. 준동사

문장의 동사	준동사(to부정사, 동명사)
1 주로 주어 뒤에 쓰여 주어의 동작, 상태를 서술한다. 단, 동사로 시작하는 명령문은 동사 앞에 주어가 생략되어 있다. 2 시제를 나타내고, 주어에 수(단수, 복수)를 일치시켜야 하며, 주어와의 관계에 따라 능동태와 수동태를 구분하여 써야 한다. **a.** The company **has spent** a lot of money on newspaper advertising. ▶ 단수명사 주어(The company) → 단수동사(has), 현재완료시제(have p.p.) **b.** Some athletes **have** recently **been caught** cheating by taking illegal drugs. ▶ 복수명사 주어(Some athletes) → 복수동사(have), 현재완료 수동태(have been p.p.)	1 **to부정사(to-v)** 문장에서 명사처럼 주어, 목적어, 보어 자리에 쓰인다. 또한 형용사나 부사처럼 명사나 동사, 문장 등을 수식하는 자리에 쓰인다. **c.** He decided **to work** on stress management. ▶ 동사(decided)의 목적어 **d.** Farmers plow more and more fields **to produce** more food. ▶ 동사구(plow ... fields)를 수식하는 부사 2 **동명사(v-ing)** 명사처럼 주어, 목적어, 보어 자리에 쓰인다. **e.** [**Using** the Internet to communicate] has become a part of our daily life. ▶ 동사(has become)의 주어 **f.** He had little interest in [**earning** lots of money]. ▶ 전치사(in)의 목적어

a. 그 회사는 신문 광고에 많은 돈을 써왔다. b. 어떤 선수들이 최근에 불법 약물을 복용하여 부정행위를 하다가 잡혔다. c. 그는 스트레스 관리를 시작하기로 결심했다. d. 농부들은 더 많은 식량을 생산하기 위해 점점 더 많은 밭을 일군다. e. 의사소통을 하기 위해 인터넷을 사용하는 것은 우리의 일상생활의 일부가 되었다. f. 그는 많은 돈을 버는 것에는 거의 관심이 없었다.

WORDS **athlete** (운동)선수 **work on** ~에 노력을 들이다, 착수하다 **plow** (밭을) 갈다, 경작하다

대표 예문 1 The use [of vibrations] [in communication] ~~depending~~(→ depends) on the ability of the sender to make a substance vibrate. 기출

문장의 주어 / 전치사구 / 전치사구 / 동사

▶ 문장의 주어는 전치사구(of vibrations / in communication)의 수식을 받는 The use이고, the ability 이하가 전치사 on의 목적어이다. 문장에 동사가 없으므로, 준동사 depending을 동사 depends로 고쳐야 한다.

대표 예문 2 The only part [of his work] [that he enjoyed] was ~~made~~(→ making) models of buildings. 기출

문장의 주어 / 전치사구 / 관계대명사절 / 동사 / 주격보어(동명사)

▶ 문장의 주어는 전치사구(of his work)와 관계대명사절(that he enjoyed)의 수식을 받는 The only part이고, was가 문장의 동사이다. was 뒤에 주격보어가 와야 하므로 made를 making으로 고쳐야 한다.

기출 예문 PLUS

정답 및 해설 p.5

1 [**Imagining** yourself totally without an audience] **would be** painful and difficult. 기출

2 We**'ve done** everything we can [**to contain** costs without **compromising** quality]. 기출

3 If you **were trained** to be a physical education teacher, [**not having** a gym] **is** not a huge problem. 기출

4 (You) **Don't wash** the broccoli before **storing** it, since moisture on its surface **encourages** the growth of mold. 기출

5 People [who **are** daring in **taking** a wholehearted stand for truth] **achieve** results [that **surpass** their expectations]. 기출

6 [**To make** the choice **to express** a feeling by **carving** a specific form from a rock], without the use of high technology or colors, **restricts** the artist significantly. 기출

WORDS vibration 진동(vibrate 떨다, 진동하다) substance 물질 contain ~이 들어있다; *억제하다 compromise 타협하다; *손상하다 mold 곰팡이 daring 대담한 wholehearted 전폭적인, 전적인 take a stand 태도를 취하다 surpass 능가하다, 뛰어넘다 expectation 기대 carve 조각하다 restrict 제한하다 significantly 상당히, 크게

기출 문장으로 PRACTICE

정답 및 해설 p.5

[01-13] 다음 문장의 네모 안에서 어법상 알맞은 것을 고르시오.

01 Our total set of values and their relative importance to us [constitute / constituting] our value system. 기출

02 To protect your camera, [keep / keeping] the lens covered when you are not using it is recommended. 기출 응용

03 The most common activity among people observed by Whyte [turned / turning] out to be watching other people. 기출

04 Therefore, [invest / investing] regularly in learning opportunities is one of the greatest gifts you can give yourself. 기출

05 It's not hard to imagine that [live / living] your life in pursuit of someone else's expectations can be a difficult way to live. 기출 응용

06 Most animals, including our ancestors and modern-day capuchin monkeys, [to live / lived] very close to the margin of survival. 기출

*capuchin monkey: 꼬리감는 원숭이

07 In fact, everything that people post [is / being] automatically licensed to E-World for its transferable use, distribution, or public display. 기출

08 Unfortunately, most of the productivity measurement schemes I have encountered [to measure / measured] effort or apparent activity. 기출

WORDS

relative 상대적인 **constitute** 구성하다 **invest** 투자하다 **in pursuit of** ~을 추구하여 **margin** 가장자리; *한계 **license** 허가하다, 인가하다 **transferable** 이전할 수 있는 **distribution** 분배, 배포 **measurement** 측정(**measure** 측정하다) **scheme** 계획, 제도 **encounter** 접하다, 마주치다 **apparent** 분명한

09 Professionals who work to convince us of certain viewpoints [study / to study] research on human decision making to determine how to exploit our weaknesses. 기출

10 Many small mammals living in cold climates, who lose heat easily by having an unfavorable surface area to body weight ratio, [tend / tending] to sleep a lot. 기출

11 A system of transporting letters and newspapers, as well as people, by canal boat [to develop / was developed] in the Dutch Republic in the seventeenth century. 기출

12 [Protect / To protect] its historic building character, the city has set detailed criteria for the installation of signs, plaques, and posters, and has revised its street signs. 기출

13 According to a study published in April in the *Journal of Personality and Social Psychology*, [recall / recalling] childhood memories can lead people to behave more ethically. 기출

[14-16] 다음 문장의 밑줄 친 부분이 어법상 바르면 O를 쓰고, 틀리면 바르게 고치시오.

14 The best way, of course, is <u>to bring</u> your phone to the customer service center as soon as possible. 기출

15 In the nineteenth century in London, the tragic conditions pointed out by many critics <u>to produce</u> measures to clean up the city. 기출 응용

16 Anyone who has spent time with a five-year-old <u>knowing</u> that children this age can test the limits of your patience by trying to get explanations for why everything works as it does. 기출

WORDS convince 납득시키다 determine 알아내다, 밝히다 exploit 이용[활용]하다 mammal 포유동물 unfavorable 호의적이 아닌; *불리한 ratio 비율, 비 canal 운하 criterion 기준(*pl.* criteria) installation 설치, 설비 plaque 명판 revise 고치다, 변경하다 ethically 윤리적으로 condition 상태; *상황 critic 비평가 measure 방안, 조치 patience 참을성

1 **다음 글의 밑줄 친 부분 중, 어법상 틀린 것은? [3점]** (2014년 6월 고3 모평)

In the twentieth century, advances in technology, from refrigeration to sophisticated ovens to air transportation ① that carries fresh ingredients around the world, contributed immeasurably to baking and pastry making. At the beginning of the twenty-first century, the popularity of fine breads and pastries ② are growing even faster than new chefs can be trained. Interestingly enough, many of the technological advances in bread making have sparked a reaction among bakers and consumers ③ alike. They are looking to reclaim some of the flavors of old-fashioned breads that ④ were lost as baking became more industrialized and baked goods became more refined, standardized, and—some would say—flavorless. Bakers are researching methods for ⑤ producing the handmade sourdough breads of the past, and they are experimenting with specialty flours in their search for flavor.

POINT 01 적용하기 **수식어구가 아닌 핵심 주어를 찾아라!**

1 동사 앞에 있는 수식어구를 찾아보자.

> …, the popularity [of fine breads and pastries] are(동사) growing even faster than new chefs can be trained.

▶ 동사 앞에 of로 시작하는 전치사구가 있다.

2 핵심 주어를 파악해보자.

▶ 전치사구(of ... pastries)의 수식을 받는 the popularity가 핵심 주어이다.

3 단수동사가 와야 하는지 복수동사가 와야 하는지 판단하자.

▶ 주어가 단수명사이면 단수동사가, 주어가 복수명사이면 복수동사가 와야한다.

정답 및 해설 p.6

2 **다음 글의 밑줄 친 부분 중, 어법상 틀린 것은? [3점]** (2016학년도 수능)

The Greeks' focus on the salient object and its attributes led to ① their failure to understand the fundamental nature of causality. Aristotle explained that a stone falling through the air is due to the stone having the property of "gravity." But of course a piece of wood ② tossed into water floats instead of sinking. This phenomenon Aristotle explained as being due to the wood having the property of "levity"! In both cases the focus is ③ exclusively on the object, with no attention paid to the possibility that some force outside the object might be relevant. But the Chinese saw the world as consisting of continuously interacting substances, so their attempts to understand it ④ causing them to be oriented toward the complexities of the entire "field," that is, the context or environment as a whole. The notion ⑤ that events always occur in a field of forces would have been completely intuitive to the Chinese.

*salient: 현저한, 두드러진 **levity 가벼움

WORDS

1 **refrigeration** 냉각, 냉장 **sophisticated** 세련된; *정교한 **contribute** 기여하다 **immeasurably** 헤아릴 수 없을 정도로 **spark** 촉발시키다, 유발하다 **reaction** 반응, 반작용 **reclaim** 되찾다 **old-fashioned** 옛날식의, 구식의 **industrialized** 산업화된 **refined** 정제된, 제련된 **standardized** 표준화된 **flavorless** 풍미 없는, 맛 없는

2 **attribute** 속성, 자질 **fundamental** 근본[본질]적인 **causality** 인과관계 **property** 성질, 속성 **gravity** 중력 **toss** (가볍게) 던지다 **float** (물에) 뜨다 **phenomenon** 현상 **exclusively** 오로지, 전적으로 **relevant** 관련 있는 **interact** 상호 작용을 하다 **orient** 지향하게 하다 **complexity** 복잡성 **field** 들판; *장(場) **context** 맥락, 전후 사정 **notion** 개념, 관념 **intuitive** 직관적인

Chapter 02

동사의 태

UNIT 03

능동태 vs. 수동태

POINT 06 ★★★★

주어와 동사의 의미 관계를 따져라!

주어와 동사의 의미가 '~이 …하다'일 경우 능동태를, '~이 …되다'일 경우 수동태(be p.p.)를 쓴다. 목적어를 취하지 않는 자동사(arrive, happen, appear, disappear, become, take place, consist 등)는 수동태로 쓸 수 없음에 유의한다.

수동태의 여러 형태

진행형 수동태 「be being p.p.」	**a.** Efforts **are being made** to improve the situation.
완료형 수동태 「have been p.p.」	**b.** His office **has been moved** to a new building.
to부정사의 수동태 「to be p.p.」	**c.** She hoped **to be invited** to their party.
동명사의 수동태 「being p.p.」	**d.** The boy doesn't like **being treated** like a child.

a. 상황을 개선하기 위해 노력이 이뤄지고 있다. b. 그의 사무실이 새 건물로 이전되었다. c. 그녀는 그들의 파티에 초대되기를 바랐다. d. 그 소년은 어린애 취급을 받는 것을 싫어한다.

대표 예문 Although the living supplies for the settlers (부사절의 주어(~이)) would ~~send~~ / be sent (동사(보내진다)) from Earth, taking the risk of exchanging life for dreams is tough. 기출

▶ 접속사 Although가 이끄는 부사절에서, 주어(the living supplies for settlers)와 동사 사이에 '~이 보내진다'라는 수동의 의미 관계가 성립하므로 수동태 be sent를 써야 한다.

기출 예문 PLUS

정답 및 해설 p.8

1 In most cases one can tell from the context what sense **is being used.** 기출

2 Concrete crosses marked the spots where careless fishermen **had been swept** into the sea. 기출

3 A currently popular attitude is to blame technology for today's environmental problems. We believe this view needs **to be changed.** 기출 응용

WORDS **supply** 공급; *(*pl.*) 보급품 **settler** 정착민 **take a risk** 위험을 무릅쓰다 **context** 문맥 **sense** 감각; *(어구의) 의미 **careless** 부주의한

기출 문장으로 PRACTICE

정답 및 해설 p.8

[01-06] 다음 문장의 네모 안에서 어법상 바른 것을 고르시오.

01 We would like to ask if you could [give / be given] a speech about your writing process. 기출

02 New technology should [develop / be developed] to reduce the dangers to the environment before drilling is allowed. 기출

03 One day a local newspaper carried a story about a rescued horse that had [abandoned / been abandoned] to die in the desert. 기출

04 Yet when these molecules [extracted / were extracted] from vegetables and made into supplements, they did not reduce cancer. 기출

05 For decades, child-rearing advice from experts has [encouraged / been encouraged] the nighttime separation of baby from parent. 기출

06 Whyte expected lovers to [find / be found] in private, isolated spaces, but most often they sat or stood right in the center of things for everyone to see. 기출

[07-08] 다음 문장의 밑줄 친 부분이 어법상 바르면 O를 쓰고, 틀리면 바르게 고치시오.

07 They entered a contest to guess how many soda cans the back of a pickup truck <u>was held</u>. 기출

08 Motorists pull up to a gas station where an attendant <u>encloses</u> in a glass booth with a tray for taking money. 기출

WORDS

drill 구멍을 뚫다; *(석유를) 시추하다 **abandon** 버리다, 유기하다 **molecule** 분자 **extract** 추출하다 **supplement** 보조식품 **rearing** 양육 **separation** 분리 **isolated** 외떨어진, 외딴 **attendant** 종업원, 안내원 **enclose** 에워[둘러]싸다

POINT 07 ★★★★★

수동태 뒤에 오는 명사(구)에 유의하라!

수동태(be p.p.)는 보통 목적어를 취할 수 없어 수동태 뒤에 명사(구)가 오지 않지만, 4형식과 5형식을 수동태로 전환할 경우에는 「be p.p.」 뒤에 명사(구)가 올 수 있다.

4형식의 수동태	주어(← 간접목적어) + be p.p. + **직접목적어**(← 주어+동사+간접목적어+직접목적어)
5형식의 수동태	주어(← 목적어) + be p.p. + **목적격보어**(← 주어+동사+목적어+목적격보어)

❗ 4형식 동사로는 give, pay, offer, send, tell 등이 있고, 5형식 동사로는 consider, call, name, elect 등이 있다.

대표 예문 They were [given / ~~giving~~] only a pistol and a rifle to protect themselves from their enemies. 기출 응용

(given: 동사(주어지다), a pistol and a rifle: 직접목적어)

▶ 주어, 동사, 명사구가 '~이 …을 지급받다'라는 수동의 의미 관계가 성립하므로 수동태 were given이 와야 한다. 보통 수동태는 뒤에 목적어를 취하지 않지만, 4형식 문장의 간접목적어를 주어로 하는 수동태 문장에서는 직접목적어(명사)가 수동태 뒤에 남음에 유의해야 한다.

기출 예문 PLUS

정답 및 해설 p.8

1 The 18th century **is called** the Golden Age of botanical painting. 기출

2 I tried to resist my mother at every opportunity, as I hated to **be told** what to do. 기출 응용

3 Soon after he returned to his home country, he **was offered** a job as the chief executive officer of a newspaper publisher. 기출 응용

4 The word "kid" **was** once **considered** slang because it came from a word whose meaning was — and is — a young goat. 기출

WORDS pistol 권총 rifle 소총 botanical 식물의 chief executive officer 최고 경영자 publisher 출판사 slang 속어, 은어

기출 문장으로 PRACTICE

정답 및 해설 p.9

[01-05] 다음 문장의 네모 안에서 어법상 바른 것을 고르시오.

01 He organized about twenty-five men into a unit, which [called / was called] the Texas Rangers. 기출

02 The flight attendants [serve / are served] the passengers free drinks once the plane reaches a cruising altitude.

03 His work has been internationally recognized. His book [awarded / was awarded] the Pulitzer Prize for History and the Bancroft Prize. 기출 응용

04 Edwin Armstrong, who first developed FM radio, [considers / is considered] the most prolific and influential inventor in radio history. 기출

05 The participants were purposely not [giving / given] any specific instructions about the sizes of the shapes or the amount of paper that they should use in the task. 기출

[06-07] 다음 문장의 밑줄 친 부분이 어법상 바르면 O를 쓰고, 틀리면 바르게 고치시오.

06 Whenever my son did what I wanted him to do, I <u>paid</u> him little attention. 기출

07 Michelangelo <u>offered</u> the project of creating the tomb of Pope Julius in 1505, but the tomb was not completed until 1545.

WORDS **flight attendant** (비행기) 승무원 **cruising altitude** 순항 고도 **recognize** 인정하다 **prolific** 다작하는 **influential** 영향력이 있는 **participant** 참가자 **purposely** 고의로, 일부러 **specific** 구체적인, 명확한 **instruction** 교육; *(*pl.*) 설명, 지시 **pope** 교황 **tomb** 무덤

1 **다음 글의 밑줄 친 부분 중, 어법상 틀린 것은? [3점]** (2017년 3월 고3 학평)

One of the simplest and most effective ways to build empathy in children ① is to let them play more on their own. Unsupervised kids are not reluctant to tell one another how they feel. In addition, children at play often take on other roles, pretending to be Principal Walsh or Josh's mom, happily forcing ② themselves to imagine how someone else thinks and feels. Unfortunately, free play is becoming rare. Boston College research professor Peter Gray has documented a continuous and ③ ultimately dramatic decline in children's opportunities to play and explore in their own chosen ways over the past fifty years in the United States and other developed countries. The effects have been especially ④ damaged, he argues, to empathy. He concludes that a decline of empathy and a rise in narcissism are exactly ⑤ what we would expect to see in children who have little opportunity to play socially.

*empathy: 공감, 감정 이입

POINT 06 적용하기 **주어와 동사의 의미 관계를 따져라!**

1 문장의 주어와 동사를 찾아보자.

The effects (S) have been especially damaged (V), he argues, to empathy.

▶ The effects가 주어, have been damaged가 동사이다.

2 주어와 동사의 의미 관계를 따져보자.

▶ 효과가(주어) / 손상되었다(수동) vs. 손상을 주었다(능동) / 공감 능력에

3 동사가 능동태여야 하는지 수동태여야 하는지 판단하자.

▶ 주어와 동사가 능동의 의미 관계이면 능동태를, 수동의 의미 관계이면 수동태를 써야 한다.

정답 및 해설 p.9

2 다음 글의 밑줄 친 부분 중, 어법상 틀린 것은? (2015년 6월 고2 학평)

The process of job advancement in the field of sports ① is often said to be shaped like a pyramid. That is, at the wide base are many jobs with high school athletic teams, while at the narrow tip are the few, highly desired jobs with professional organizations. Thus there are many sports jobs altogether, but the competition becomes ② increasingly tough as one works their way up. The salaries of various positions reflect this pyramid model. For example, high school football coaches are typically teachers who ③ paid a little extra for their after-class work. But coaches of the same sport at big universities can earn more than $1 million a year, causing the salaries of college presidents ④ to look small in comparison. One degree higher up is the National Football League, ⑤ where head coaches can earn many times more than their best-paid campus counterparts.

WORDS

1 **unsupervised** 감독되지 않는 **reluctant** 꺼리는, 주저하는 **pretend** ~인 척하다, ~인 것처럼 굴다 **document** (상세한 내용을) 기록하다 **ultimately** 궁극적으로, 결국 **dramatic** 극적인 **damage** 손상을 주다, 피해를 입히다 **narcissism** 나르시시즘, 자기 도취증 **socially** 사회적으로

2 **advancement** 발전; *승진, 출세 **pyramid** 피라미드 **base** (사물의) 맨 아래 부분 **athletic** 체육의, 운동 경기의 **tip** (뾰족한) 끝 **desired** 바랐던, 훌륭한 **reflect** 비추다; *반영하다 **in comparison** 비교해 보면 **counterpart** 상대

Chapter 03

문장의 구조

UNIT 04

병렬구조

POINT 08 ★★★★★

등위접속사나 상관접속사가 연결하는 요소는 대등해야 한다!

접속사는 두 개 이상의 어구(단어, 구, 절)를 연결한다. 그 중 등위접속사나 상관접속사로 연결되는 요소들은 형태나 문법적 기능이 일치하는 병렬구조를 이뤄야 한다.

등위접속사와 상관접속사

등위접속사	상관접속사
1 and, or, but 등이 있다. 2 3가지 이상을 나열할 경우, 「A, B, and[or] C」 구조로 쓴다. 3 동사를 병렬 연결하는 경우, 동사의 태와 수에 주의해야 한다. 4 병렬 연결 시, 반복을 피하기 위해 공통어구(to부정사의 to, 「전치사+동명사」의 전치사, 수동태의 be동사 등)는 생략하기도 한다. **a.** He is smart, good-looking, **and** fashionable. (A, B, and C) **b.** Flowers are often presented for celebrations **and** given to moms on Mother's Day. 기출 ▶ 수동태가 병렬 연결됨. are는 공통어구이고, 과거분사(presented, given)가 연결됨	**〈자주 나오는 상관접속사〉** • 「both A and B」: A와 B 둘 다 • 「not only A but (also) B」: A뿐만 아니라 B도 • 「either A or B」: A이거나 B • 「neither A nor B」: A도 아니고 B도 아닌 • 「not A but B」: A가 아니라 B **c.** Serious mistakes were made, and these were costly **both** in terms of direct losses **and** in respect of the company's image. 기출 응용 **d.** She **not only** wrote the novel **but also** designed the book cover. **e.** It is not easy to show moral courage in the face of **either** indifference **or** opposition. 기출

a. 그는 똑똑하고, 잘생기고, 패션감각이 있다. b. 꽃은 보통 축하를 위해 선물되고 어머니의 날에 어머니께 선사된다. c. 중대한 실수가 저질러졌고, 이것들은 직접적인 손실 면에서와 회사 이미지 면에서 모두 손해가 컸다. d. 그녀는 그 소설을 썼을 뿐만 아니라, 책 표지를 디자인하기도 했다. e. 무관심이나 반대에 직면하여 도덕적 용기를 보여주는 것은 쉽지 않다.

WORDS **good-looking** 잘생긴, 아름다운 **celebration** 기념, 축하 **costly** 값이 비싼; *손해가 많은 **in terms of** ~ 면에서 **in respect of** ~에 대해 **moral** 도덕적인 **indifference** 무관심, 무심 **opposition** 반대, 항의

대표 예문 1 I saw a woman **trying** to turn onto the main street and ~~had~~ / having very little luck because of the constant stream of traffic. 기출

동사 / 목적어 / 목적격보어1 / 등위접속사 / 목적격보어2

▶ 등위접속사 and에 의해 지각동사 saw의 목적격보어가 병렬 연결된 구조로, 앞에 나온 현재분사 trying과 병렬구조를 이루는 having이 와야 한다. 과거형 동사 saw와 병렬구조를 이루는 것으로 혼동하여 had를 쓰지 않아야 한다.

대표 예문 2 The purpose of laughter is not only **to communicate** [that one is in a playful state], but actually ~~induces~~ / to induce this state in others as well. 기출

주어 / 상관접속사 / 주격보어1 / 주격보어2

▶ 상관접속사 「not only A but (also) B」에 의해 주격보어가 병렬 연결된 구조로, 앞에 나온 to부정사 to communicate와 병렬구조를 이루는 to induce가 와야 한다.

기출 예문 PLUS

정답 및 해설 p.11

1 In fact, however, the effects of art are neither **so certain** nor **so direct.** 기출

2 Whether she **was** a slave or **came** from a wealthier class made a great deal of difference. 기출

3 A human is much more capable of **operating** the instruments correctly and **placing** them in appropriate and useful positions. 기출

4 The objects in front of my eyes include some pieces of fruit and a bowl, but no object corresponding to the word 'and' exists either **in the world** or **in my visual image.** 기출

WORDS **constant** 끊임없는 **stream** 연속, 이어짐 **laughter** 웃음 **communicate** 의사소통을 하다; *(느낌 등을) 전하다 **playful** 장난스러운, 명랑한 **induce** 유도하다 **be capable of** ~할 수 있다 **appropriate** 적절한 **correspond to** ~와 일치하다

기출 문장으로 PRACTICE

정답 및 해설 p.11

[01-12] 다음 문장의 네모 안에서 어법상 바른 것을 고르시오.

01 Gabby calmed down and [remembering / remembered] clearly what she had to say. 기출

02 I responded to his comments by bending my knees more and [to run / running] faster when I got back in the game. 기출

03 If you're going to write a thank-you note, take a minute to purchase a nice card and [use / using] a pen that gives you a decent flow. 기출 응용

04 They'll go to the edge of a difficult slope, look all the way down to the bottom, and [determine / to determine] that the slope is too steep for them to try. 기출

05 The purser accepted the responsibility for the valuables and [remarking / remarked], "It's all right. I'll be very glad to take care of them for you." 기출

06 Charity means not only providing immediate assistance to the poor but also [helps / helping] them in ways that will enable them to support themselves. 기출 응용

07 Child-rearing experts always caution parents not to tell children they're bad when they misbehave, but rather [scolds / to scold] them for doing bad things. 기출

08 Researchers asked 32 people to watch a brief computer animation of white bars drifting over a black background and [say / said] which way they were moving. 기출

WORDS **decent** 괜찮은; *품위 있는 **edge** 가장자리 **slope** 경사면 **steep** 가파른 **purser** 사무장 **valuables** (*pl.*) 귀중품 **remark** 언급하다, 말하다 **charity** 자선 **immediate** 즉각적인 **assistance** 도움, 원조 **rearing** 양육 **caution** 주의[경고]를 주다 **misbehave** 못된 짓을 하다, 비행을 저지르다 **scold** 야단치다 **drift** (물에) 떠가다; *(서서히) 이동하다

09 Their next goal is to provide enough energy for the entire city without increasing the use of fossil fuels and eventually [become / becoming] self-sufficient in terms of energy.

10 The gift of time can sometimes be more satisfying than money. You can see this by watching those who have volunteered at homeless shelters or [bring / brought] meals to seniors. 기출

11 Tory Higgins had university students read a personality description of someone and then [summarize / summarized] it for someone else who was believed either to like or to dislike this person. 기출

12 A country must begin to make the transition from a welfare state to a workfare state, with an emphasis on creating a more highly skilled labor force and [improve / improving] access to the labor market for women and low-income youth. 기출

[13-15] 다음 문장의 밑줄 친 부분이 어법상 바르면 O를 쓰고, 틀리면 바르게 고치시오.

13 After high school, I gave up on my dream of going to college and <u>getting</u> a part-time job instead. 기출

14 As a reviewer, you analyze the book for how it tells a story and <u>to evaluate</u> the quality of writing and organization. 기출

15 Above the television is a large picture of Neil Armstrong standing on the surface of the moon and <u>salutes</u> a stiff American flag. 기출

WORDS **fossil fuel** 화석 연료 **self-sufficient** 자급자족할 수 있는 **shelter** 쉼터, 보호소 **senior** 연장자 **personality** 성격, 인격 **description** 서술, 묘사 **summarize** 요약하다 **transition** (다른 상태로의) 이행 **workfare** 근로 복지 제도 **emphasis** 강조, 주안점 **labor force** 노동력 **access** 접근 **analyze** 분석하다 **evaluate** 평가하다 **salute** 경례를 하다 **stiff** 뻣뻣한, 빽빽한

POINT 09 ★★★★★

비교 대상은 병렬구조를 이뤄야 한다!

둘 이상의 대상을 비교하는 표현에서, 비교 대상은 형태나 문법적 기능이 같아야 한다. 비교구문에 쓰이는 than, to, as 앞뒤 비교 대상이 병렬구조를 이루는지 확인한다.

비교구문에 쓰이는 than, to, as

than	•「비교급 + than」: ~보다 더 …한 •「A rather than B」: B라기보다 차라리 A
to	•「prefer A to B」: B보다 A를 더 좋아하다[선호하다]
as	•「as + 원급 + as」: ~만큼 …한

대표 예문 For instance, it requires **more** energy to make water vibrate (비교 대상(A)) **than** ~~vibrating~~ / to vibrate (비교 대상(B)) air. 기출

▶ 비교구문의 비교 대상은 병렬구조를 이루므로, than 앞의 to부정사구(to make water vibrate)와 대등하도록 to부정사 to vibrate가 오는 것이 적절하다.

기출 예문 PLUS

정답 및 해설 p.12

1 Some students say that **getting** a few extra minutes of sleep is more important than **eating** a bowl of oatmeal, but they're wrong. 기출

2 A given amount of food is used more efficiently by the body if it is **spaced** throughout the day rather than **eaten** at one sitting. 기출

3 Introverts seem to prefer **working** alone or in small groups to **being** in a role requiring a high degree of social interaction.

4 **When you eat** is almost as important as **what you eat**, because the same nutrients have different effects on the body when consumed at different times. 기출

WORDS **vibrate** 진동하다 **space** 간격을 두다 **sitting** 착석; *식사 시간 **introvert** 내성[내향]적인 사람 **interaction** 상호작용 **nutrient** 영양소, 영양분 **consume** 소모하다; *먹다

기출 문장으로 PRACTICE

정답 및 해설 p.12

[01-03] 다음 문장의 네모 안에서 어법상 바른 것을 고르시오.

01 It's much easier for wartime spies to wear the enemy's uniform than [imitating / to imitate] the enemy's language and pronunciation convincingly. 기출

02 The expectation of future interaction motivates people to find positive qualities in others so that they will look forward to future interactions rather than [dread / to dread] them. 기출 응용

03 To predict whether students will achieve their goals, seeing their attitude towards the task may be more useful than [to know / knowing] their score on a measure of conscientiousness. 기출 응용

[04-05] 다음 문장의 밑줄 친 부분이 어법상 바르면 O를 쓰고, 틀리면 바르게 고치시오.

04 The evidence suggests that early human populations preferred consuming the fat and organ meat of the animal to <u>eat</u> its muscle meat. 기출 응용

05 Members share their ideas during regularly scheduled meetings, and information and knowledge are open rather than <u>protected</u> and <u>controlled</u>. 기출 응용

WORDS imitate 흉내내다 pronunciation 발음 convincingly 납득이 가도록 dread 몹시 무서워하다 measure 조치; *척도, 기준 conscientiousness 양심적임, 성실함

1 **다음 글의 밑줄 친 부분 중, 어법상 틀린 것은?** (2016년 6월 고2 학평)

Architecture is generally conceived, designed, and realized in response to an existing set of conditions. These conditions may be ① purely functional in nature, or they may also reflect in varying degrees the social, political, and economic climate. In any case, it is assumed that the existing set of conditions is ② much less satisfactory and that a new set of conditions would be desirable. The initial phase of any design process is the recognition of a problematic condition and the decision ③ to find a solution to it. Design is above all a purposeful endeavor. A designer must first document the existing conditions of a problem and ④ collecting relevant data to be analyzed. This is the critical phase of the design process since the nature of a solution is related to how a problem ⑤ is defined.

POINT 08 적용하기 **등위접속사나 상관접속사가 연결하는 요소는 대등해야 한다!**

1 문장의 구조를 파악해보자.

... must [first document the existing conditions of a problem] and [collecting relevant data to be analyzed].

▶ 등위접속사 and가 동사구를 연결하는 병렬구조이다.

2 접속사 앞에 오는 요소의 형태를 살펴보자.

▶ 조동사 must 뒤에 오는 동사구로, 동사원형으로 시작한다.

3 접속사 뒤에 연결되는 요소의 형태가 대등한지 판단하자.

▶ and 뒤의 요소는 and 앞의 요소와 형태나 문법적 기능이 일치해야 한다.

2 다음 글의 밑줄 친 부분 중, 어법상 틀린 것은? (2017년 6월 고3 모평)

Though most bees fill their days visiting flowers and collecting pollen, some bees take advantage of the hard work of others. These thieving bees sneak into the nest of an ① unsuspecting "normal" bee (known as the host), lay an egg near the pollen mass being gathered by the host bee for her own offspring, and then sneak back out. When the egg of the thief hatches, it kills the host's offspring and then eats the pollen meant for ② its victim. Sometimes called brood parasites, these bees are also referred to as cuckoo bees, because they are similar to cuckoo birds, which lay an egg in the nest of another bird and ③ leaves it for that bird to raise. They are more ④ technically called *cleptoparasites*. Clepto means "thief" in Greek, and the term *cleptoparasite* refers specifically to an organism ⑤ that lives off another by stealing its food. In this case the *cleptoparasite* feeds on the host's hard-earned pollen stores.

*brood parasite: (알을 대신 기르도록 하는) 탁란 동물

WORDS

1 **conceive** (계획 등을) 생각해 내다, 마음속으로 하다 **in response to** ~에 응하여, ~에 답하여 **existing** 기존의, 현재 사용되는 **purely** 순전히, 전적으로 **functional** 기능 위주의 **climate** 기후; *경향, 추세, 풍조 **assume** 추정하다 **satisfactory** 만족스러운, 흡족한 **initial** 초음의, 초기의 **phase** 단계 **purposeful** 목적이 있는, 의도를 가진 **endeavor** 노력, 애씀 **relevant** 관련 있는

2 **pollen** 꽃가루, 화분 **thieve** 도둑질하다 **sneak** 슬그머니 움직이다, 몰래 가다 **unsuspecting** 의심하지 않는, 이상한 낌새를 못 챈 **host** (기생 생물의) 숙주 **mass** 덩어리 **offspring** (사람의) 자식; *(짐승의) 새끼 **hatch** 부화하다 **cuckoo** 뻐꾸기 **technically** 전문적으로는, 엄밀히 말하면 **organism** 생물, 유기체 **live off** ~에 기생하다, ~에 의지해서 살다

Chapter 04

관계사, 접속사, 전치사

UNIT 05

관계사의 쓰임

UNIT 06

관계사, 접속사와 전치사 구분

POINT 10 관계대명사의 쓰임

★★★★

관계대명사는 접속사 역할과 대명사 역할을 한다. 절과 절을 연결하는 자리이고, 뒤에 문장 성분이 빠진 불완전한 절이 올 때는 관계대명사를 써야 한다. 또한 관계대명사의 격은 이어지는 절에 빠져있는 문장 성분과 일치시켜야 한다.

절	+ 관계대명사	+ 불완전한 절
	주격 • 선행사가 사람: who, that • 선행사가 사물, 동물: which, that	주어가 빠진 절
	목적격 • 선행사가 사람: who(m), that • 선행사가 사물, 동물: which, that	목적어가 빠진 절
	소유격 • 선행사가 사람: whose • 선행사가 사물, 동물: whose, of which	소유격 대명사가 빠진 절

❗ 「전치사+관계대명사」 뒤에는 완전한 절이 오는 것에 주의한다.

관계대명사절에서 관계대명사가 전치사의 목적어 역할을 하는 경우, 전치사가 관계대명사 앞으로 와서 「전치사+관계대명사」의 순서로 쓸 수 있으며, 이때 「전치사+관계대명사」 뒤에는 완전한 절이 온다.

❗ 제한적 용법 vs. 계속적 용법

제한적 용법	계속적 용법
관계대명사절이 선행사를 수식하는 형용사절의 역할을 한다. **a.** My brother is in a band [**that** is popular with teenage girls]. **b.** He couldn't find the notebook [**which** he had left on his desk].	**1** 선행사에 대한 부가적인 정보를 제공하며, 관계대명사 앞에 콤마(,)를 써서 나타낸다. **2** 관계대명사 what과 that은 계속적 용법으로 쓸 수 없다. **c.** He met the new secretary**, who** had been hired to replace Tom. **d.** She said she had returned the books, ~~that~~ (→ **which**) turned out to be a lie.

a. 내 남동생은 십 대 소녀들에게 인기가 있는 밴드에 속해 있다. b. 그는 책상 위에 놓아 두었던 공책을 찾을 수 없었다. c. 그는 새 비서를 만났는데, 그 사람은 Tom을 대신하기 위해 고용되었다. d. 그녀는 책을 반납했었다고 말했지만, 그것은 거짓말임이 드러났다.

WORDS secretary 비서 hire 고용하다 replace 대체하다

대표 예문 1 My dream school had offered me a full scholarship, it / which was worth more money than I could even imagine. 기출 응용

선행사 / 주격 관계대명사 / 주어가 빠진 절

▶ 절과 절을 연결하는 접속사 역할을 하면서, 뒤에 오는 절에서 선행사 a full scholarship을 대신하여 주어 역할을 하는 관계대명사 which가 와야 한다.

대표 예문 2 One of the bosses ~~whom~~ / for whom I worked strongly resisted the movement that was popular at the time. 기출 응용

선행사 / = whom[that] I worked for

▶ 선행사 One of bosses는 관계대명사절의 동사 worked의 직접적인 목적어가 아니라 동사가 수반하는 전치사 for의 목적어 역할을 하므로 「전치사+관계대명사」로 써야 한다.

기출 예문 PLUS

정답 및 해설 p.14

1 We can make fur clothing, shelters, and weapons [**with which** we can hunt and defend ourselves]. 기출

2 Andrew, [**who**(**m**) nobody had noticed before the tournament this year], made it to the final match. 기출

3 Consumers buy produce and other goods from local farmers, [**who** buy farm supplies from local businesses]. 기출

4 The person will tend to feel guilty when his or her own conduct violates that principle and to disapprove of others [**whose** behavior conflicts with it]. 기출

WORDS **scholarship** 장학금 **resist** 저항하다, 반대하다 **fur** 털, 모피 **tournament** 경기, 토너먼트 **produce** 농산물, 수확물 **supply** 물품 **guilty** 죄책감이 드는 **conduct** 행위, 처신 **violate** 위반하다 **principle** 원칙, 원리 **disapprove** 못마땅해하다 **conflict** 충돌하다, 대립하다

기출 문장으로 PRACTICE

정답 및 해설 p.14

[01-11] 다음 문장의 네모 안에서 어법상 바른 것을 고르시오.

01 The person on the stage is an average-looking man [his / whose] teeth are not straight. 기출 응용

02 The researchers lengthened the period of daylight [which / to which] the peach trees were exposed. 기출 응용

03 You may lose your job for countless reasons, some of [them / which] you may not even be responsible for. 기출

04 The man riding a pony passed by without stopping, [that / which] caused me to break into a flood of tears. 기출 응용

05 Note-taking is one of the activities [which / by which] students attempt to stay attentive, but it is also an aid to memory. 기출

06 The violinists and pianists [who / whose] names you've heard regularly earn between $30,000 and $50,000 for a single performance. 기출

07 To help kids cut down on lunch bag waste, I have invented a reusable lunch bag, [which / whom] I am now selling on my website. 기출

08 Many people believe that it is critical to share similar, if not identical, beliefs and values with someone [whom / with whom] they have a relationship. 기출

WORDS **straight** 곧은 **lengthen** 길게 하다, 늘이다 **expose** 노출시키다 **countless** 셀 수 없이 많은 **responsible** 책임이 있는 **pony** 조랑말 **attentive** 주의를 기울이는 **reusable** 재사용할 수 있는 **critical** 대단히 중요한 **identical** 동일한

09 I recently saw a news interview with an acquaintance [who / whom] I was certain was going to lie about a few particularly sensitive issues. 기출

10 The train arrived at my destination ten minutes early, [that / which] was perfect, as I was due to present my new idea to the company at 10 a.m. 기출

11 The state of Louisiana voted to outlaw cockfighting. This victory represents a historic achievement for the animal rights movement, [it / which] has fought long and hard to ban cockfighting throughout the country. 기출

*cockfighting: 닭싸움, 투계

[12-15] 다음 문장의 밑줄 친 부분이 어법상 바르면 O를 쓰고, 틀리면 바르게 고치시오.

12 The skillful mechanic has been replaced by a teenager in a uniform <u>which</u> doesn't know anything about cars and couldn't care less. 기출

13 The cooperative herders limit the size of their individual herds, <u>it</u> allows them to maintain a sustainable food supply. 기출

14 The most successful employees are those <u>whom</u> keep their tasks in line with what's most important to the company and its future. 기출

15 An X Games competition is held each summer in Rhode Island. It features sports like sky surfing, <u>which</u> people jump from airplanes with surfboards attached to their feet. 기출

WORDS **acquaintance** 아는 사람, 지인 **sensitive** 세심한; *민감한 **be due to-v** ~할 예정이다 **outlaw** 불법화하다 **represent** 대표하다; *해당[상응]하다 **ban** 금지하다 **cooperative** 협력하는 **herder** 목동 **sustainable** 지속 가능한 **feature** 특별히 포함하다, 특징으로 삼다 **attach** 붙이다

POINT 11 ★★★

관계부사의 쓰임

관계부사는 절과 절을 연결하는 접속사 역할과 동시에 부사 역할을 하므로, 관계부사 뒤에는 빠진 문장 성분이 없는 완전한 절이 와야 한다. 관계부사와 선행사 중 하나는 종종 생략되며, 특히 관계부사 how는 선행사와 함께 쓸 수 없다.

! 관계부사 where은 선행사가 추상적인 의미의 장소일 때도 사용할 수 있다.

a. She found herself in a hopeless situation **where** she didn't know what to do.

a. 그녀는 자신이 어찌 해야 할지 모르는 절망적인 상황에 있음을 알았다.

대표 예문 When Einstein was ten, his family enrolled him in the Luitpold Gymnasium, (장소를 나타내는 선행사) ~~there~~ / where (관계부사) he developed a suspicion of authority. (완전한 절) 기출

▶ 절(his family ... the Luitpold Gymnasium)과 절(he ... authority)을 연결하는 자리이고, 뒤에 완전한 절이 이어지고 있으므로 관계부사 where이 와야 한다. 부사는 절과 절을 연결할 수 없다.

기출 예문 PLUS

정답 및 해설 p.15

1 Aristotle was particularly fascinated with [**how** the masons on the Isle of Lesbos used rulers]. 기출

2 Beginning in the 2nd Century A.D., Taoist and Confucian scholars engaged in a practice known as 'pure talk', [**where** they debated spiritual and philosophical issues].
*Taoist: 도교의 **Confucian: 유교의

3 Life can be like riding a roller coaster. There are ups and downs, fast and slow parts, bumps and shaky parts, and even times [**when** you're upside down]. 기출

4 This effect, which is often overlooked, is a primary reason **why** people doing aerobic exercises establish a new metabolism and a leaner body. 기출

WORDS enroll 입학시키다 suspicion 의심 authority 권위 fascinate 마음을 사로잡다, 매료시키다 mason 석수, 석공 isle 섬 engage in ~에 관여[참여]하다 practice 실행; *관행 spiritual 정신의, 정신적인 philosophical 철학의 overlook 간과하다 primary 주된, 주요한 aerobic 유산소의 metabolism 신진대사 lean 야윈, 마른

기출 문장으로 PRACTICE

정답 및 해설 p.15

[01-06] 다음 문장의 네모 안에서 어법상 바른 것을 고르시오.

01 The riddle was not solved until the 1970s, [when / then] the deep ocean openings were discovered. 기출

02 Life and sports present many situations [there / where] critical and difficult decisions have to be made. 기출

03 In 1887, [then / when] the land was up for sale, Grandpa bought two hundred acres from the Granger family. 기출

04 In Candeal, [there / where] Brown was born, local kids were encouraged to join drum groups, sing, and stage performances. 기출

05 There is absolutely no reason [how / why] any e-commerce enterprise should limit itself to marketing and selling one maker's products. 기출

06 All we have to do nowadays is drive to the supermarket or the fast-food restaurant, [where / there] for a very low price we can obtain nearly all of our daily calories. 기출

[07-08] 다음 문장의 밑줄 친 부분이 어법상 바르면 O를 쓰고, 틀리면 바르게 고치시오.

07 Dr. Paul Odland and his friend Bob travel frequently to South America, <u>there</u> they provide free medical treatment for disabled children from poor families. 기출

08 Fieldwork is the hallmark of cultural anthropology. It is <u>how</u> we explore and learn about the vast detailed intricacy of human culture and individual behavior. 기출

WORDS **riddle** 수수께끼 **opening** 구멍, 틈 **stage** (공연 등을) 무대에 올리다 **e-commerce** 전자 상거래 **enterprise** 기업, 회사 **disabled** 장애를 가진 **fieldwork** 현장 연구 **hallmark** (전형적인) 특징 **anthropology** 인류학 **vast** 어마어마한 **intricacy** 복잡한 사항[내용]

POINT
12 관계대명사 vs. 관계부사

★★★★★

절과 절을 연결하는 자리에 관계대명사를 써야 하는지 관계부사를 써야 하는지를 판단해야 할 경우, 관계사 뒤에 오는 절을 살펴야 한다. 뒤에 불완전한 절이 오면 관계대명사를, 완전한 절이 오면 관계부사를 쓴다. 「관계사+-ever」 형태의 복합관계대명사와 복합관계부사도 뒤에 각각 불완전한 절과 완전한 절이 온다.

! 시간, 장소 등을 나타내는 선행사를 보고 무조건 관계부사를 고르지 않도록 주의한다.

대표 예문 It was a long day, [~~when~~ / which] included picking up my teenager]. 기출

선행사: a long day / 주격 관계대명사: which / 주어가 빠진 불완전한 절: included picking up my teenager

▶ 관계사 뒤에 주어가 없는 불완전한 절이 이어지므로 주격 관계대명사인 which를 써야 한다. 시간을 나타내는 선행사 a long day를 보고 관계부사 when을 고르지 않아야 한다.

기출 예문 PLUS

정답 및 해설 p.16

1 Sometimes we make bad decisions [**which** are irreversible]. 기출

관계대명사 / 불완전한 절(주어가 빠짐)

2 We are entering a time [**when** people will have all of their own medical data and the computing power to process it]. 기출

관계부사 / 완전한 절

3 After enjoying the memorable victory, Andrew headed straight to the nursing home, [**where** his sick grandad had been staying]. 기출

관계부사 / 완전한 절

4 If you are willing to volunteer, there are many organizations [**that** will be glad to welcome you]. [**Whatever** you do], it will almost certainly be rewarding. 기출

관계대명사 / 불완전한 절(주어가 빠짐)
복합관계대명사 / 불완전한 절(목적어가 빠짐)

WORDS irreversible 되돌릴 수 없는 memorable 기억에 남을 head 가다, 향하다 straight 곧장 nursing home 양로원 rewarding 보람 있는

[01-06] 다음 문장의 네모 안에서 어법상 바른 것을 고르시오.

01 Starting next year, the public can tour the house, [where / which] the duke built for his wife in the 17th century. 기출

02 He designed one of his most famous buildings, Fallingwater, [which / where] was built on top of a waterfall. 기출

03 Soy milk is thickened with a mineral salt, forming curds — that's [why / which] tofu's other popular name is "bean curd." 기출

04 During this lengthy process, [whoever / whenever] he feels threatened, he turns back toward the safety of his parents' love and authority. 기출

05 Hurrying doesn't just give us less time; it can also steal the pleasure and benefit from the time [when / which] we do have. 기출

06 For most of recorded history, people lived (A) [where / which] they were born, did (B) [how / what] their parents had done, and associated with those (C) [when / who] were doing the same. 기출

[07-08] 다음 문장의 밑줄 친 부분이 어법상 바르면 O를 쓰고, 틀리면 바르게 고치시오.

07 It is quite a different situation after the loss of a close family member, <u>when</u> some mourning is required to prove your humanity. 기출

08 One domain <u>which</u> this is of considerable significance is music's potentially damaging effects on the ability to drive safely. 기출

WORDS **duke** 공작 **thicken** 걸쭉하게 만들다 **curd** 응유(우유가 응고된 것) **lengthy** 너무 긴 **threatened** 위협당한 **associate** 사귀다, 교제하다 **mourning** 애도 **humanity** 인간성 **domain** 영역, 분야 **considerable** 상당한, 많은 **significance** 중요성 **potentially** 잠재적으로 **damaging** 손상을 주는

POINT 13 ★★★★

what vs. which vs. that

절과 절을 연결하는 자리에서, 관계대명사 what/which/that, 그리고 접속사 that의 쓰임을 구분해야 한다.

관계대명사 what vs. 관계대명사 which[that]	선행사 있음 → 관계대명사 which[that]
	선행사 없음 → 관계대명사 what (선행사 포함)
접속사 that vs. 관계대명사 what/which	뒤에 완전한 절이 이어짐 → 접속사 that
	뒤에 불완전한 절이 이어짐 → 관계대명사 what/which

❗ 관계사 바로 앞에 있는 명사가 항상 선행사는 아니라는 사실에 유의한다!

대표 예문 As the Internet is a familiar resource for young people, it is logical ~~what~~ / **that** (접속사) they would seek assistance from it. (완전한 절) 기출

▶ 절(it is logical)과 절(they ... it)을 연결하는 자리이고, 뒤에 문장 성분이 완전한 절이 이어지고 있으므로, 접속사 that이 와야 한다. 이 문장에서 접속사 that이 이끄는 명사절은 앞의 가주어 it에 대한 진주어 역할을 한다.

기출 예문 PLUS

정답 및 해설 p.17

1 There is probably a supermarket (선행사) close to your home [**that** (관계대명사) sells just {**what** (관계대명사) you want (불완전한 절(목적어가 빠짐))}] (불완전한 절(주어가 빠짐)). 기출 응용

2 Many social scientists have believed for some time [**that** (접속사) birth order directly affects both personality and achievement in adult life (완전한 절)]. 기출

3 Armed only with a book on electricity and some plastic pipes, Kamkwamba built his first windmill (선행사), [**which** (관계대명사) generated enough power to run a light in his room (불완전한 절(주어가 빠짐))]. 기출

WORDS **resource** 자원; *수단 **assistance** 도움, 지원 **arm A with B** A에게 B를 주다[공급하다] **windmill** 풍차 **generate** 발생시키다, 만들어내다

기출 문장으로 PRACTICE

정답 및 해설 p.17

[01-06] 다음 문장의 네모 안에서 어법상 바른 것을 고르시오.

01 The one lesson I have learned is [what / that] there is no substitute for paying attention.

02 Indeed, living things are made of the same tiny particles [that / what] make up nonliving things. 기출

03 When a robot scans a room, it sees nothing but a vast collection of straight and curved lines, [which / what] it converts to pixels. 기출

04 The earliest map is thought to have been made in 7000 B.C. in an ancient city that was in [what / which] is now present-day Turkey. 기출

05 One of the reasons cars have been getting safer is [that / what] we can conduct well-established crash tests with test dummies. 기출

06 The two men were walking up a path, when Conan Doyle heard the other fall behind him. He judged by the sound [that / which] the fall was a mere slip. 기출 응용

[07-08] 다음 문장의 밑줄 친 부분이 어법상 바르면 O를 쓰고, 틀리면 바르게 고치시오.

07 There are things <u>what</u> I remembered about her, but which did not strike me as strange or interesting until quite recently. 기출 응용

08 Even though well over a billion dollars is spent every year on promoting new movies, people talking to people is <u>which</u> really counts. 기출

WORDS substitute 대체물 particle 입자 scan 살피다 vast 광대한 curved 곡선 모양의 convert 전환시키다 conduct (특정한 활동을) 하다 dummy 인체 모형 mere 단지 ~에 불과한 slip 미끄러짐 strike 치다, 부딪치다; *(~하다는) 인상을 주다 promote 촉진하다; *홍보하다 count 중요하다

POINT 14 ★★★★★

전치사 vs. 접속사

일부 전치사와 접속사는 의미가 비슷하더라도 뒤에 이어지는 말의 구조가 완전히 다르다. 전치사 뒤에는 명사(구)가, 접속사 뒤에는 문장 성분이 완전한 절이 와야 한다.

의미	전치사	접속사
~ 때문에	because of + 명사(구)	because + 절
~ 동안에	during + 명사(구)	while + 절
~에도 불구하고	despite[in spite of] + 명사(구)	although[(even) though] + 절

❗ as, after, before, since는 전치사와 접속사로 모두 쓰인다.

대표 예문 ~~Despite~~ / **Though** (접속사) it is true that the overall use of energy is reduced during sleep, (완전한 절) just resting quietly causes almost as much of a reduction. 기출

▶ 전치사 despite와 접속사 though는 모두 '~에도 불구하고'라는 의미를 나타내지만, 뒤에 주어와 동사를 갖춘 완전한 절이 이어지므로, Despite가 아닌 Though가 와야 한다.

기출 예문 PLUS

정답 및 해설 p.18

1 Keith was giving the performance of a lifetime **despite** (전치사) the shortcomings of the piano (명사구). 기출

2 Jessica listened **while** (접속사) the band teacher played the different musical instruments (완전한 절). 기출

3 **During** (전치사) his childhood (명사구), Wright lived in the country and fell in love with the rolling landscape. 기출 응용

4 He started his lecture by saying, "We study philosophy **because of** (전치사) the mental skills (명사구) that it develops." 기출 응용

5 Farmers don't have to worry that their livelihood will be stolen in the night, **because** (접속사) crops can't easily be stolen (완전한 절). 기출

WORDS overall 전반적인 shortcoming 결점, 단점 rolling 완만하게 경사진 landscape 풍경 philosophy 철학 livelihood 생계(의 수단)

기출 문장으로 PRACTICE

정답 및 해설 p.18

[01-05] 다음 문장의 네모 안에서 어법상 바른 것을 고르시오.

01 It's a common practice [during / while] creativity seminars to give participants a bag full of materials and then a problem to solve. 기출

02 It is [because / because of] their communicative properties that intense debates continue over the true role of the arts in today's world. 기출

03 One's memories grow much sharper even after a long passage of time. This is [because / because of] one is looking at the past with fresh eyes. 기출

04 Midsize cars recorded the highest percentage of retail car sales in each of the given years [despite / though] a decrease from 1995 to 2005. 기출

05 [Although / Despite] there are numerous explanations for the fall of the Roman Empire, the deeper cause lies in the declining fertility of its soil and the decrease in agricultural yields. 기출

[06-07] 다음 문장의 밑줄 친 부분이 어법상 바르면 O를 쓰고, 틀리면 바르게 고치시오.

06 The dummy's job is to simulate a human being <u>during</u> a crash is conducted, collecting data that would not be possible to collect from a human occupant. 기출 응용

07 Workers can use their "golden years" to do many of the things they had always hoped to do, but never had the opportunity to do <u>because</u> their 40-plus-hour workweeks. 기출

WORDS **participant** 참가자 **communicative** 통신의, 의사 전달의 **property** 재산; *속성, 특성 **intense** 극심한; *격렬한 **passage** (시간의) 흐름[경과] **retail** 소매 **numerous** 수많은 **fertility** 비옥함 **agricultural** 농업의 **yield** 산출[수확]량 **simulate** ~인 척하다, 흉내내다 **occupant** 사용자; *차에 타고 있는 사람

1 **(A), (B), (C)의 각 네모 안에서 어법에 맞는 표현으로 가장 적절한 것은?** (2012년 6월 고3 모평)

Deseada is a small island which belongs to the Lesser Antilles. This island is said to have obtained its name from the desire Christopher Columbus felt of seeing land on his second voyage in 1493. It is twelve miles in length and six miles in width. The part which looks to the north is lower than (A) [it / that] which looks to the south. The island abounds greatly in iguanas, and in a species of birds called *fragatas*. There is a deep cavern on the island, containing the bones and arms of the Indians, who, it is supposed, (B) [was / were] buried there. In 1762, this island was taken by the English, (C) [who / where] restored it the following year to the French by the Peace of Paris, and since that time it has been in the possession of the latter.

	(A)		(B)		(C)
①	it	……	was	……	who
②	it	……	were	……	where
③	that	……	was	……	who
④	that	……	were	……	who
⑤	that	……	were	……	where

POINT 12 적용하기 **관계대명사 vs. 관계부사**

1 관계사 뒤에 이어지는 절을 살펴보자.

In 1762, this island was taken by the English, [who / where] [restored (동사) it the following year to the French by the Peace of Paris], ...

▶ 동사로 시작하고, 주어가 없는 불완전한 절이 이어진다.

2 관계대명사의 자리인지 관계부사의 자리인지 판단하자.

▶ 관계대명사 뒤에는 불완전한 절이, 관계부사 뒤에는 완전한 절이 이어져야 한다.

2 **(A), (B), (C)의 각 네모 안에서 어법에 맞는 표현으로 가장 적절한 것은? [3점]** (2015년 4월 고3 학평)

Leonardo da Vinci was one of the most learned and well-rounded persons ever to live. The entire universe from the wing of a dragonfly to the birth of the earth (A) [was / were] the playground of his curious intelligence. But did Leonardo have some mystical or innate gift of insight and invention, or was his brilliance learned and earned? Certainly he had an unusual mind and an uncanny ability to see (B) [that / what] others didn't see. But the six thousand pages of detailed notes and drawings present clear evidence of a diligent, curious student—a perpetual learner in laborious pursuit of wisdom who was constantly exploring, questioning, and testing. Expanding your mind is vital to being creative. Therefore, (C) [invest / investing] regularly in learning opportunities is one of the greatest gifts you can give yourself.

(A)		(B)		(C)
① was	……	what	……	investing
② was	……	that	……	invest
③ was	……	what	……	invest
④ were	……	what	……	invest
⑤ were	……	that	……	investing

WORDS

1 **obtain** 얻다, 구하다 **voyage** 항해 **length** 길이 **width** 폭, 너비 **abound** 아주 많다, 풍부하다 **cavern** 동굴 **restore** 회복시키다; *반환하다 **possession** 소유 **latter** (둘 중에서) 후자

2 **well-rounded** 다재다능한 **intelligence** 지능; *지성 **mystical** 신비로운 **innate** 타고난, 선천적인 **insight** 통찰력 **invention** 발명품; *독창성, 창의력 **brilliance** 탁월함 **uncanny** 불가사의한; *뛰어난, 예리한 **perpetual** 끊임없이 계속되는, 영원한 **laborious** 부지런한 **expand** 확대[확장]시키다 **vital** 필수적인

Chapter 05

준동사

UNIT 07

분사와 분사구문

UNIT 08

to부정사와 동명사

POINT 15 ★★★★★

의미가 '~하는'이면 현재분사를, '~되는'이면 과거분사를 써라!

분사는 형용사처럼 명사를 수식하거나 보어로 쓰이고, 분사구문에 쓰여 부사구를 이끌기도 한다. 분사와 분사의 의미상 주어 사이의 관계가 능동(~하는)이나 진행(~하고 있는)의 의미이면 현재분사(v-ing)를, 수동(~되는)이나 완료(~한)의 의미이면 과거분사(p.p.)를 쓴다.

분사가 명사를 수식하는 경우	분사와 명사의 관계가 능동 → 현재분사 분사와 명사의 관계가 수동 → 과거분사 **a.** Who is the boy **weeping** quietly in the corner of the room? **b.** They were asked to fix the **damaged** wall immediately.
분사가 주격[목적격]보어인 경우	분사와 주어[목적어]의 관계가 능동 → 현재분사 분사와 주어[목적어]의 관계가 수동 → 과거분사 **c.** Tommy sat **swinging** his legs. **d.** He has left the door to the attic **closed** since then.
분사구문인 경우	분사와 의미상 주어의 관계가 능동 → 현재분사 분사와 의미상 주어의 관계가 수동 → 과거분사 **e.** **Finding** some clues, the police were able to solve the case. **f.** **Treated** with great care, his bike was as good as new.
「with+(대)명사+분사」 구문인 경우	분사와 (대)명사와의 관계가 능동 → 현재분사 분사와 (대)명사와의 관계가 수동 → 과거분사 **g.** She sat on the sofa **with** her cat **sitting** on her lap. **h.** **With** the TV **turned** off, they could focus on the conversation.

a. 방 구석에서 조용히 울고 있는 소년은 누구인가? b. 그들은 파손된 벽을 즉시 고쳐달라고 요청 받았다. c. Tommy는 다리를 흔들며 앉아 있었다. d. 그는 그 이후로 다락방으로 이어지는 문을 닫아두었다. e. 몇 가지 단서를 찾아서, 경찰은 그 사건을 해결할 수 있었다. f. 아주 주의 깊게 다뤄져서, 그의 자전거는 새것만큼 좋았다. g. 그녀는 고양이가 그녀의 무릎에 앉아있는 채로 소파에 앉아있었다. h. 텔레비전이 꺼진 채로, 그들은 대화에 집중할 수 있었다.

WORDS weep 울다, 눈물을 흘리다 immediately 즉시 attic 다락(방) clue 단서, 실마리 case 경우; *(경찰이 조사 중인) 사건

대표 예문 John Wooden, a basketball coach, often described his team as a finely ~~tuning~~ / tuned automobile. 기출

▶ 뒤에 오는 명사 automobile을 수식하는 분사이고, automobile은 '조율되는' 대상이므로, 수동의 의미를 나타내는 과거분사 tuned가 오는 것이 적절하다.

기출 예문 PLUS

정답 및 해설 p.20

1 He felt the dreadful, cold sweat **running** down his back. 기출

2 He spent so much of his lifetime **involved** in art that he ignored his official duties. 기출 응용

3 **Asked** to recall what they had read, they remembered the description as being more positive than it was. 기출

4 People pay attention to information that supports their viewpoints, while **ignoring** evidence to the contrary. 기출

5 Adolescents have been quick to immerse themselves in technology, **with** most **using** the Internet to communicate. 기출

6 Picture two programmers working side by side. One man is leaning back in his chair **with** his eyes **closed** and his feet on the desk. 기출

7 The court clerk usually shows a movie **outlining** what is going to happen throughout the day as the jury is chosen for a particular trial. 기출

WORDS **finely** 정교하게 **tune** 조율하다, 최고 상태로 조정하다 **dreadful** 불쾌한 **involve** 수반하다; *몰두하다 **recall** 기억해내다 **description** 설명, 묘사 **viewpoint** 관점, 시각 **evidence** 증거, 근거 **to the contrary** 그와 반대의, 그 반대를 보여주는 **adolescent** 청소년 **immerse** 몰두하다 **lean** 기대다 **court clerk** 법원서기 **outline** 개요를 서술하다 **jury** 배심원단

기출 문장으로 PRACTICE

정답 및 해설 p.20

[01-12] 다음 문장의 네모 안에서 어법상 바른 것을 고르시오.

01 With Bob [acting / acted] as his interpreter, Paul offered $300 and his opponent proposed $450. 기출 응용

02 It will enable you to see opportunities and utilize resources which may otherwise have remained [hiding / hidden]. 기출

03 When [installing / installed] in a window frame, the glass would be placed with the thicker side down for the sake of stability. 기출

04 He described his daily routine of strolling through the village [observing / observed] the intimate details of family life. 기출

05 With the phone number of a professional surfer [folding / folded] in her pocket, she felt the promise of an exciting new life. 기출

06 In the Paleolithic age, the hunters [arming / armed] only with primitive weapons were no real match for an angry mammoth. 기출 응용
*Paleolithic: 구석기 시대의

07 Remove all residual moisture by drawing it away with a vacuum cleaner [holding / held] over the affected areas for up to 20 minutes. 기출

08 [Assuming / Assumed] to possess a substantial amount of water, Mars is probably most habitable of all the planets in our solar system. 기출

WORDS
interpreter 통역자 **opponent** 상대 **utilize** 활용하다, 이용하다 **install** 설치하다 **for the sake of** ~을 위해서 **stability** 안정(성) **stroll** 거닐다, 산책하다 **intimate** 친밀한; *사적인 **surfer** 파도타기를 하는 사람 **promise** 약속; *(좋은 일이 있을) 징조 **arm** 무장시키다 **primitive** 원시적인 **match** 경기; *맞수 **residual** 남은, 잔여의 **assume** 추정하다 **substantial** 상당한 **habitable** 거주할 수 있는, 살기에 적합한

09 It is said that when babies watch their mom [experiencing / experienced] sad feelings, they can recognize it by instinct.

10 Birth order may define your role within a family, but as you mature into adulthood, [accepted / accepting] other social roles, birth order becomes insignificant. 기출

11 After the conquests, the enormous wealth [bringing / brought] back to Italy allowed middle- and upper-class women to run things with more independence and power. 기출

12 We hope you will consider contributing generously to our fund. You'll get a great feeling [known / knowing] you're helping support the formation of future leaders in the profession. 기출

[13-15] 다음 문장의 밑줄 친 부분이 어법상 바르면 O를 쓰고, 틀리면 바르게 고치시오.

13 <u>Situating</u> at an elevation of 1,350 m, the city of Kathmandu enjoys a warm climate year-round. 기출

14 The rule sounded sensible and quickly caught on, with over a hundred other local councils <u>followed</u> it within a few years. 기출

15 The habit of reading newspapers has been on the decline, and some of the dollars previously <u>spending</u> on newspaper advertising have migrated to the Internet. 기출

WORDS **experience** 경험하다; *(감정 · 느낌을) 느끼다 **instinct** 본능 **define** 정의하다 **mature** 다 자라다, 어른이 되다 **insignificant** 중요하지 않은 **conquest** 정복 **enormous** 막대한 **independence** 독립, 자립 **contribute** 기부하다 **fund** 기금 **formation** 형성, 육성 **profession** (전문적인) 직업[직종] **situate** 두다, 위치시키다 **elevation** 승진; *고도, 해발 높이 **year-round** 연중 계속되는 **sensible** 합리적인 **catch on** 유행하다 **council** 의회 **migrate** 이동하다

POINT 16 ★★★★★

감정을 나타내는 분사: v-ing vs. p.p.

감정을 나타내는 동사는 분사 형태로 자주 쓰는데, '(의미상 주어가) ~한 감정을 유발하는'의 의미일 경우 현재분사를 쓰고, '(의미상 주어가) ~한 감정을 느끼는'의 의미일 경우 과거분사를 쓴다. 감정을 나타내는 동사로는 excite, interest, surprise, bore, shock, annoy, depress, satisfy, please, embarrass, confuse, amaze, disappoint, frighten 등이 있다.

대표 예문 Thus pets are important in the treatment of ~~depressing~~ / depressed (과거분사(~한 감정을 느끼는)) or chronically ill patients (분사의 의미상 주어). 기출

▶ 감정을 나타내는 분사가 명사 patients를 수식하고 있는데, patients가 '우울한 감정을 느끼는'이라는 의미이므로, 과거분사 depressed를 쓴다.

기출 예문 PLUS

정답 및 해설 p.21

1 It should not be **surprising** that students learn better when they cooperate. 기출

2 The presentation went better than expected, and my manager seemed particularly **pleased**. 기출

3 It started out like any other day. I had no idea that I was in for one of the most **terrifying** experiences of my life. 기출

4 A flock of **frightened** children was standing close behind Amy Brown, who was about to confront the intruder.

WORDS chronically 만성적으로 cooperate 협력하다, 협동하다 particularly 특히 be in for ~을 당할[겪게 될] 상황이다 flock 무리, 떼 confront 직면하다; *맞서다 intruder 침입자

기출 문장으로 PRACTICE

정답 및 해설 p.21

[01-05] 다음 문장의 네모 안에서 어법상 바른 것을 고르시오.

01 Andrew was greatly [delighting / delighted] with the fact that his grandad was recovering. 기출 응용

02 Most readers of reports and papers are reading the documents because they are [interesting / interested] in the subject. 기출

03 Being musicians and playing together in a group looked like more fun and was more [satisfying / satisfied] than being criminals. 기출 응용

04 When you are feeling [overwhelming / overwhelmed] by presentations, paper deadlines, or tests, you will spend all your time dealing with the pressure. 기출

05 In one study, chimps had to choose between two plates holding a different number of treats. If a chimp pointed to the plate with more treats, that plate would be given to another chimp, and the [frustrating / frustrated] subject would receive the smaller amount. 기출 응용

[06-07] 다음 문장의 밑줄 친 부분이 어법상 바르면 O를 쓰고, 틀리면 바르게 고치시오.

06 Acknowledge your feelings, good or bad. Just saying to yourself, or someone else, "I was <u>frightening</u>" is a great start. 기출 응용

07 If you've ever gone snorkeling, you may have seen an <u>amazed</u> sight: an entire school of fish suddenly changing direction as one unit. 기출

WORDS **document** 서류, 문서 **subject** 주제, 화제; 연구 대상, 피실험자 **overwhelm** (감정이) 압도하다 **deadline** 기한, 마감 시간 **plate** 접시 **treat** 즐거움을 주는 것; *간식 **acknowledge** 인정하다 **school** 떼, 무리

POINT 17 ★★★★★

동사의 목적어로 쓰이는 to부정사 vs. 동명사

to부정사와 동명사는 명사처럼 동사의 목적어로 쓰일 수 있다. 목적어로 to부정사를 써야 하는지 동명사를 써야 하는지는 동사에 따라 결정되므로, 동사를 파악하여 알맞은 형태의 목적어를 써야 한다.

1 to부정사를 목적어로 취하는 동사: agree, want, decide, hope, expect, refuse, plan, wish 등

2 동명사를 목적어로 취하는 동사: avoid, mind, enjoy, consider, deny, finish, give up, suggest, stop 등

※ 「stop to-v」: stop 뒤에 오는 to부정사는 부사적 용법의 to부정사로, '~하기 위해 멈추다'라는 의미이다.

3 to부정사와 동명사를 모두 목적어로 취하는 동사

- 의미 차이가 없는 경우: love, like, start, begin, hate, continue
- 의미 차이가 있는 경우: remember, forget, regret, try

❗ 목적어로 쓰인 to부정사는 주로 미래의 일(~할 것)을, 동명사는 주로 과거의 일(~한 것)을 나타낸다.

대표 예문 Legend has it that a poor public official was so honest that he refused (to부정사를 목적어로 취하는 동사) ~~taking~~ / to take (목적어) bribes. 기출

▶ refuse는 to부정사를 목적어로 취하는 동사이므로, to take가 오는 것이 알맞다.

기출 예문 PLUS

정답 및 해설 p.22

1 Before long, he regretted **leaving** the sunny weather and exciting lifestyle of Los Angeles. 기출

2 These caravans can be moved, and many people **enjoy** traveling from place to place with them. 기출

3 Though he tried **to ignore** their troubles, Paul soon found himself caring for them and sharing his home with them. 기출

4 He remembered **seeing** a pocket compass when he was five years old and **marveling** that the needle always pointed north. 기출

WORDS bribe 뇌물 caravan 이동식 주택 care for ~을 보살피다 compass 나침반 marvel ~에 놀라다, 경탄하다

기출 문장으로 PRACTICE

정답 및 해설 p.22

[01-05] 다음 문장의 네모 안에서 어법상 바른 것을 고르시오.

01 If you ever do fall into quicksand, remember (A) [staying / to stay] calm and not to move until you've stopped (B) [to sink / sinking]. 기출

*quicksand: 유사(아래로 흘러내리는 모래)

02 She had a very good voice, although some of her high notes tended to sound like a gate which someone had forgotten [oiling / to oil]. 기출

03 As he had decided (A) [to do / doing] something about the stubborn extra pounds he'd been carrying, he considered (B) [to take / taking] up various sports. 기출 응용

04 I was feeling pretty good until, a couple of blocks later, she stopped [to let / letting] a few more cars into the line, causing both of us to miss the next light. 기출

05 Everyone who heard the story wanted (A) [to congratulate / congratulating] the man, but he shied away from the media and avoided (B) [to be / being] filmed. 기출

[06-07] 다음 문장의 밑줄 친 부분이 어법상 바르면 O를 쓰고, 틀리면 바르게 고치시오.

06 The next day, he regretted <u>to fight</u> with his best friend but hesitated about whether he should call Paul first. 기출 응용

07 If you want to suck the liquid out of the inner parts of a phone that has fallen into the water, try <u>using</u> a vacuum cleaner. 기출 응용

WORDS sink 가라앉다, 빠지다 stubborn 고집스러운; *없애기 어려운 take up ~을 시작하다 shy away from ~을 피하다 hesitate 망설이다, 주저하다 suck 빨아내다

POINT 18 ★★★★★

명사 vs. 동명사

문장의 주어, 목적어, 보어 자리에는 명사와 동명사가 모두 올 수 있다. 하지만, 동명사는 동사적 성질을 가지고 있어서 목적어를 취할 수 있고 부사의 수식을 받을 수 있는 반면, 명사는 전치사 없이 뒤에 명사를 취할 수 없다.

대표 예문 Traditionally, intellectual property has only played a small role in(전치사) ~~promotion~~ / promoting(동명사(전치사의 목적어)) basic science(동명사의 목적어). 기출

▶ 전치사 in의 목적어 역할을 하면서 동시에 목적어(basic science)를 취할 수 있는 동명사 promoting이 와야 한다.

기출 예문 PLUS

정답 및 해설 p.23

1 Ultrasound, an imaging technique, produces an image by **bouncing** sound waves off an object inside the body. 기출

2 However, **increasing** the frequency of advertising costs more money, and advertising is most expensive where it is most effective. 기출

3 The brown tree snake is infamous for **causing** the extinction of the majority of native bird species in Guam. 기출

4 As the sea conditions will be rough along and off the eastern coast, the weather office has suggested the **suspension** of all fishing operations.

WORDS intellectual property 지적 재산 ultrasound 초음파 bounce 튀어오르게 하다 frequency 빈도 infamous 악명 높은 extinction 멸종 suspension 정지, 보류

기출 문장으로 PRACTICE

정답 및 해설 p.23

[01-07] 다음 문장의 네모 안에서 어법상 바른 것을 고르시오.

01 I would like to thank you for [approval / approving] my request that the company pay for my college tuition. 기출

02 A forest fire in Brazil can affect the weather in Moscow by [creation / creating] huge dust clouds that eventually float over Russia. 기출

03 College life is busy. Activities, friends, and pastimes may cause some difficulties in your [performance / performing] the real job at hand. 기출

04 As a system for [transmission / transmitting] specific factual information, the sign system of honeybees may be superior to that of human beings. 기출

05 Since the fifteenth century, this tradition has been concerned with [recognition / recognizing] individual achievements. 기출

06 By comparison, the [evaluating / evaluation] of performances in events such as gymnastics and figure skating is more subjective, although elaborate scoring rules help make it more objective. 기출 응용

07 Instead of [avoidance / avoiding] one another and hiding from predators through camouflage and inactivity, desert locusts gather in vast groups and overwhelm their predators simply through numbers. 기출

*desert locust: 이집트 땅메뚜기

WORDS **approval** 인정; *승인 **tuition** 수업료 **pastime** 오락 **at hand** 가까이에 (있는) **transmit** 전송하다 **factual** 사실에 입각한 **superior** 우수한 **gymnastics** 체조 **subjective** 주관적인 **elaborate** 정교한 **objective** 객관적인 **predator** 포식자 **camouflage** 위장 **overwhelm** 제압하다

POINT 19 ★★★★★

to부정사와 「전치사 to+동명사」를 구분하라!

to부정사를 쓸지 「전치사 to+동명사」를 쓸지는 to 앞의 어구에 따라 결정된다. 주로 「be+형용사」 뒤에 부사적 용법의 to부정사가 오며, 일부 동사나 표현은 뒤에 「전치사 to+동명사」를 수반한다.

to부정사를 쓰는 경우	「전치사 to + 동명사」를 쓰는 경우
• be used to-v: ~하는 데 사용되다 • be likely to-v: ~할 것 같다 • be willing to-v: 기꺼이 ~하다 • be inclined to-v: ~하고 싶다, ~하는 경향이 있다 • be reluctant to-v: ~하기를 꺼리다 • be sure[certain] to-v: 반드시 ~하다 • be eager to-v: ~하고 싶어 하다 • be due to-v: ~할 예정이다	• be used to v-ing: ~하는 것에 익숙하다 • be opposed to v-ing: ~하는 것에 반대하다 • object to v-ing: ~하는 것에 반대하다 • look forward to v-ing: ~하는 것을 고대하다 • devote oneself to v-ing: ~하는 것에 헌신하다 • adjust to v-ing: ~하는 것에 적응하다 • when it comes to v-ing: ~하는 것에 관한 한

❗ 「be used」 뒤에는 to부정사(~하는 데 사용되다)와 「to+동명사」(~하는 것에 익숙하다)가 모두 올 수 있으나 의미가 달라지는 것에 주의한다.

대표 예문 In India, debate was used to [settle / ~~settling~~] religious controversies and was a very popular form of entertainment. 기출
(was used: 사용되다 / settle: to부정사)

▶ '토론이 논란을 해결하는 데 사용되었다'라는 의미가 적절하므로, to부정사인 to settle이 되어야 한다.

기출 예문 PLUS

정답 및 해설 p.23

1 I look forward **to hearing** from you soon. 기출

2 In the modern world, people are not used **to living** with discomfort. 기출

3 Motivated by feelings of guilt, they are inclined **to make** amends for their actions. 기출

4 He was willing **to fight** in response to even the slightest challenge to his reputation. 기출

WORDS settle 해결하다 religious 종교의 controversy 논란 discomfort 불편 amends (*pl.*) 변상, 보상 reputation 명성

기출 문장으로 PRACTICE

정답 및 해설 p.24

[01-07] 다음 문장의 네모 안에서 어법상 바른 것을 고르시오.

01 The term "multitasking" didn't exist until the 1960s. At first it was used to [describe / describing] computers, not people. 기출 응용

02 I know a father who devoted himself earnestly to [photograph / photographing] the birth of his first and only child. 기출

03 Large animals such as elephants are more likely than small animals to [use / using] vibrations in the soil for communication. 기출

04 When I got back to my hotel room after taking a lot of pictures, I was eager to [upload / uploading] the photos to my blog. 기출

05 Some people are so used to [hear / hearing] their inner critics that they don't even notice when they're putting themselves down. 기출 응용

06 When people try to control situations that are essentially uncontrollable, they are inclined to [experience / experiencing] high levels of stress. 기출

07 When it comes to [plan / planning] the talk you intend to have with others, choosing words carefully becomes even more important. 기출 응용

WORDS **earnestly** 진지하게, 진정으로 **vibration** 진동 **put down** 깎아내리다, 비하하다 **essentially** 근본적으로 **uncontrollable** 통제할 수 없는 **intend** 의도하다, (~하려고) 생각하다

1 **다음 글의 밑줄 친 부분 중, 어법상 틀린 것은? [3점]** (2014년 6월 고2 학평)

Jack Welch is considered to be one of the USA's top business leaders. In a gesture ① that was at once symbolic and real, Welch directed the ceremonial burning of the old-fashioned GE Blue Books. The Blue Books were a series of management training manuals that told how GE managers were to get tasks ② done in the organization. Despite the fact that these books for training ③ had not been used for some 15 years, they still had great influence over the actions of GE managers. ④ Cited the need for managers to write their own answers to day-to-day management challenges, Welch swept away the old order by removing the Blue Books from the organization's culture. Now, GE managers are taught to find their own solutions rather than ⑤ look them up in a dusty old book.

POINT 15 적용하기 **의미가 '~하는'이면 현재분사를, '~되는'이면 과거분사를 써라!**

1 분사의 의미상 주어를 파악하자.

> [Cited the need for managers to write their own answers …], Welch swept away the old order ….
> (Welch: 분사의 의미상 주어)

▶ Cited 이하는 접속사와 주어가 생략된 분사구문으로, 분사의 의미상 주어는 뒤에 이어지는 주절의 주어와 같다.

2 분사의 의미상 주어와 분사와의 관계를 따져보자.

▶ 주어와 분사의 관계가 능동(~하는)이면 현재분사를, 수동(~되는)이면 과거분사를 쓴다.

정답 및 해설 p.24

2 **(A)~(C)에서 어법에 맞는 표현을 바르게 짝지은 것은?** (2012년 4월 고3 학평)

Double Dutch is a style of jumping rope in which there are two participants turning two ropes while either one or two participants jump through the ropes. Double Dutch is a dynamic form of jumping rope that kids really love. In addition to its (A) [is / being] a beneficial cardiovascular exercise, Double Dutch also improves coordination and quickness. Furthermore, because it requires three to four participants working closely together, it is also great for (B) [development / developing] cooperative skills among children. At the most advanced levels, Double Dutch is also being done as an extreme competition sport (C) [where / which] groups of kids are doing high-energy dancing routines that are truly amazing.

*cardiovascular: 심장 혈관의

	(A)		(B)		(C)
①	is	……	development	……	where
②	is	……	developing	……	which
③	being	……	development	……	which
④	being	……	developing	……	which
⑤	being	……	developing	……	where

WORDS

1 **gesture** 몸짓; *표현 **symbolic** 상징적인 **direct** 지시[명령]하다 **ceremonial** 의식의 **cite** 인용하다, 언급하다 **sweep away** ~을 완전히 없애다

2 **dynamic** 역동적인 **beneficial** 유익한, 이로운 **coordination** (신체 동작의) 조정력 **quickness** (움직임 등이) 빠름 **cooperative** 협력[협동]하는 **routine** 정해진 동작

Chapter

06

동사 I

UNIT 09

시제

UNIT 10

가정법

POINT 20 ★★★★★

단순 과거 시제 vs. 완료 시제

단순히 과거에 일어난 일은 단순 과거 시제로 나타낸다. 과거에 일어난 일이 현재(기준 시점)까지 영향을 미칠 때는 현재완료(have p.p.)를 쓴다. 대과거를 나타내거나 과거 이전의 일이 과거(기준 시점)까지 영향을 미칠 때는 과거완료(had p.p.)를 쓴다.

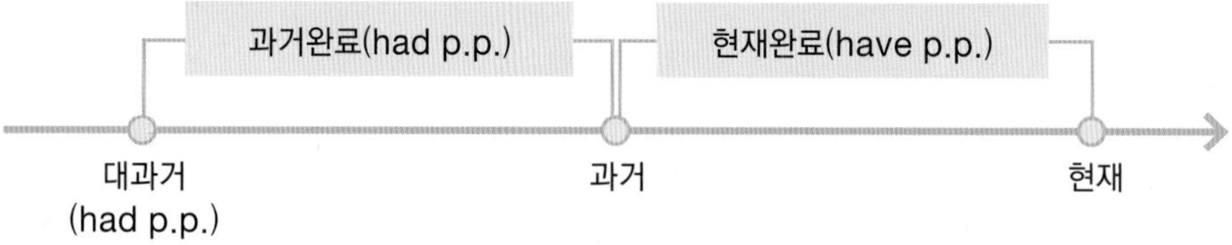

❗ 완료 시제는 시간 부사의 사용을 주의해야 한다.

완료 시제와 함께 쓰이는 부사(구/절)	완료 시제와 쓸 수 없는 부사(구/절)
「since+과거 시점」, 「for+기간」, how long, once, already, ever, never, before 등	yesterday, ~ ago, last week/night, 「in+연도」, when절 등 분명한 과거를 나타내는 표현

대표 예문 **Since** its debut in 2000 (since + 과거 시점), an American drama (주어) [centered around crime scene investigation] **has become** / ~~became~~ (동사(현재완료 시제)) very popular. 기출

▶ 과거 시점(its debut in 2000)부터 현재까지 계속되는 상태를 말하고 있으므로, 현재완료 시제인 has become이 알맞다.

기출 예문 PLUS

정답 및 해설 p.26

1 Twenty thousand years ago (과거를 나타내는 부사구), sea level **was** so low that dry land **joined** what are now separate continents. 기출

2 Kate and Joan, who **had** not **seen** each other for three months (for + 기간), **were** chatting happily in Joan's apartment.

3 Since the introduction of automotive crash testing (since + 과거 시점), the number of people killed and injured by motor vehicles **has decreased** in many countries. 기출

WORDS **debut** 첫 공개[등장] **center** 집중시키다 **investigation** 수사 **separate** 분리된 **continent** 대륙 **introduction** 도입 **automotive** 자동차의 **vehicle** 차량, 탈것

기출 문장으로 PRACTICE

정답 및 해설 p.26

[01-04] 다음 문장의 네모 안에서 어법상 바른 것을 고르시오.

01 It [has rained / had rained] earlier that week and the river was brown and swollen. 기출

02 James, you [have been / had been] with us for six years now. How would you feel if I were to offer you the Sales Director position in London? 기출

03 Since the 1980's, zoos [strived / have strived] to reproduce the natural habitats of their animals, replacing concrete floors and steel bars with grass, rocks, and pools of water. 기출

04 Human beings [discovered / have discovered] how to form a thread by twisting fibers thousands of years ago, and they have invented several devices to make it easier and faster. 기출 응용

[05-06] 다음 문장의 밑줄 친 부분이 어법상 바르면 O를 쓰고, 틀리면 바르게 고치시오.

05 It was only in 1837, with the invention of the electric telegraph, that the traditional link between transport and the communication of messages <u>has been</u> broken. 기출

06 In January 2000, J. K. Rowling sent an email to Catie Hoch, an eight-year-old girl suffering from cancer, who she <u>had heard</u> about. 기출

WORDS **swollen** 불어난 **strive** 분투하다 **reproduce** 재생[재현]하다 **habitat** 서식지 **thread** 실 **fiber** 섬유 **telegraph** 전신 **transport** 운송, 수송

POINT 21 ★★★★★

「조동사+동사원형」 vs. 「조동사+have p.p.」

「조동사+동사원형」은 현재나 미래의 일에 대한 추측, 가능성 등을 나타내는 반면, 「조동사+have p.p.」는 과거의 일에 대한 추측, 가능성, 후회 등을 나타낸다. 과거의 일에 대해 말하고 있다면, 조동사 뒤에는 「have p.p.」가 와야 한다.

❗ 「조동사+have p.p.」의 의미

- 「may[might] have p.p.」: ~했을지도 모른다(약한 추측)
- 「could have p.p.」: ~했을 수도 있다(불확실한 추측)
- 「should have p.p.」: ~했어야 했다(후회)
- 「would have p.p.」: ~했을 것이다(확실한 추측)
- 「must have p.p.」: ~했음이 틀림없다(강한 추측)
- 「cannot have p.p.」: ~했을 리가 없다(강한 부정적 추측)
- 「shouldn't have p.p.」: ~하지 말았어야 했다(후회)

대표 예문 The Rust Belt's thick fog may [~~help~~ / have helped] (과거의 일에 대한 추측) slow down the effects of climate change, particularly when it **was** thickest (과거 시제). 기출

▶ 과거의 일에 대한 추측을 나타내고 있으므로, 조동사 may 뒤에 have helped가 오는 것이 알맞다.

기출 예문 PLUS

정답 및 해설 p.26

1 The worker with his feet up on the desk **could be** thinking, and the other one **may be** too busy typing to pay attention. 기출 응용

2 No Stone Age ten-year-old **would have been** living on tender foods like modern potato chips, hamburgers, and pasta. 기출

3 There are lots of myths about preventing bad breath. Here are two things you **might have heard** about bad breath that are not true. 기출 응용

WORDS type 타자 치다 live on ~을 먹고 살다 tender 부드러운, 씹기 쉬운 myth 신화; *(근거 없는) 이야기 bad breath 입 냄새

기출 문장으로 PRACTICE

정답 및 해설 p.27

[01-04] 다음 문장의 네모 안에서 어법상 바른 것을 고르시오.

01 When you finished shopping, you may [leave / have left] the parking spot with a certain hesitation, particularly if someone else was waiting for it. 기출

02 In an ancient tribe living in small huts in a tiny village settlement, a mother would [be / have been] able to hear any of the babies crying in the night. 기출

03 First, everyone who has been summoned to appear at jury duty must [arrive / have arrived] by nine o'clock in the morning and assemble in the jury room. 기출

04 The man riding a pony said, "I've been looking all over for your house. I should [be / have been] here at 7. Your father told me to bring the pony here and leave him for you." 기출 응용

[05-06] 다음 문장의 밑줄 친 부분이 어법상 바르면 O를 쓰고, 틀리면 바르게 고치시오.

05 Like most parents, you might <u>spend</u> money on a toy that your child didn't play with very much. 기출 응용

06 Australia was colonized 45,000 years ago by pioneers spreading east from Africa. The vanguard of such a migration must <u>be</u> small in number. 기출

WORDS **hesitation** 주저, 망설임 **tribe** 부족 **hut** 오두막 **settlement** 정착지 **summon** 소환하다 **jury** 배심원 **assemble** 모이다 **pony** 조랑말 **colonize** 식민지로 만들다 **pioneer** 개척자 **vanguard** 선두, 선봉 **migration** 이주

POINT 22 ★★★★★

가정법 과거 vs. 가정법 과거완료

가정법 과거와 가정법 과거완료는 가정하는 시점과 동사의 시제가 다르므로, 문맥을 통해 가정하는 시점을 파악하여 알맞은 형태의 동사를 써야 한다.

「가정법 과거」	1 현재 사실과 반대되는 일을 가정 2 「If+주어+**동사의 과거형**, 주어+조동사의 과거형+**동사원형**」: '(만약) ~라면 …할 텐데'
「가정법 과거완료」	1 과거 사실과 반대되는 일을 가정 2 「If+주어+**had p.p.**, 주어+조동사의 과거형+**have p.p.**」: '(만약) ~했더라면 …했을 텐데'

「I wish 가정법」과 「as if[though] 가정법」

「I wish 가정법」과 「as if[though] 가정법」은 주절과 같은 시점의 일을 가정할 경우 「가정법 과거(주어+동사의 과거형)」를 쓰고, 주절보다 앞선 시점의 일을 가정할 경우 「가정법 과거완료(주어+had p.p.)」를 쓴다.

대표 예문 **If** the fleeing Nazis ~~destroyed~~ / had destroyed the bridge, the Ponte Vecchio, she **would have** never **seen** it. 기출 응용

if절 동사 형태: had p.p.

주절의 동사 형태: 조동사의 과거형+have p.p.

▶ 과거 사실과 반대되는 일을 가정하는 가정법 과거완료로, 주절의 동사가 「조동사의 과거형 + have p.p.」의 형태이므로 if절의 동사로 과거완료 형태인 had destroyed가 와야 한다.

기출 예문 PLUS

정답 및 해설 p.27

1 **If** someone **told** you that the Chinese Emperor Qin Shi Huang was a cruel ruler, **would** you simply **accept** this as the truth? 기출

2 When your friend scores the winning goal during a critical soccer match, you take delight in her victory celebrations **as if**, by association, it **were** your victory too. 기출

3 He knew the person who fell down was sensitive and easily embarrassed, so he did not turn; instead, he strode on **as if** he **had heard** nothing. 기출 응용

WORDS flee 도망치다 emperor 황제 cruel 잔인한 ruler 통치자 take delight in ~에 기쁨을 느끼다 association 연관, 연상 stride 성큼성큼 걷다

기출 문장으로 PRACTICE

정답 및 해설 p.27

[01-05] 다음 문장의 네모 안에서 어법상 바른 것을 고르시오.

01 If the people [knew / had known] they were being tested, everyone would instantly come to the aid of the stranger. 기출

02 If you heard someone say your name, even if you were being pushed around in a big noisy crowd, you would [pay / have paid] attention and listen. 기출

03 The fire destroyed an entire block of homes in the suburbs. It would not have spread so far and so quickly if our firefighters [were / had been] able to arrive at the scene in time. 기출 응용

04 If our ancestors hadn't agonized over losses and instead had taken too many chances in going after the big gains, they'd [be / have been] more likely to lose out and never become anyone's ancestor. 기출

05 When two different species use the same resource and the resource is scarce, the two species must compete against each other just as if they [were / have been] members of the same population. 기출 응용

WORDS **instantly** 즉각, 즉시 **come to the aid of** ~을 돕기 위해 찾아오다 **suburb** 교외 **agonize** 몹시 괴로워하다 **take a chance** 위험을 감수하다 **lose out** 멸망하다 **scarce** 부족한, 드문 **population** 개체군, 집단

1 **다음 글의 밑줄 친 부분 중, 어법상 틀린 것은?** (2011년 3월 고3 학평)

Archaeologist Mark Aldenderfer set out last year to explore remote cliffside caves in Nepal's Mustang district, aiming to find human remains near an ancient settlement ① high in the Himalayas. Almost at once, he came face-to-face with ② what he was seeking: Sticking out from the rock, a skull was looking at him right ③ as he was looking at it. The skull, dating back perhaps 2,500 years, was among many human bones ④ piled inside several burial caves. Aldenderfer and his team hope that DNA analysis will pinpoint the origins of this isolated region's inhabitants, who may ⑤ migrate from the Tibetan Plateau or southern points.

POINT 21 적용하기 「조동사+동사원형」 vs. 「조동사+have p.p.」

1 동사 앞의 조동사의 의미를 파악하자.

… DNA analysis will pinpoint the origins of this isolated region's inhabitants, who may migrate from the Tibetan Plateau or southern points.

▶ 동사 may는 '~일지도 모른다'라는 추측의 의미를 나타낸다.

2 현재 시점의 일인지, 과거 시점의 일인지를 파악하자.

The skull, dating back perhaps 2,500 years, was among many human bones piled inside several burial caves. … DNA analysis will pinpoint the origins of this isolated region's inhabitants, who may migrate from the Tibetan Plateau or southern points.

▶ 동사(migrate)의 주어는 선행사 this isolated region's inhabitants로, 약 2천5백 년 전에 동굴에 매장된 사람들이므로 과거 시점의 일을 이야기하고 있다.

3 조동사 뒤에 오는 동사의 형태가 바른지 판단하자.

▶ 현재의 일에 대한 추측은 「조동사(may)+동사원형」을 쓰고, 과거의 일에 대한 추측은 「조동사(may)+have p.p.」를 써서 나타낸다.

2

(A), (B), (C) 각 네모 안에서 어법에 맞는 표현으로 가장 적절한 것은? (2009년 6월 고2 학평)

It was a cold winter morning in a busy subway station in Washington, D.C. There, clothed in jeans and a T-shirt, was a young man (A) [playing / played] his violin with great passion. He played for almost an hour, during which time at least a thousand people must have passed by. It seemed that hardly anyone recognized him. Most people were busily hurrying along and probably thought he was just another musician trying to make money. Even though most of the passers-by were most likely rushing to work, the scene might (B) [be / have been] quite different if they had known that the young musician was Tony Adamson, a world famous violinist. However, those who showed any surprise or appreciation of their good fortune (C) [was / were] so few that you could have counted them on one hand.

	(A)		(B)		(C)
①	playing	……	be	……	was
②	playing	……	have been	……	were
③	playing	……	be	……	were
④	played	……	have been	……	were
⑤	played	……	be	……	was

WORDS

1 **archaeologist** 고고학자 **set out** 출발하다, (여행을) 시작하다 **remote** 외진 **district** 지구, 지역 **aim** ~을 목표하다 **remains** (*pl.*) 유골, 유해 **settlement** 정착지 **seek** 찾다 **stick out** ~에서 툭 튀어나오다 **skull** 두개골 **date back** ~까지 거슬러 올라가다 **pile** 쌓다 **burial** 매장 **pinpoint** 정확히 찾아내다 **isolated** 고립된 **inhabitant** 주민, 거주자 **migrate** 이주하다 **plateau** 고원

2 **clothe in** ~을 입히다 **passion** 열정 **passer-by** 행인 **appreciation** 감상, (진가의) 이해

Chapter

07

동사 II

UNIT 11
목적격보어의 형태

UNIT 12
주의해야 할 동사

POINT 23 ★★

목적격보어의 형태는 동사가 결정한다!

일부 동사는 「동사+목적어+목적격보어」의 구조를 취하는데, 목적격보어의 형태는 동사에 따라 달라진다. 각각의 동사에 따라 알맞은 형태의 목적격보어를 써야 한다.

형태와 의미	동사
「동사+목적어+to부정사」: (목적어)가 ~하도록[할 것을] (동사)하다	want, ask, like, order, teach, allow, cause, enable, expect, convince, advise, encourage, force 등
「동사+목적어+동사원형」: **1** (목적어)가 ~하는 것을 (동사)하다 **2** (목적어)가 ~하게 (동사)하다	**1** 지각동사 see, hear, feel, listen to, watch, notice, observe 등 ※ 동작이 진행 중인 경우, 목적격보어로 현재분사(v-ing)가 올 수 있다. **2** 사역동사 let, make, have 등

❗ 동사 help는 목적격보어로 to부정사와 동사원형을 모두 쓸 수 있다.

대표 예문 Mr. Meredith suffered from an unusual disease [that caused(동사) him(목적어) ~~fall~~ / to fall(목적격보어(to부정사)) occasionally]. 기출

▶ 동사 cause는 목적격보어로 to부정사를 취하므로, to fall이 오는 것이 알맞다.

기출 예문 PLUS

정답 및 해설 p.30

1 It is wrong to think that proper institutions, knowledge, methods of consultation, or participatory mechanisms can **make** disagreement **go** away. 기출

2 While working at the cash register in a shop, a young college student **saw** an elderly couple **come[coming]** in with their granddaughter in a wheelchair. 기출

3 The experiences of his past had **helped** him **develop[to develop]** a belief: Receiving praise for doing what was obviously right would be inappropriate. 기출 응용

WORDS **occasionally** 가끔 **institution** 제도, 기관 **consultation** 협의 **participatory** 참여의 **mechanism** 방법, 장치 **obviously** 분명히, 명백히 **inappropriate** 부적절한, 부적합한

기출 문장으로 PRACTICE

정답 및 해설 p.30

[01-06] 다음 문장의 네모 안에서 어법상 바른 것을 고르시오.

01 At that moment, she noticed an anxious expression suddenly [come / to come] over the driver's face. 기출 응용

02 Feedback that simply makes you [feel / to feel] great will not help you develop tennis skills in the long run. 기출

03 Furthermore, people having private conversations would stand in the middle of the sidewalk, forcing people [step / to step] around them. 기출

04 Even books that provide only pleasure will increase the confidence of students and encourage them [try / to try] to read more technical materials in school. 기출

05 Tourism allows people from different places and cultures [come / to come] together, which enables tourists and host communities to learn about each other. 기출 응용

06 Whether it is a piece of paper, or a product, if you want to let your audience [know / to know] what you are holding is important, handle it with respect and care. 기출

[07-08] 다음 문장의 밑줄 친 부분이 어법상 바르면 O를 쓰고, 틀리면 바르게 고치시오.

07 At the hospital, Tom served ice cream while he watched his friend <u>did</u> magic tricks. 기출 응용

08 Learning more about animals by attaching small cameras to them helps people <u>understanding</u> more about their behaviors and habitats. 기출 응용

WORDS **sidewalk** 보도, 인도 **confidence** 신뢰; *자신감 **technical** 기술적인; *전문적인 **material** 자료 **attach** 붙이다, 첨부하다 **habitat** 서식지

POINT 24 ★★★★★

목적어와 목적격보어의 능동/수동 관계를 따져라!

일부 동사는 여러 형태의 목적격보어를 취할 수 있다. 목적어와 목적격보어가 '(목적어가) ~하는'이라는 능동의 관계일 경우 to부정사, 동사원형, 현재분사를 목적격보어로 쓰고, '(목적어가) ~되는'이라는 수동의 관계일 경우에는 과거분사를 쓴다.

목적어와 목적격보어가 능동 관계: to-v, v, v-ing	목적어와 목적격보어가 수동 관계: p.p.

a. The rescue team **heard** an avalanche **come**[**coming**] toward them. (능동: 동사원형/현재분사)
b. Fred **heard** his name **called** in the distance. (수동: 과거분사)
c. The teacher **had** his students **read** a sentence aloud. (능동: 동사원형)
d. They had to **have** their tickets **stamped** at the entrance. (수동: 과거분사)
e. She **found** her baby daughter **giving** out odd little cries. (능동: 현재분사) 기출 응용
f. Jenny **found** her cat **covered** in mud. (수동: 과거분사)
g. How did you **get** the dolphin **to do** all these tricks? (능동: to부정사)
h. I went to the service center to **get** my camera **repaired**. (수동: 과거분사)

a. 구조대는 눈사태가 그들을 향해 오는[오고 있는] 것을 들었다. b. Fred는 멀리서 그의 이름이 불리는 것을 들었다. c. 선생님은 학생들에게 한 문장을 소리 내어 읽게 했다. d. 그들은 입구에서 입장권에 도장을 받아야 했다. e. 그녀는 딸 아이가 이상하고 작은 소리를 내고 있는 것을 발견했다. f. Jenny는 그녀의 고양이가 진흙으로 덮여있는 것을 발견했다. g. 당신은 어떻게 돌고래가 이 모든 묘기를 하게 했나요? h. 나는 카메라를 수리받기 위해 서비스센터에 갔다.

대표 예문 Examine your thoughts, and you will **find**(동사) them(목적어) wholly [~~to occupy~~ / occupied](목적격보어(과거분사)) with the past or the future. 기출

▶ 목적어(them)와 목적격보어가 '그것들이 사로잡힌'이라는 수동의 관계이므로, 과거분사 occupied를 써야 한다.

기출 예문 PLUS

정답 및 해설 p.30

1 The room was painted a bright red, which **kept** the people **excited** or even **agitated**. 기출 응용

2 Stepping up to the microphone, Gabby could **feel** the sweat **run**[**running**] down her face and neck. 기출 응용

3 Mammals and birds commonly **make** their presence **felt** by sound, but birds are far better at it. 기출

WORDS **avalanche** (눈·산)사태 **odd** 이상한 **examine** 검토하다 **wholly** 완전히, 전적으로 **occupy** 차지하다 **agitate** 동요시키다, 격앙시키다 **presence** 존재(함)

기출 문장으로 PRACTICE

정답 및 해설 p.31

[01-06] 다음 문장의 네모 안에서 어법상 바른 것을 고르시오.

01 One day last summer, the lock on the bathroom's door jammed. I couldn't get it [unlocking / unlocked] however hard I tried. 기출 응용

02 I was surprised to see trainers on their lunch hour [sunbathing / sunbathed] in a pile with their sea lions. 기출

03 Customer responses like this complimentary letter keep us [motivating / motivated] and guide us to improve our service. 기출 응용

04 According to one researcher, the brain has a kind of built-in defense system that works to make us [satisfy / satisfied] with choices that cannot be undone. 기출

05 By the end of the Roman Imperium, Italy had been stripped of forest cover. Unfortunately, deforestation left the soil [exposing / exposed] to harsh weather. 기출
*imperium: 지배권, 주권

06 The public wants to have the service [render / rendered] to them in a manner that pleases them; they want not only efficiency but courtesy and consideration. 기출

[07-08] 다음 문장의 밑줄 친 부분이 어법상 바르면 O를 쓰고, 틀리면 바르게 고치시오.

07 He tried to deliver his lines as best as he could, but he could feel his voice <u>shaken</u>. 기출

08 If he would have only taken a few minutes to get the nail <u>to remove</u>, he most likely would not have gotten a flat tire on that particular day. 기출

WORDS **jam** 밀어 넣다; *움직이지 못하게 되다 **unlock** 열다 **sunbathe** 일광욕을 하다 **complimentary** 무료의; *칭찬하는 **built-in** 붙박이의; *본래 갖추어진, 고유한 **undo** 풀다; *원상태로 돌리다 **strip** 벗기다, 떼어내다 **deforestation** 산림 벌채[파괴] **render** 제공하다 **manner** 방식 **efficiency** 효율(성), 능률 **courtesy** 공손함, 정중함 **consideration** 배려 **line** 대사 **flat tire** 바람 빠진 타이어

POINT 25 ★★★★★

「동사+it+목적격보어+to-v」 형태에 주의하라!

think, make, find, consider, believe와 같은 5형식 동사의 목적어로 to부정사가 올 때, 「동사+가목적어 it+목적격보어+진목적어 to-v」의 형태로 쓴다. think 등의 동사 뒤에 it이 오면 목적격보어 뒤에 진목적어 to부정사가 쓰였는지 확인한다. 또한, 목적격보어 뒤에 진목적어 to부정사가 오면 앞에 가목적어 it이 쓰였는지도 확인한다.

대표 예문 Modern medicine lets us live longer, but governments are finding **it** hard [~~look~~ / to look after the increasing number of old people]. 기출

(동사: are finding / 가목적어: it / 목적격보어: hard / 진목적어(to부정사): to look)

▶ 동사(are finding) 뒤에 가목적어 it이 쓰였으므로, 목적격보어(hard) 뒤에 진목적어 역할을 하는 to부정사 to look이 와야 한다.

기출 예문 PLUS

정답 및 해설 p.31

1 Oddly enough, while making individual zebras indistinguishable to other animals, zebra stripes actually make **it** easier for zebras [**to recognize** one another]. 기출

2 They thought **it** better [**to use** their limited resources on the younger, more productive generation], which accounts for how the tribe survived in the harsh environment.

3 One 35-year-old woman used to rub her eyes with her hands until they became sore and infected. She found **it** helpful [**to put** on makeup] when she was tempted to rub. 기출 응용

WORDS indistinguishable 구분이 안 되는 stripe 줄무늬 productive 생산적인 account for ~을 설명하다 sore 아픈 infected 감염된 be tempted to-v ~하고 싶어지다

기출 문장으로 PRACTICE

정답 및 해설 p.32

[01-04] 다음 문장의 네모 안에서 어법상 바른 것을 고르시오.

01 Some people consider it extremely rude [call / to call] others by their first names when they aren't close.

02 Inflation can be a major life concern for most people. It makes [it / this] difficult for households to plan ahead. 기출

03 Children raised in households that foster communication find it easier [talk / to talk] to others about their disappointments, fears, frustrations, and other emotions later in life. 기출

04 His habit of skepticism made [him / it] easy for him to question many long-standing scientific assumptions. 기출

[05-06] 다음 문장의 밑줄 친 부분이 어법상 바르면 O를 쓰고, 틀리면 바르게 고치시오.

05 Some wildflower books arrange all white-flowered species or all yellow-flowered species together. However, such groupings do not reflect natural relationships and make it difficult <u>recognize</u> family characteristics. 기출

06 All living languages change, but the rate of change varies from time to time and from language to language. For example, the modern Icelander does not <u>find very difficult</u> to read the Icelandic sagas from the Middle Ages. 기출

*saga: 영웅전설

WORDS **inflation** 인플레이션, 물가 상승(률) **concern** 우려, 걱정 **household** 가정 **foster** 촉진[조장]하다 **frustration** 좌절 **skepticism** 회의적인 태도, 의심 **long-standing** 오래 계속[지속]되는 **assumption** 가정 **arrange** 정리하다, 배열하다 **grouping** 그룹으로 나누기, 분류 **reflect** 반영하다 **living** 살아있는; *현재 사용되는 **rate** 정도

POINT 26 ★★★★★

형태가 유사한 자동사와 타동사를 구분하라!

타동사와 달리 자동사는 뒤에 바로 목적어(명사)를 취할 수 없고 전치사를 써서 목적어를 취할 수 있으며, 수동태로 쓸 수 없다. 뒤에 바로 목적어가 오거나 수동태로 쓰였다면 타동사를 써야 한다.

자동사(+전치사+목적어) / 수동태 불가	타동사+목적어 / 수동태 가능
lie(–lied–lied / lying): 거짓말하다 lie(–lay–lain / lying): 놓여[누워] 있다	lay(–laid–laid / laying): ~을 놓다; (알을) 낳다
rise(–rose–risen): 오르다; 뜨다	raise(–raised–raised): ~을 들어올리다; 키우다[기르다]
arise(–arose–arisen): 발생하다	arouse(–aroused–aroused): ~을 불러일으키다

❗ 의미상 자동사인지 타동사인지 혼동되는 경우, 전치사의 사용에 주의해야 한다.

자동사처럼 보이는 타동사 (전치사가 필요 없음)	discuss(~을 논의하다), enter(~에 들어가다), attend(~에 참석하다[다니다]), reach(~에 이르다, 닿다), marry(~와 결혼하다), resemble(~와 닮다), approach(~에 접근하다)
타동사처럼 보이는 자동사 (전치사와 함께 쓰임)	arrive at(~에 도착하다), graduate from(~을 졸업하다), participate in(~에 참여하다), succeed[fail] in(~에 성공[실패]하다), wait for(~을 기다리다), consist of(~로 구성되다)

대표 예문 Namibia, Botswana, and Zimbabwe(주어) ~~lay~~ / lie(자동사) [to the north of the Republic of South Africa](부사구(전치사구)). 기출 응용

▶ 동사 뒤에 목적어가 없고, 의미상 '놓여 있다'가 자연스러우므로, 자동사인 lie가 오는 것이 적절하다.

기출 예문 PLUS

정답 및 해설 p.32

1 He immediately **rose** and went down the hall of the hospital to her room. 기출

2 When a company releases a new product, it **raises** [the prices of its existing products]. 기출

3 Families in Egypt mourned the death of cats and had their bodies wrapped in cloth before they were finally **laid** to rest. 기출

WORDS **release** 풀어주다; *공개하다, 발매[출시]하다 **existing** 기존의, 현재 사용되는 **body** 몸, 신체; *(인간 · 동물의) 사체 **lay ~ to rest** ~을 매장하다

기출 문장으로 PRACTICE

정답 및 해설 p.32

[01-06] 다음 문장의 네모 안에서 어법상 바른 것을 고르시오.

01 Some fish [lay / lie] their eggs in or near a current, which may then carry the eggs into an environment favorable for growth. 기출

02 Originally sheep and goats were [risen / raised] mainly for their meat; these animals later became valuable also for their milk and wool as well. 기출 응용

03 Why would the pot of hot soup cause more damage than a spoonful of it? The answer to the question [lies / lays] in the difference between temperature and heat. 기출 응용

04 When the garbage man yelled "Ready," the dumpster began to (A) [raise / rise] from the ground. It soon (B) [reached / arrived] its peak, and the trash fell into the truck. 기출 응용

05 The origins of contemporary Western thought can be traced back to the golden age of ancient Greece, when Greek thinkers [lay / laid] the foundations for modern Western politics, philosophy, science, and law. 기출

06 The "uncanny valley" is the idea that when artificial humans such as robots and computer animations look almost, but not exactly, like real human beings, this human likeness [arises / arouses] certain unpleasant feelings.

WORDS **current** 흐름, 해류 **favorable** 호의적인; *유리한 **spoonful** 한 숟가락 **temperature** 온도, 기온 **dumpster** 쓰레기 수집 용기 **peak** 꼭대기, 정상 **contemporary** 동시대의; *현대의 **trace back to** (기원이) ~까지 거슬러 올라가다 **uncanny** 이상한, 묘한 **artificial** 인공[인조]의 **likeness** 유사성, 닮음

POINT 27 do동사의 쓰임

★★★★★

do동사는 앞에 나온 일반동사(구)를 대신하는 대동사 역할과, 일반동사 앞에서 동사의 의미를 강조하는 역할을 한다. do동사는 문장이나 절의 주어의 인칭이나 수, 시제에 따라 do, does, did의 형태로 써야 한다.

대동사 do	동사를 강조하는 do
1 앞에 나온 일반동사(구)의 반복을 피하기 위해 쓴다. 2 접속사 as, than 절에 자주 쓰인다. a. Food goes bad much faster in summer *than* it **does** in winter. b. They assumed early human beings ate mainly the muscle flesh of animals, *as* we **do** today. 기출	1 일반동사를 강조하기 위해 쓴다. 2 「do/does/did + 동사원형」 형태로 쓴다. c. Many animals, including dolphins, **do** indeed communicate with one another. 기출

a. 음식은 겨울에 그러는 것보다 여름에 훨씬 더 빠르게 상한다. b. 그들은 초기 인류가 오늘날 우리가 그러는 것처럼, 주로 동물의 살코기를 먹었을 것이라고 추정했다. c. 돌고래를 포함한 많은 동물들이 정말로 서로서로 의사소통을 한다.

대표 예문 You are under the false impression that you don't have as many items to pack as you really [do / are] 기출 응용

(have as many items to pack: 일반동사구(반복어구); do: 대동사)

▶ 앞에 오는 일반동사구 have items to pack을 대신하는 대동사 do가 와야 한다.

기출 예문 PLUS

정답 및 해설 p.33

1 The Greeks traded with each other far more often than they **did** with Persians or other non-Greeks. 기출

2 A sort of group consciousness emerges in which no single member of the group can be said to know the song, but the group itself **does**. 기출

3 Studies **do** show that motorists are more likely to yield to pedestrians in marked crosswalks than at unmarked crosswalks. 기출

WORDS indeed 정말, 확실히 a sort of 일종의 consciousness 생각[의식] emerge 나오다, 드러나다 motorist 운전자 yield 양보하다 pedestrian 보행자 crosswalk 횡단보도

기출 문장으로 PRACTICE

정답 및 해설 p.33

[01-05] 다음 문장의 네모 안에서 어법상 바른 것을 고르시오.

01 Many users probably spend more time on the Internet than they [do / are] in their cars. 기출

02 People moving from more expensive cities sink the same amount of money into their new housing situations as they [were / did] in the past. 기출

03 Most amateur speakers (A) [do / does] have some idea that they should speak with more power on stage than they (B) [are / do] on a one-to-one basis. 기출

04 "Art does not solve problems, but it makes us aware of their existence," a sculptor once said. Art education, on the other hand, [does / do] solve problems.

05 You have probably heard Luciano Pavarotti sing the song once or twice. However, it has never had so much meaning as it [did / was] on a stage in Great Britain, being sung by a mobile phone salesman named Paul Potts. 기출

[06-07] 다음 문장의 밑줄 친 부분이 어법상 바르면 O를 쓰고, 틀리면 바르게 고치시오.

06 Organic farmers grow crops that are no less plagued by pests than those of conventional farmers; insects generally do not discriminate between organic and conventional crops as we <u>are</u>. 기출

07 It was once considered an amazing achievement to reach the summit of Mount Everest. But now that almost 4,000 people have reached its summit, the achievement means less than it <u>does</u> half a century ago. 기출

WORDS **sink** 가라앉히다; *투자하다 **housing** 주거 **basis** 근거; *기준, 단위 **existence** 존재, 실재 **sculptor** 조각가 **plague** 괴롭히다 **pest** 해충, 유해 동물 **conventional** 전통적인, 종래의 **discriminate** 구분하다 **summit** 정상, 산꼭대기

POINT 28 ★★★★★

당위성을 내포한 that절의 동사는 「(should+) 동사원형」으로 쓴다!

요구, 제안, 주장, 권유, 명령 등을 나타내는 동사가 이끄는 that절이 당위성(~해야 한다)을 내포할 때, that절의 동사는 「(should+) 동사원형」 형태로 쓰는데, should는 보통 생략되고 동사원형만 남는다.

※ 동사: (요구, 요청) demand, require, request, ask / (제안) suggest, propose / (주장) insist / (명령) order / (권유, 충고) recommend, advise, urge 등

❗ that절이 당위성을 내포하지 않고 객관적인 사실을 나타낼 때는 직설법으로 쓴다.

당위성을 나타내는 that절: 「(should+) 동사원형」	사실을 나타내는 that절: 직설법
a. The customer insisted that she (**should**) **get** a full refund for the defective product.	**b.** The man insisted that he **had witnessed** the accident. ▶ that절의 동사는 적절한 시제를 사용해야 함

a. 그 고객은 자신이 결함이 있는 제품에 대해 전액 환불을 받아야 한다고 주장했다. b. 그 남자는 자기가 그 사고를 목격했다고 주장했다.

대표 예문 The rule of reciprocation requires [that one person try / ~~tries~~ to repay, in kind, what another person has provided]. 기출 응용

(requires: 동사(요구) / that one person: 당위성을 나타내는 that절 / try: (should+) 동사원형)

▶ 요구를 나타내는 동사 requires가 이끄는 that절이 당위성을 나타내므로, 동사를 「(should+) 동사원형」 형태로 써야 한다. 따라서 동사원형인 try가 와야 한다. 이때 주어인 one person과 수를 일치시켜야 하는 것으로 혼동하지 않아야 한다.

기출 예문 PLUS

정답 및 해설 p.34

1 When consumers lack adequate information to make an informed choice, the government may step in to require that a firm (should) **provide** information. 기출 응용

2 My job now has me traveling most weeks, and I simply cannot keep up with a daily paper. So I would like to request that you (should) **stop** delivering it to my home. 기출

3 Recent evidence suggests that the common ancestor of Neanderthals and modern people probably **used** (직설법) pretty sophisticated language about 400,000 years ago. 기출 응용

WORDS defective 결함이 있는 witness 목격하다 reciprocation 교환; *보답 in kind 동일한 것으로, 마찬가지로 adequate 충분한, 적절한 step in 개입하다 firm 회사 sophisticated 세련된

기출 문장으로 PRACTICE

정답 및 해설 p.34

[01-04] 다음 문장의 네모 안에서 어법상 바른 것을 고르시오.

01 A new study suggests that the number of people texting while driving [is / be] actually on the rise despite various campaigns to prevent it. 기출 응용

02 Due to my foot problems, I've asked that I [was / be] given a clerical job in the warehouse rather than continuing my duties of loading and unloading trucks. 기출

03 William's father felt that his son's late-night reading would cut into his energy for the next day's work. He insisted that William [retire / retires] for the night when the rest of the family did. 기출

04 A study recommends that babies [are / be] moved into their own room by three months of age. "Children who regularly sleep in their parents' room are likely to have become dependent on this arrangement," reports the study. 기출 응용

[05-06] 다음 문장의 밑줄 친 부분이 어법상 바르면 O를 쓰고, 틀리면 바르게 고치시오.

05 We should hope for exposure to failure, early and often. The sociologist Glen Elder proposed that there <u>be</u> a sensitive period for growth — late teens through early 30s — during which failures are most beneficial. 기출

06 American experts wrote guidelines suggesting that patients with mild blood pressure elevation (A) <u>were</u> encouraged to take medicine. But in Europe, experts advised that people with the same symptoms (B) <u>avoid</u> taking medicine. 기출 응용

WORDS **clerical** 사무직의 **warehouse** 창고 **load** (~에 짐을) 싣다[적재하다] **retire for the night** 잠자리에 들다 **exposure** 노출 **sociologist** 사회학자 **beneficial** 유익한, 이로운 **elevation** (정도의) 증가 **symptom** 증상

1 **(A), (B), (C)의 각 네모 안에서 어법에 맞는 표현으로 가장 적절한 것은?** (2012년 7월 고3 학평)

Empathy is made possible by a special group of nerve cells called mirror neurons. These special cells enable us to "mirror" emotions. Mirror neurons were first discovered by Italian scientists who, while looking at the activity of individual nerve cells inside the brains of monkeys, (A) [noticed / noticing] that neurons in the same area of the brain were activated whether the animals were performing a particular movement or simply observing another monkey perform the same action. It appeared as though the cells in the observer's brain "mirrored" the activity in the performer's brain. A similar phenomenon takes place when we watch someone (B) [experiencing / experienced] an emotion and feel the same emotion in response. The same neural systems get activated in a part of the insula, (C) [it / which] is part of the mirror neuron system, and in the emotional brain areas associated with the observed emotion.

	(A)		(B)		(C)
①	noticed	……	experiencing	……	it
②	noticed	……	experiencing	……	which
③	noticed	……	experienced	……	which
④	noticing	……	experiencing	……	it
⑤	noticing	……	experienced	……	it

POINT 24 적용하기 **목적어와 목적격보어의 능동/수동 관계를 따져라!**

1 절의 동사, 목적어, 목적격보어를 먼저 파악하자.

A similar phenomenon takes place [when we watch(동사) someone(목적어) [experiencing / experienced](목적격보어) an emotion ...].

2 목적어와 목적격보어의 의미 관계를 따져보자.

▶ '누군가가 감정을 느끼다'라는 의미로, 목적어와 목적격보어는 능동의 관계이다.

3 현재분사를 써야 하는지 과거분사를 써야 하는지 판단하자.

▶ 목적어와 목적격보어가 능동의 관계일 때는 현재분사를 쓰고, 수동의 관계일 때는 과거분사를 쓴다.

정답 및 해설 p.34

2 (A), (B), (C)의 각 네모 안에서 어법에 맞는 표현으로 가장 적절한 것은? [3점] (2016년 3월 고3 학평)

Water has no calories, but it takes up a space in your stomach, which creates a feeling of fullness. Recently, a study found (A) [that / what] people who drank two glasses of water before meals got full sooner, ate fewer calories, and lost more weight. You can put the same strategy to work by choosing foods that have a higher water content over those with less water. For example, the only difference between grapes and raisins (B) [is / are] that grapes have about 6 times as much water in them. That water makes a big difference in how much they fill you up. You'll feel much more satisfied after eating 100 calories' worth of grapes than you would after eating 100 calories' worth of raisins. Salad vegetables like lettuce, cucumbers, and tomatoes also have a very high water content, as (C) [are / do] broth-based soups.

*broth: 묽은 수프

	(A)		(B)		(C)
①	that	……	is	……	are
②	that	……	is	……	do
③	that	……	are	……	do
④	what	……	is	……	are
⑤	what	……	are	……	do

WORDS

1 **empathy** 공감 **nerve cell** 신경 세포 **mirror** 거울; 반영하다 **neuron** 뉴런, 신경 세포 **activate** 활성화시키다 **phenomenon** 현상 **experience** 경험하다; *(감정을) 느끼다 **neural** 신경(계통)의 **insula** 뇌섬엽 **associate** 연관짓다

2 **take up** (공간을) 차지하다 **fullness** 충만; *포만 **strategy** 전략 **content** 내용물; *함유량, 함량 **fill up** ~을 가득 채우다

Chapter 08

형용사와 부사

UNIT 13
형용사와 부사

UNIT 14
비교구문

POINT 29 ★★★★★

형용사 자리와 부사 자리를 구분하라!

형용사는 명사를 수식하고, 보어의 역할을 하는 반면, 부사는 동사(구)나 형용사, 다른 부사 등을 수식한다. 형용사와 부사가 모두 들어갈 수 있는 구조일 경우, 수식하는 대상이나 문장 안에서의 역할을 따져 형용사 자리인지 부사 자리인지 판단한다.

형용사	부사
1 명사를 앞이나 뒤에서 수식한다. 2 주어나 목적어를 설명하는 보어 역할을 한다.	동사, 형용사, 다른 부사, 구나 절을 앞이나 뒤에서 수식한다.
a. Do you have any **fragile** items in your bag?	**h.** You need to drive **carefully**. (동사 수식)
b. Something **strange** happened that night.	**i.** The test was **unbelievably** difficult. (형용사 수식)
c. Air pollution in Seoul is getting **serious**. ▶ 주어(Air pollution)를 설명하는 보어	**j.** The rumor spread **extremely** quickly. (부사 수식)
d. This blanket will keep you **warm**. ▶ 목적어(you)를 설명하는 보어	**k.** The movie was a failure **partly** because of the bad acting. (구 수식)
e. The town was *as* **silent** *as* the grave. ▶ 주어(The town)를 설명하는 보어	**l.** **Unfortunately**, my flight has been canceled. (절 수식)
f. [*How* **good** your report is] depends on your research. ▶ 의문사절에서 주어(your report)를 설명하는 보어	**m.** She walks *as* **silently** *as* a cat. ▶ 동사(walks)를 수식하는 부사
g. The traffic was *so* **slow** *that* I was late for school. ▶ 주어(The traffic)를 설명하는 보어	**n.** Please tell me [*how* **well** you know Damon]. ▶ 의문사절에서 동사(know)를 수식하는 부사
	o. The water flows *so* **slowly** *that* its surface looks still. ▶ 동사(flows)를 수식하는 부사

a. 가방에 부서지기 쉬운 물건이 들어있습니까? b. 그날 밤 이상한 일이 일어났다. c. 서울의 대기오염이 심각해지고 있다. d. 이 담요는 당신을 따뜻하게 해줄 것이다. e. 그 마을은 무덤처럼 조용했다. f. 당신의 보고서가 얼마나 좋은가는 당신의 연구에 달려 있다. g. 교통이 너무 느려서 나는 학교에 지각했다. h. 당신은 조심히 운전할 필요가 있다. i. 그 시험은 믿을 수 없을 정도로 어려웠다. j. 그 소문은 엄청나게 빠르게 퍼졌다. k. 그 영화는 부분적으로는 형편없는 연기 때문에 실패작이었다. l. 불행하게도, 나의 항공편이 취소되었다. m. 그녀는 고양이만큼 조용히 걷는다. n. 당신이 Damon을 얼마나 잘 아는지 저에게 말해주세요. o. 물이 아주 느리게 흘러서 수면이 정지한 것처럼 보인다.

WORDS **fragile** 부서지기 쉬운 **grave** 무덤 **rumor** 소문 **partly** 부분적으로 **flight** 항공편 **still** 고요한, 정지한 **surface** 표면, 수면

대표 예문 Psychologists have a lot of theories about [why people are so sensitive / ~~sensitively~~ to hearing about their own imperfections]. 기출

(people: 주어, sensitive: 주격보어(형용사))

▶ 의문사절에서 주어를 설명하는 주격보어 자리이므로, 형용사 sensitive가 오는 것이 적절하다.

기출 예문 PLUS

정답 및 해설 p.36

1 We anticipate the future as if we found it too **slow** in coming and we were trying to hurry it up. 기출

2 It is no accident that fish have bodies [which are **streamlined** and **smooth**], with fins and a powerful tail. 기출

3 These days, young people **increasingly** access social networking websites using their mobile phones or other digital devices. 기출 응용

4 This semester's courses are arranged **alphabetically** by each department so that students may choose which courses they want to take. 기출

5 You have to pay close attention to someone's normal pattern in order to notice a deviation from it when he or she lies. Sometimes the variation is as **subtle** as a pause. 기출

WORDS **psychologist** 심리학자 **theory** 이론 **sensitive** 예민한, 민감한 **imperfection** 불완전, 결함 **anticipate** 예상하다; *기대하다, 고대하다 **streamlined** 유선형의 **fin** 지느러미 **access** 접속하다 **arrange** 배열하다 **deviation** (기준에서) 벗어남, 탈선 **variation** 변화, 차이 **subtle** 미묘한, 감지하기 힘든 **pause** (말 등의) 멈춤

정답 및 해설 p.36

[01-13] 다음 문장의 네모 안에서 어법상 바른 것을 고르시오.

01 If advertising is on television, the more [frequent / frequently] a commercial is run, the more people it will reach. 기출

02 People with depression find it [easy / easily] to interpret large images or scenes, but struggle to "spot the difference" in fine details. 기출

03 In an [increasing / increasingly] globalized world, literature in translation has an especially important role as a bridge between cultures. 기출

04 Masks are too heavy to uphold indefinitely, and no matter how [good / well] you believe you are disguising yourself, others always know. 기출

05 Louisiana was the only state where cockfighting remained [legal / legally], because chickens were not defined as animals according to state law. 기출

*cockfighting: 닭싸움, 투계

06 Gold is a (A) [relative / relatively] soft metal, so much so that rings are very rarely made from pure gold because they (B) [quick / quickly] get scratched. 기출

07 More information is now exchanged via text than ever before, making it [extreme / extremely] important that you can communicate effectively in writing. 기출

08 The negative impact on local wildlife inhabiting areas [close / closely] to the fish farms continues to be an ongoing public relations problem for the industry. 기출

WORDS

commercial 광고(방송) **interpret** 해석[이해]하다 **spot** 발견하다, 찾다 **fine** 질 높은; *미세한 **translation** 번역, 통역 **uphold** (법 등을) 옹호하다; *지탱하다 **indefinitely** 무기한으로 **disguise** 위장하다, 숨기다 **legal** 법률과 관련된; *합법적인 **relative** 비교상의, 상대적인 **so much so that** 매우 그러하므로 ~하다 **via** ~을 통해 **ongoing** 계속 진행 중인 **public relations** (*pl.*) (기관의) 대민관계

09 Knowledge is amoral — not immoral but morality neutral. There is nothing [inherent / inherently] in knowledge that dictates any specific social or moral application. 기출 응용

10 From the point of view of research into motor behavior, it is important to use performances in the laboratory for which the scoring can be as [objective / objectively] as possible. 기출

11 The pull effect of a destination can be (A) [positive / positively] influenced by the introduction and reinforcement of pro-tourism policies that make the destination more (B) [accessible / accessibly]. 기출

12 She gazed (A) [happy / happily] out the window, looking at the palm trees and sidewalks full of athletic people running, skateboarding, and (B) [casual / casually] hanging out with friends. 기출

13 Mourning a dead pet provides children with a useful "rehearsal" for the death of human family members, but it is not considered [appropriate / appropriately] for adults because there is a lack of social support for the mature person going through such grief. 기출

[14-15] 다음 문장의 밑줄 친 부분이 어법상 바르면 O를 쓰고, 틀리면 바르게 고치시오.

14 Our immune systems are not functioning as <u>effective</u> as they do when we are well rested, so we get sick. 기출

15 Farmers turn and loosen the soil, leaving it in the best condition for farming. However, this process removes the important plant cover that holds soil particles in place, making soil <u>defenselessly</u> to wind and water erosion. 기출

WORDS **amoral** 도덕 관념이 없는 **immoral** 비도덕적인 **morality** 도덕성 **neutral** 중립적인 **inherent** 내재하는 **dictate** 받아쓰게 하다; *좌우하다 **application** 적용, 응용 **motor behavior** 운동행위 **pull effect** 유인 효과 **destination** 목적지; *관광지 **reinforcement** 강화 **pro-** ~에 호의적인 **accessible** 접근 가능한 **athletic** 원기 왕성한, 건강한 **mourn** 애도하다 **mature** 어른스러운; *성인이 된 **go through** ~을 겪다 **function** 기능하다 **defenselessly** 무방비로 **erosion** 침식

POINT 30 ★

수량형용사는 뒤에 오는 명사의 수에 주목하라!

수를 나타내는 형용사(many, few 등)는 셀 수 있는 명사의 복수형과 함께 쓰고, 양을 나타내는 형용사(much, little 등)은 셀 수 없는 명사와 함께 쓴다.

셀 수 있는 명사의 복수형과 쓰이는 형용사	셀 수 없는 명사(단수형)와 쓰이는 형용사
many(많은) / a few(약간 있는) / few(거의 없는) / several(몇몇의)	much(많은) / a little(약간 있는) / little(거의 없는)

❗ a lot of, lots of, plenty of(많은)은 셀 수 있는 명사, 셀 수 없는 명사를 모두 수식할 수 있다.

대표 예문 You may think that moving a short distance is so easy that you can do it with [few / little] effort. 기출

셀 수 없는 명사

▶ 뒤에 셀 수 없는 명사 effort가 이어지고 있으므로, 셀 수 없는 명사를 수식하는 수량형용사 little을 쓰는 것이 적절하다. few는 셀 수 있는 명사의 복수형과 쓰인다.

기출 예문 PLUS

정답 및 해설 p.37

1 Around the cottage, there wasn't **much** vegetation in the stark, rocky landscape. 기출 응용

2 Although Gullah has been spoken for hundreds of years, until recently there were **few** attempts to write it down. 기출

3 Trees do indeed have **a few** small roots which penetrate to great depth, but most of their roots are in the top half-meter of the soil. 기출

4 With all the passion for being slim, it is no wonder that **many** people view even **a little** fat on the body as something to get rid of. 기출 응용

WORDS cottage 작은 집, 오두막 vegetation 초목, 식물 stark 삭막한, 황량한 rocky 바위 투성이의 penetrate 뚫고 들어가다 passion 열정

기출 문장으로 PRACTICE

정답 및 해설 p.37

[01-04] 다음 문장의 네모 안에서 어법상 바른 것을 고르시오.

01 After some years of carving, he completed Moses, one of the most famous statues of the tomb. However, the next pope, Leo X, had [few / little] interest in continuing the project. 기출

02 Promise yourself that no matter how [many / much] work you have, you will always relax for one whole evening. You will work better if you take time off for relaxation. 기출

03 In earlier times, people traded crops or objects they had made in exchange for the goods they needed. The first shops sold just [a few / a little] products such as meat and bread. 기출

04 People were not particularly motivated to produce more goods for stockpiling, as there wasn't (A) [many / much] incentive to do so where there was (B) [few / little] security from raids. 기출

[05-06] 다음 문장의 밑줄 친 부분이 어법상 바르면 O를 쓰고, 틀리면 바르게 고치시오.

05 If advertising is placed in a high-traffic zone, more people will see it. If it is placed in a low-traffic zone, <u>less</u> people will see it. 기출 응용

06 A strategic vision has <u>few</u> value to the organization unless it's effectively communicated down the line to lower-level managers and employees. 기출

WORDS carve 조각하다 statue 조각상 pope 교황 relaxation 휴식 in exchange for ~와 교환으로, ~대신에 stockpiling 저장, 비축 incentive 유인책, 동기 raid 약탈, 급습 strategic 전략적인 communicate 의사소통을 하다, (정보를) 전달하다 down the line 완전히

POINT 31 ★★★★★

형태가 유사한 형용사, 부사, 전치사를 구분하라!

형태나 의미가 유사한 형용사와 부사, 그리고 전치사는 혼동하기 쉬우므로 각각의 의미와 쓰임을 구분해야 한다.

혼동하기 쉬운 형용사와 부사, 전치사
1 late(㊢ 늦은 ㊕ 늦게) – lately(㊕ 최근에)
2 high(㊢ 높은 ㊕ 높이, 높게) – highly(㊕ 매우, 대단히)
3 near(㊢ 가까운 ㊕ 가까이 ㊖ ~ 가까이에) – nearly(㊕ 거의)
4 hard(㊢ 단단한; 어려운 ㊕ 열심히) – hardly(㊕ 거의 ~ 않다)
5 most(㊢ 대부분의) – mostly(㊕ 대개) – almost(㊕ 거의)
6 alike(㊢ 비슷한 ㊕ 비슷하게) – like(㊖ ~와 같이, ~처럼) – likely(㊢ ~할 것 같은)

대표 예문 Researchers have determined that there is no leader or controlling force. Rather, each individual bird is reacting ~~most~~ / almost instantly to the movements of its neighbors in the flock. 기출 응용

▶ '거의'라는 의미로 뒤에 오는 부사 instantly를 수식할 수 있는 부사 almost가 와야 한다. most는 형용사로 '대부분의'이라는 의미이다.

기출 예문 PLUS

정답 및 해설 p.38

1 The city of Pompeii is a partially buried Roman town-city **near** modern Naples. 기출

2 Whatever circumstance you are dealing with, it is **highly likely** that a year from now you are not going to care. 기출 응용

3 You may decide to use your own car instead of the services of a moving company. But you might find out too **late** that your car cannot carry as much as you thought it could. 기출 응용

WORDS instantly 즉각, 즉시 flock (새의) 떼, 무리 partially 부분적으로 circumstance 환경, 상황

기출 문장으로 PRACTICE

정답 및 해설 p.38

[01-05] 다음 문장의 네모 안에서 어법상 바른 것을 고르시오.

01 I know you've been having a hard time [late / lately] and aren't feeling positive about your life. 기출

02 Every place on the earth is different. Just like people, no two places can be exactly [like / alike]. 기출

03 I remembered the small window on the back wall. The basin [near / nearly] the window provided an easy step up. 기출

04 Some coaches erroneously believe that mental skills training can only help perfect the performance of [high / highly] skilled competitors. 기출

05 A friend of mine and his wife were in Hawaii, standing on a beach, watching a beautiful sunset— [hard / hardly] able to believe how magnificent the sight was. 기출

WORDS **basin** 대야, 세면기 **erroneously** 잘못되게 **perfect** 완벽한; *완벽하게 하다 **competitor** 경쟁자; *선수 **magnificent** 웅장한

POINT 32 ★★★★★

비교구문의 형태와 의미를 파악하라!

비교구문과 비교구문을 이용한 관용 표현의 형태 및 의미를 파악해두어야 한다.

비교구문	
「**as+원급+as**」: …만큼 ~한[하게]	a. Driving this car is **as complicated as** flying a plane.
「**비교급+than**」: …보다 더 ~한[하게]	b. The economic situation is **worse than** last year.
「**the+최상급**(+in/of+명사)」: (…중) 가장 ~한[하게]	c. Becoming a parent was **the most memorable** moment of her life.

비교 구문을 이용한 관용 표현

1 「**as+원급+as possible**」: 가능한 한 ~한[하게] (= **as+원급+as+주어+can**)
2 「**비교급+and+비교급**」: 점점 더 ~한[하게]
3 「**the+비교급, the+비교급**」: ~하면 할수록 더 …한[하게]
4 「**one of the+최상급+복수명사**」: 가장 ~한 …중 하나

a. 이 차를 운전하는 것은 비행기를 조종하는 것만큼 복잡하다. b. 경제 상황은 작년보다 더 나쁘다. c. 부모가 된 것은 그녀의 인생에서 가장 기억할 만한 순간이었다.

대표 예문 Today, young athletes want risk and excitement — the [closer / ~~close~~] (the+비교급) to the edge, the better. (the+비교급) 기출

▶ '~하면 할수록 더 …한'의 의미인 「the+비교급, the+비교급」 구문이므로, 비교급 형태인 closer가 와야 한다.

기출 예문 PLUS

정답 및 해설 p.38

1 The only way to avoid ambiguity is to spell things out **as explicitly as possible.** 기출

2 We are too busy trying to squeeze **more and more** activities into **less and less** time. 기출

3 Whether in flower or in fruit, the coral bean is **one of the most striking plants** in the American Southwest. 기출

WORDS **complicated** 복잡한 **memorable** 기억할 만한 **excitement** 흥분; *자극 **edge** 모서리; *위기 **ambiguity** 모호함 **spell out** ~을 분명히[상세히] 설명하다 **explicitly** 솔직하게, 명시적으로 **squeeze** (좁은 곳에) 밀어[집어] 넣다 **striking** 눈에 띄는

정답 및 해설 p.38

[01-04] 다음 문장의 네모 안에서 어법상 바른 것을 고르시오.

01 In quicksand, the more you struggle, the [deeper / deepest] you'll sink. But if you remain still, you'll start to float. 기출

*quicksand: 유사(아래로 흘러내리는 모래)

02 No animal on earth can lift as much weight [as / than] the African elephant, which can carry up to 25% of its own weight on its back.

03 Sometimes the wind blows soil from a plowed field. Soil erosion in many places occurs at a [faster / fastest] rate than the natural processes of weathering can replace it. 기출

04 Although the effect of party size on campsites has never been formally studied, it makes sense that a large group can cause impacts on an undisturbed site more rapidly [as / than] a small group. 기출

[05-07] 다음 문장의 밑줄 친 부분이 어법상 바르면 O를 쓰고, 틀리면 바르게 고치시오.

05 With a power gap, the <u>hierarchical</u> your culture or background, the greater the power gap is apt to be. 기출

06 Gila monsters are one of only two kinds of venomous lizards in the world. Their venom is about as <u>poisonous</u> diamondback rattlesnake venom. 기출

*diamondback rattlesnake: 등에 마름모꼴 무늬가 있는 방울뱀

07 Changing our food habits is one of the <u>hardest</u> things we can do, because the impulses governing our preferences are often hidden, even from ourselves. 기출

WORDS **struggle** 몸부림치다, 허우적거리다 **plow** (밭을) 갈다, 경작하다 **erosion** 부식; *침식 **rate** 비율; *속도 **weathering** 풍화(작용) **party** 정당; *단체 **undisturbed** 누구도 건드리지 않은, 그대로 있는 **hierarchical** 계급제의 **venomous** 독이 있는 **lizard** 도마뱀 **venom** 독 **poisonous** 독이 있는 **impulse** 충동, 욕구 **govern** 지배하다, 좌우하다 **preference** 선호, 애호

POINT **33** ★★★★★

비교급을 수식하는 부사와 수식할 수 없는 부사를 구분하라!

비교급 앞에 쓰여 '훨씬'이라는 의미로 비교급을 강조하는 부사로는 much, still, even, far, a lot 등이 있다. 부사 very는 비교급을 수식할 수 없다.

❗ 최상급은 much, by far, the very, quite 등의 수식을 받는다.

대표 예문 In fact, robots can see [much / ~~very~~] better than humans, but they don't understand what they are seeing. 기출

(much: 비교급 강조부사, better: 비교급)

▶ 비교급 better를 수식하는 비교급 강조 부사 much가 와야 한다. very는 비교급을 수식할 수 없다.

기출 예문 PLUS

정답 및 해설 p.39

1 There is no right way to draw. Keeping this in mind, you'll have **a lot** more fun drawing the unique art that comes from you. 기출

2 How can you make the person you are talking to on the phone feel special? Just use your caller's name **far** more often than you would in person. 기출

3 There are many good things in your life waiting for you to fully enjoy them. If you do, these positive things will grow **even** stronger. 기출 응용

WORDS unique 유일무이한, 독특한 in person 직접, 몸소

기출 문장으로 PRACTICE

정답 및 해설 p.39

[01-04] 다음 문장의 네모 안에서 어법상 바른 것을 고르시오.

01 Fast muscle fibers are cells that can contract more quickly and powerfully than slow muscle fibers but fatigue [very / much] more easily. 기출

02 I think it's (A) [more / much] nicer to send a physical card than an email. A personal note written by your own hand matters (B) [far / very] more than a few lines of typing on a screen. 기출

03 After applying it to 34 people, the researchers confirmed the original finding and pushed back the frontiers of knowledge [still / very] further by showing that males were more ticklish than females. 기출

04 It might cost the farmer very little to grow a tomato, so the farmer might be able to sell it to you for [much / very] less than it would cost in the supermarket and still make a nice profit. 기출

[05-06] 다음 문장의 밑줄 친 부분이 어법상 바르면 O를 쓰고, 틀리면 바르게 고치시오.

05 Some of the lesser-known musicians are full of talent and energy, and they play <u>a lot</u> better than some of the famous musicians. 기출 응용

06 "He was a fiercely proud old man," Conan Doyle later explained, "and my instincts told me that his humiliation in being helped up would be <u>very</u> greater than any relief I could give him." 기출

WORDS **fiber** 섬유 **contract** 수축하다 **fatigue** 피로해지다, 지치다 **personal** 개인의; *직접[몸소] 한 **apply** 지원하다; *적용하다 **confirm** 확정하다 **finding** (연구 등의) 결과, 결론 **push back a frontier** 경계를 넓히다 **ticklish** 간지럼을 잘 타는 **fiercely** 사납게, 지독하게 **instinct** 직감 **humiliation** 창피, 굴욕 **relief** 안도, 안심

1 **다음 글의 밑줄 친 부분 중, 어법상 틀린 것은?** (2012년 3월 고3 학평)

We do not hear with our eyes, but sometimes it almost seems as if we do. An environment–agency official tells a surprising incident about some people ① who lived in an apartment building close to a busy state highway. The families were made ② miserably by the noise, and they complained to the city government. City officials went to the state capital again and again to ask that something ③ be done about quieting the highway noise. They were put off repeatedly. At last the city officials had an idea. They planted a single row of trees in front of the apartment house. The trees made hardly any difference in the amount of noise, but they ④ did block the view of the highway. After that, there were very ⑤ few complaints from the people in the building.

POINT 29 적용하기 **형용사 자리와 부사 자리를 구분하라!**

1 형용사 또는 부사가 문장 안에서 어떤 역할을 하는지 확인하자.

The families(주어) were made(동사) miserably(주격보어) by the noise, and they complained to the city government.

▶ 주어(The families)의 상태를 설명하는 주격보어 역할을 한다.

2 형용사 자리인지 부사 자리인지 판단하자.

▶ 형용사는 보어의 역할을 할 수 있지만 부사는 보어의 역할을 할 수 없다.

2

(A), (B), (C)의 각 네모 안에서 어법에 맞는 표현으로 가장 적절한 것은? (2012학년도 수능)

On January 10, 1992, a ship (A) [traveled / traveling] through rough seas lost 12 cargo containers, one of which held 28,800 floating bath toys. Brightly colored ducks, frogs, and turtles were set adrift in the middle of the Pacific Ocean. After seven months, the first toys made landfall on beaches near Sitka, Alaska, 3,540 kilometers from (B) [what / where] they were lost. Other toys floated north and west along the Alaskan coast and across the Bering Sea. Some toy animals stayed at sea (C) [even / very] longer. They floated completely along the North Pacific currents, ending up back in Sitka.

	(A)		(B)		(C)
①	traveled	……	what	……	even
②	traveled	……	what	……	very
③	traveling	……	what	……	even
④	traveling	……	where	……	even
⑤	traveling	……	where	……	very

WORDS

1 **official** 공무원, 관리, 임원 **incident** 일, 사건 **quiet** 조용해지게 하다, 진정시키다 **put off** 미루다, 연기하다; *발뺌하다 **row** 열, 줄 **complaint** 불평, 항의

2 **rough** 거친 **cargo** (선박·비행기의) 화물 **container** 용기; *(화물 수송용) 컨테이너 **adrift** 표류하는 **make landfall** 상륙하다, 육지에 닿다 **current** 해류, 조류

Chapter 09

대명사

UNIT 15

대명사의 쓰임

POINT 34 ★★★★★

대명사는 그것이 대신하는 명사와 수·격이 일치해야 한다!

대명사는 그것이 대신하는 명사의 수와 일치하도록 단수대명사 또는 복수대명사로 써야 하며, 문장에서의 역할에 따라 주격, 목적격, 소유격 형태로 쓴다. 소유대명사는 '~의 것'이라는 의미로, 「소유격 대명사+명사」를 대신한다.

대명사 it의 쓰임

1 앞에 오는 단수명사, 혹은 구나 절을 대신한다.
2 뒤에 오는 진주어, 진목적어를 대신하여 가주어, 가목적어 역할을 한다.

a. One benefit of our new system is that **it** can help you save a lot of time.
b. The flight suddenly disappeared into thin air, and **it** was headline news for a month.
c. **It** is nice to have what you want when you want it. 기출

a. 우리의 새 시스템의 한 가지 장점은 그것이 당신이 많은 시간을 절약하도록 도울 수 있다는 것이다. b. 비행기가 갑자기 흔적도 없이 사라졌고, 그것은 한 달간 뉴스의 헤드라인이었다. c. 당신이 원하는 것을 당신이 원할 때 가지는 것은 즐거운 일이다.

대표 예문 If you found a dead bird or mosquito (단수명사), you could guess by looking at ~~their~~ / its (소유격 대명사(단수)) wings that flying was its normal mode of transport. 기출

▶ 단수명사인 a dead bird or mosquito를 대신하는 대명사이므로, 단수형 소유격 대명사인 its를 써야 한다.

기출 예문 PLUS

정답 및 해설 p.41

1 Living things exist in a nonliving universe and depend on **it** in many ways. 기출

2 He made a number of fascinating findings, and he had the evidence to back **them** up. 기출

3 Sissi was not discouraged by the boys who wouldn't let **her** play soccer. Eventually, **she** got **her** way on the streets of Salvador, Brazil, because the soccer ball that the boys wanted to play with was **hers**. 기출
= her soccer ball

WORDS disappear into thin air 흔적도 없이 사라지다 mode 방식, 방법 fascinating 대단히 흥미로운 back up ~을 뒷받침하다 discouraged 낙담한

기출 문장으로 PRACTICE

정답 및 해설 p.41

[01-05] 다음 문장의 네모 안에서 어법상 바른 것을 고르시오.

01 Halfhearted individuals are seldom distinguished for courage, even when it involves [its / their] own welfare. 기출

02 Brazil had larger proven oil reserves than Mexico in 2011, but the daily oil production of Brazil was lower than [that / those] of Mexico in 2010. 기출

03 If the standards you set were not [your / yours], it may be time to define your personal expectations for yourself and make self-fulfillment your goal. 기출

04 To make the choice to express a feeling by carving a specific form from a rock, without the use of high technology or colors, restricts the artist significantly. Such choices are not made to limit creativity, but rather to cultivate [it / them]. 기출

05 Because of his injury, Jim wasn't able to play on the basketball team during the rest of that year, but the coach did make [his / him] equipment manager so that he could come and practice. 기출

[06-07] 다음 문장의 밑줄 친 부분이 어법상 바르면 O를 쓰고, 틀리면 바르게 고치시오.

06 In fact, all complex organisms, especially <u>those</u> with brains, suffer from information overload. 기출

07 In order for a great company to serve the public, it must have a philosophy of doing business which will insure that <u>their</u> people serve the public efficiently and in a pleasing manner. 기출

WORDS **halfhearted** 냉담한 **distinguish** 눈에 띄다, 유명하다 **welfare** 복지, 행복 **reserve** 비축(물); 《*pl.*》 *매장량 **standard** 기준 **self-fulfillment** 자기 달성, 자기 실현 **significantly** 상당히 **cultivate** 경작하다; *기르다, 육성하다 **organism** 유기체, 생물(체) **overload** 과부하 **philosophy** 철학 **insure** 보장하다

POINT 35 ★★★★★

인칭대명사 vs. 재귀대명사

동사의 주어, 혹은 의미상의 주어와 동사의 동작을 받는 목적어가 동일한 대상일 때, 목적어 자리에 재귀대명사를 써야 한다.

재귀대명사의 용법

재귀 용법(주어 = 목적어)	강조 용법(명사, 대명사 강조)
a. After they give their presentation, they are going to evaluate **themselves**.	**b.** The manager (**himself**) told me about our new London branch. ▶ 강조 용법의 재귀대명사는 생략 가능

a. 발표를 한 뒤에, 그들은 스스로를 평가할 것이다. b. 부장이 직접 내게 우리의 새 런던 지사에 대해 말했다.

대표 예문 You don't have to be Shakespeare, but you do need to know how to express (동사의 의미상 주어는 you) ~~you~~ / yourself (주어 = 목적어) properly in written form. 기출

▶ 동사 express의 의미상 주어와 목적어가 동일한 대상이므로 목적어로 재귀대명사 yourself가 와야 한다.

기출 예문 PLUS

정답 및 해설 p.41

1 I find **myself** laughing at things that I used to take far too seriously. 기출

2 A fire badly burned Glenn's legs. Though in unbearable pain, he forced **himself** to exercise daily and finally took a few painful steps. 기출

3 If you insist on always having a plan, you cut **yourself** off from your intuitive self and the inner joy it provides. To break planning addiction, (you) allow **yourself** one freedom. 기출

WORDS evaluate 평가하다 branch 지사, 분점 unbearable 견딜 수 없는 intuitive 직관적인 addiction 중독

기출 문장으로 PRACTICE

정답 및 해설 p.42

[01-05] 다음 문장의 네모 안에서 어법상 바른 것을 고르시오.

01 Jake was supposed to introduce [him / himself], but as soon as he opened his mouth, everyone started to laugh. 기출 응용

02 I am tired, physically and emotionally, and I sit down to enjoy a cold drink, trying to make [me / myself] comfortable. 기출

03 Don't keep telling [you / yourself] you can't do this or you can't do that. You can do ANYTHING if you think you can! 기출

04 During the day Louise Wilkinson works as a librarian. Once the sun goes down, she transforms [her / herself] into a vampire. 기출

05 People were more responsive and reacted more favorably to messages and proposals that were self-oriented and that allowed [them / themselves] to elevate their individualism. 기출

[06-07] 다음 문장의 밑줄 친 부분이 어법상 바르면 O를 쓰고, 틀리면 바르게 고치시오.

06 One night, my wife surprised <u>myself</u> by packing up the kids and dinner and coming to see me at work. 기출

07 The Greeks, far more than their contemporaries, speculated about the nature of the world they found <u>them</u> in and created models of it. 기출

WORDS **transform** 변형시키다 **vampire** 흡혈귀 **responsive** 즉각 반응하는; *관심을 보이는 **favorably** 호의적으로 **oriented** 지향적인 **elevate** 승격시키다 **individualism** 개인주의 **contemporary** 《*pl.*》 동시대인 **speculate** 사색하다, 심사숙고하다

POINT 36 ★★★★★

부정대명사는 주변 명사와 동사의 수를 살펴라!

부정대명사는 뒤에 오는 (대)명사나 동사의 수에 영향을 준다. 부정대명사는 명사를 수식하는 부정형용사로도 쓰인다.

부정대명사의 쓰임(one, some, other, another)

1 **one(s)**: 앞에 언급된 명사(구)를 받아 같은 종류의 불특정한 것을 나타냄
2 「**one ~ the other ...**」: 둘 중 '하나'는 one, '나머지 하나'는 the other
3 「**one ~ the others ...**」: 셋 이상에서 '하나'는 one, '나머지 전부'는 the others
4 「**one ~ another ...**」: 셋 이상에서 '하나'는 one, '다른 막연한 하나'는 another
5 「**some ~ (the) others ...**」: 여러 대상 중 '일부'는 some, '다른 막연한 일부'는 others, '나머지 전부'는 the others

부정대명사/부정형용사의 수 일치

• both (of+복수명사)+복수동사	• both+복수명사+복수동사
• either (of+복수명사)+단수동사	• either+단수명사+단수동사
• each (of+복수명사)+단수동사	• each+단수명사+단수동사
	• other+복수명사+복수동사
	• another+단수명사+단수동사
	• the other+단수/복수명사+단수/복수동사

대표 예문 Dozens of wildflowers of countless varieties cover the ground on [both / ~~either~~](부정형용사) sides(복수명사) of the path. 기출

▶ 뒤에 복수명사 sides가 이어지고 있으므로 both가 와야 한다. either은 단수명사와 쓰인다.

기출 예문 PLUS

정답 및 해설 p.42

1 On the table were two bowls—**one** held fresh cookies and **the other** contained radishes. 기출

2 When he went on board, he found **another** passenger was to share the cabin with him. 기출

3 Planning involves only the half of your brain that controls your logical thinking. **The other** half of your brain is left out of this planning process. 기출

WORDS **countless** 무수한, 셀 수 없이 많은 **path** 길 **radish** 무 **on board** 승선한 **cabin** (배의) 객실, 선실 **involve** 포함하다; *관여하게 하다

기출 문장으로 PRACTICE

정답 및 해설 p.42

[01-04] 다음 문장의 네모 안에서 어법상 바른 것을 고르시오.

01 The walls on [either / both] side of the front window are lined with pictures from her father's job. 기출

02 Pointing your lens directly at the sun may hurt the camera. The lens is similar to the human eye; [both / each] are damaged by directly peering at the light. 기출

03 When a lecturer presents a succession of new concepts, students' faces begin to show signs of frustration; some write furiously in their notebooks, while [other / others] give up writing in complete discouragement. 기출

04 As literature works as a bridge between cultures, particularly Western and Arab societies, the growing interest is driving a boom in translation. However, most translations are from English into (A) [other / another] languages, not from (B) [other / another] language, such as Arabic, into English. 기출 응용

[05-06] 다음 문장의 밑줄 친 부분이 어법상 바르면 O를 쓰고, 틀리면 바르게 고치시오.

05 Would you please establish a new fire station in our area, since you are mayor of our city? We are in urgent need of <u>one</u>. 기출

06 Tourism allows people from different places and cultures to learn new ways of thinking. <u>Other</u> positive effect of tourism is that it supports the survival of other cultures. 기출

WORDS **line** 줄을 세우다 **peer** 응시하다 **lecturer** 강사 **succession** 연속적인 것, 잇따름 **frustration** 불만, 좌절감 **furiously** 맹렬히 **discouragement** 낙심, 좌절 **translation** 번역 **urgent** 긴급한, 시급한

1 **(A), (B), (C)의 각 네모 안에서 어법에 맞는 표현으로 가장 적절한 것은? [3점]** (2015년 11월 고2 학평)

If we create a routine, we don't have to expend precious energy every day prioritizing everything. We must simply expend a small amount of initial energy to create the routine, and then all that is left to do is follow it. There is a huge body of scientific research to explain the mechanism (A) [which / by which] routine enables difficult things to become easy. One simplified explanation is that as we repeatedly do a certain task the neurons, or nerve cells, (B) [make / making] new connections through communication gateways called 'synapses.' With repetition, the connections strengthen and it becomes easier for the brain to activate them. For example, when you learn a new word it takes several repetitions at various intervals for the word to be mastered. To recall the word later you will need to activate the same synapses until eventually you know the word without consciously thinking about (C) [it / them].

	(A)		(B)		(C)
①	which	……	make	……	them
②	which	……	making	……	them
③	by which	……	make	……	them
④	by which	……	making	……	it
⑤	by which	……	make	……	it

POINT 34 적용하기 **대명사는 그것이 대신하는 명사와 수·격이 일치해야 한다!**

1 대명사가 지칭하는 대상을 우선 파악하자.

... you will need to activate the same synapses until eventually you know the word without consciously thinking about [it / them].

▶ about 뒤의 대명사는 앞의 단수명사 the word를 지칭한다.

2 지칭하는 명사의 수에 대명사의 수를 일치시키자.

▶ 단수명사를 지칭할 때는 단수형 대명사를, 복수명사를 지칭할 때는 복수형 대명사를 써야 한다.

정답 및 해설 p.43

2 (A), (B), (C)의 각 네모 안에서 어법에 맞는 표현으로 가장 적절한 것은? (2009년 3월 고2 학평)

Aging is a result of the gradual failure of the body's cells and organs to replace and repair (A) [them / themselves]. This is because there is a limit to the number of times that each cell can divide. As the body's cells begin to near this limit, the rate at which they divide slows down. Sometimes the new cells that are produced have defects or do not carry out their usual task (B) [effective / effectively]. Organs can then begin to fail, tissues change in structure, and the chemical reactions that power the body (C) [become / becoming] less efficient. Sometimes the blood supply to the brain is not effective. The brain cells become short of oxygen and nutrients, leading to forgetfulness.

	(A)		(B)		(C)
①	them	……	effective	……	become
②	themselves	……	effectively	……	become
③	them	……	effectively	……	become
④	themselves	……	effectively	……	becoming
⑤	themselves	……	effective	……	becoming

WORDS

1 **routine** 정해진 순서[과정] **expend** 쏟다, 들이다 **precious** 귀중한, 값비싼 **prioritize** 우선순위를 정하다 **initial** 처음의, 초기의 **mechanism** 방법, 메커니즘 **simplified** 쉽게 한, 간소화한 **gateway** 입구; *관문 **repetition** 반복 **activate** 활성화시키다 **interval** 간격 **master** ~에 숙달[통달]하다 **recall** 기억해내다 **consciously** 의식[자각]하여, 의식적으로

2 **aging** 노화 **gradual** 점진적인, 조금씩의 **replace** 대신하다, 대체하다 **near** (시간·거리상) 가까워지다 **rate** 비율; *속도 **defect** 결함 **carry out** ~을 수행하다 **tissue** (세포) 조직 **supply** 공급 **oxygen** 산소 **nutrient** 영양소, 영양분 **forgetfulness** 건망증

Chapter 10

Actual TEST **01**

Actual TEST **02**

Actual TEST **03**

Actual TEST **04**

Actual TEST **05**

1 **다음 글의 밑줄 친 부분 중, 어법상 틀린 것은?**

The minimum wage is the lowest hourly wage that employers are legally allowed to pay their employees. It is formulated to ensure that employees are living above the poverty line. The prospect of raising the minimum wage ① has become a social issue in recent years. Proponents argue that the minimum wage has not kept up with inflation, leaving workers and their families ② impoverished. Paying employees more would likely improve the quality of their lives. On a larger scale, it would encourage them to spend more, which would strengthen the economy. On the other hand, opponents of an increase in the minimum wage ③ claims that this increase would burden businesses by creating additional expenses, ④ leading to lower profits. What's more, the employment rate could also be decreased by a higher minimum wage, and businesses might feel the need to compensate by ⑤ increasing the prices of their products.

2 **(A), (B), (C)의 각 네모 안에서 어법에 맞는 표현으로 가장 적절한 것은?**

Both 'tone' and 'mood' are important for understanding and analyzing literary works, but many do not know the difference between the two terms. The tone of a work, whether it is sarcastic, optimistic, ironic, or humorous, (A) [convey / conveys] the writer's attitude toward what is being written about. The words that the writer chooses determine the tone, (B) [it / which] affects the reader's mood; fear, irritation, happiness, and relief are possible examples of a reader's mood. By creating the tone, the writer aims at helping the reader (C) [understand / understanding] the context of the work. The tone, however, may change depending on the plot of the novel as well as the characters' development. In some cases, the tone becomes progressively more serious throughout a book or a book series where the characters age or experience traumatic events.

	(A)		(B)		(C)
①	convey	……	it	……	understand
②	convey	……	which	……	understanding
③	conveys	……	it	……	understand
④	conveys	……	which	……	understand
⑤	conveys	……	which	……	understanding

3

다음 글의 밑줄 친 부분 중, 어법상 틀린 것은?

Polycarbonate is a durable, scratch-resistant material that is used to ① make bottles, eyeglass lenses and coatings for a variety of products. The process currently employed to manufacture polycarbonate ② requiring a synthetic compound known as bisphenol-A (BPA). Unfortunately, studies have shown that BPA has an adverse effect on the brain and reproductive system development of humans. In response to these findings, scientists have developed an alternative polycarbonate made with sugar and carbon dioxide that is ③ much safer. Its physical properties are similar to those of polycarbonates ④ derived from petrochemicals. What is different is ⑤ that it can be degraded back into its original ingredients by using a special enzyme. This new material is expected to eventually replace traditional polycarbonates in baby bottles and food containers.

4

(A), (B), (C)의 각 네모 안에서 어법에 맞는 표현으로 가장 적절한 것은?

One of the best known science-fiction series, *Star Trek* clearly illustrates the sentiments and beliefs of its time, as (A) [is / does] *Star Wars*. Both of these series created universes that reflect contemporary society, which makes them such useful tools for understanding the social landscape. The world of *Star Trek* began with a television series that first aired in 1966. This was when the economies of Europe and North America were as (B) [strong / strongly] as any in modern history. Accordingly, *Star Trek* features not only futuristic technology but also a utopian society of idealism and lawfulness, where racism and sexism are noticeably absent. *Star Wars*, on the other hand, premiered in the late 1970s, a time when people were becoming increasingly aware of the toll (C) [that / what] economic growth had taken on the environment. In contrast to the bright colors and optimism of *Star Trek*, *Star Wars* offers a darker view of the future.

	(A)		(B)		(C)
①	is	……	strong	……	that
②	is	……	strongly	……	what
③	does	……	strong	……	that
④	does	……	strong	……	what
⑤	does	……	strongly	……	what

1 **다음 글의 밑줄 친 부분 중, 어법상 틀린 것은?**

Accounts of childhood bullying often describe children being physically abused by classmates or ① having to suffer various taunts and insults. In addition to these two types of bullying, there's a third and equally insidious form: intellectual bullying. It begins when students are placed in an intellectual hierarchical structure ② which is determined by their grades. However, the real trouble starts when intellectual bullies, ③ recognizing for being smarter than their peers, are unjustly allowed to humiliate those who have received lower grades and fewer awards than they have. In other words, students suffer emotional harassment imposed by ④ their supposedly superior peers. While intellectual bullying generally receives ⑤ much less attention than other forms of bullying, it has similar lasting effects. If one is on the receiving end of this abuse, it can cause feelings of inferiority and a lack of self-esteem that may continue well into adulthood.

2 **(A), (B), (C)의 각 네모 안에서 어법에 맞는 표현으로 가장 적절한 것은?**

Bitcoins are a form of virtual currency (A) [designing / designed] to have self-contained value. Each bitcoin contains a digital ledger called a blockchain. It records every transaction that an individual coin is involved in. This helps blockchains prevent transactions from being duplicated and stop people from counterfeiting bitcoins. Although they have no physical representation, bitcoins can be used as if they (B) [were / had been] actual coins in your pocket. Bitcoins are popular with investors and are commonly used to purchase goods and services online. However, many offline establishments now accept bitcoins as well. The worth of a single bitcoin fluctuates on a daily basis and can be tracked online. New bitcoins will stop (C) [to be / being] produced once a total of 21 million coins has been reached. This is expected to occur sometime around the year 2040.

	(A)		(B)		(C)
①	designing	……	were	……	to be
②	designing	……	have been	……	being
③	designed	……	have been	……	to be
④	designed	……	were	……	being
⑤	designed	……	have been	……	being

3 **다음 글의 밑줄 친 부분 중, 어법상 틀린 것은?**

Benzo[α]pyrene, commonly referred to as BaP, is a type of hydrocarbon that is formed ① during incomplete combustion at temperatures between 300 °C and 600 °C. It is believed that BaP molecules ② may have created the conditions for life on Earth long ago. Unfortunately, BaP poses a serious health threat to humans. Everyday situations in which combustion occurs, such as grilling steaks on a barbecue, ③ cause BaP to enter our air, soil and food. However, nothing creates more of a BaP risk for humans than cigarettes. When toxic hydrocarbons enter our body, ④ they are broken down into smaller molecules. This process creates a compound that bonds tightly with our DNA, ⑤ what means that the DNA can't duplicate properly and causes mutations. This can potentially lead to the occurrence of cancer.

4 **(A), (B), (C)의 각 네모 안에서 어법에 맞는 표현으로 가장 적절한 것은?**

During the First Industrial Revolution, steam power was used to (A) [mechanize / mechanizing] the production process. In the Second Industrial Revolution, it was electrical power that enabled mass production in industry. Information technology was the key to the Third Industrial Revolution, allowing companies to fully automate the production process. And now the Fourth Industrial Revolution is underway, based on the third. It is characterized by a new form of technology that blurs the boundaries between digital, physical and biological components. (B) [Comparing / Compared] to its predecessors, the Fourth Industrial Revolution is moving at breakneck speed, extensively transforming systems not only in production but also in management and governance. The possibilities of billions of people who are connected by shared knowledge and processing power (C) [is / are] limitless. It is expected that the Fourth Industrial Revolution will eventually lead to breakthroughs in artificial intelligence, nanotechnology and quantum computing.

	(A)		(B)		(C)
①	mechanize	……	Comparing	……	is
②	mechanize	……	Comparing	……	are
③	mechanize	……	Compared	……	are
④	mechanizing	……	Comparing	……	is
⑤	mechanizing	……	Compared	……	are

Actual TEST 3

1 **다음 글의 밑줄 친 부분 중, 어법상 틀린 것은?**

Some people are ashamed of their bodies—they constantly compare ① themselves to others and then criticize their own appearance. Although it is sometimes said that feeling ashamed can motivate overweight people to live a healthier lifestyle, there isn't any evidence to support this. Rather than encouraging them to make better decisions, shame makes people ② to want to cut off interpersonal connections and avoid social activities. In fact, it has been shown that people who are ashamed of their bodies are more likely to admit to ③ deliberately avoiding exercise. This means that shame actually makes ④ it more difficult to overcome weight issues. Therefore, people should be encouraged to view their bodies in the same way that they view the people they care about — imperfect but inherently worthy of ⑤ being treated with respect.

2 **(A), (B), (C)의 각 네모 안에서 어법에 맞는 표현으로 가장 적절한 것은?**

Brain-computer interfaces (BCIs) are direct communication links between the human brain and electronic devices. To date, the main focus of BCI research has been on (A) [restoration / restoring] human bodily functions—such as vision, hearing, and muscle movement—that have been damaged. However, BCIs have also drawn the interest of the gaming industry. A cutting-edge field known as neurogaming is currently utilizing BCI technology to allow players to interact with games without the use of controllers. Specially designed software monitors players' brainwaves, facial expressions and heart rates to determine what happens within the game. There is even BCI technology (B) [what / that] senses the mood of each player and adjusts the game's music and images accordingly. This allows the users' reactions to be directly reflected in the game's virtual environment in real time. There are only (C) [a few / a little] basic neurogames currently available, but they are expected to improve and increase in number in the near future.

	(A)		(B)		(C)
①	restoration	……	what	……	a few
②	restoration	……	that	……	a little
③	restoring	……	what	……	a little
④	restoring	……	that	……	a few
⑤	restoring	……	that	……	a little

3 **다음 글의 밑줄 친 부분 중, 어법상 틀린 것은?**

Evidence suggests that music played an important role in prehistoric human culture. Some of the oldest artifacts ever uncovered ① are musical instruments, such as bone flutes estimated to be approximately 40,000 years old. Of course, our auditory and vocal abilities date back ② even further; therefore, it is reasonable to speculate that vocal music preceded the instrumental variety, as Darwin and Helmholtz did. This vocal music includes songs ③ sung by parents to their offspring. While such songs do not leave behind fossils, they do appear all across the globe. The ubiquity of these songs, ④ which have a stereotyped style, supports the belief that this is universal human behavior. In fact, it is believed that the ability of infants to recognize vocal music is genetically imprinted. Although humans produce music at all stages of development and ⑤ enjoys it as well, music perception is strongest during infancy.

4 **(A), (B), (C)의 각 네모 안에서 어법에 맞는 표현으로 가장 적절한 것은?**

When trying to foster a creative environment, companies often put an emphasis on making their employees happier. However, Mark Davis, an American psychologist, (A) [believes / believing] this may not be the most efficient path to greater creativity. After reviewing research on the subject, he came to the conclusion that a positive mood does help people with the initial stage of creativity—brainstorming, information processing, and coming up with ideas—but not with the second stage, which mainly focuses on overcoming challenges. Most scientists agree that this next stage relies more on problem-solving skills than on positivity. And solving problems (B) [is / are] a process that involves things that generally don't feel good, such as critiquing, experimenting and failing. These negative feelings actually make us more creative than positive ones, as the unpleasant stress caused by problems can motivate us (C) [complete / to complete] tasks.

	(A)		(B)		(C)
①	believes	……	is	……	complete
②	believes	……	are	……	to complete
③	believes	……	is	……	to complete
④	believing	……	is	……	to complete
⑤	believing	……	are	……	complete

1 **다음 글의 밑줄 친 부분 중, 어법상 틀린 것은?**

Words have power — they frame our perspectives, and by doing so, they can change our behavior. Take cancer, for example. It's a vicious, often fatal disease, ① one that most people would rather not talk about. Because a cure for cancer remains ② elusively, the focus has been on treatments. Interestingly, the language used to describe the disease can affect the way it is treated. You may have noticed ③ that some violent words and military terms are sometimes used to discuss cancer. People who are diagnosed with it are described as being in a "battle" or "fighting" for their lives. When such language is used, it is likely to persuade doctors to consider ④ using more aggressive treatments. On the other hand, when ⑤ hearing people speak about cancer in a more peaceful way, such as using the metaphor that it is a long journey, doctors will be less likely to take an aggressive approach.

2 **(A), (B), (C)의 각 네모 안에서 어법에 맞는 표현으로 가장 적절한 것은?**

The term "cultured meat" refers to meat that is grown from cell cultures by using tissue engineering techniques. Producing meat in this fashion provides several advantages, including environmental benefits. Raising livestock consumes a high amount of energy and adversely (A) [impacts / impacting] the environment. Producing cultured meat, however, can reduce energy consumption by as much as 45% and requires only 2% of the land that the meat industry currently does, making it a sensible alternative for our overpopulated world. Furthermore, cultured meat is potentially healthier than traditional meat (B) [because / because of] the fact that it is grown in a strictly controlled setting and experiences little or no exposure to pesticides, pollutants, or disease. Finally, cultured meat is said to taste as if it (C) [were / had been] normal meat from a farm animal. Although commercial production is not yet underway, cultured meat is expected to be on supermarket shelves within a decade.

	(A)		(B)		(C)
①	impacts	……	because	……	were
②	impacts	……	because	……	had been
③	impacts	……	because of	……	were
④	impacting	……	because	……	had been
⑤	impacting	……	because of	……	were

3

다음 글의 밑줄 친 부분 중, 어법상 틀린 것은?

In 2013, the world became aware that the NSA, an intelligence agency ① located in the United States, had been spying on millions of people. Little information was known about these surveillance programs until Edward Snowden, a former employee of the NSA, released classified documents. Judging from what ② was disclosed, these surveillance programs seem to have accessed people's personal information by tapping their phones, breaking into their email accounts, and ③ track their Internet activities. Understandably, these methods appear ④ unethical and undemocratic to many citizens. Even worse, it was revealed that U.S. intelligence agencies also spied on allied countries during international summits. This revelation caused quite a stir throughout the world. To some degree, the uproar was simply an attempt to gain diplomatic leverage in an ongoing competition between countries. However, the situation has also led to a serious heightening of tensions between the United States and ⑤ other countries.

*leverage: 영향력

4

(A), (B), (C)의 각 네모 안에서 어법에 맞는 표현으로 가장 적절한 것은?

There is an old saying that goes "Two heads are better than one." It's true in almost every situation, but it's especially true for students. (A) [Few / Little] learning strategies are as beneficial to students as collaborative learning, for it teaches real-world skills, such as communication, teamwork, and cooperation. Collaborative learning occurs when students form groups and need to solve problems as a team rather than as individuals. When the teacher (B) [to assign / assigns] a complicated group task which requires teamwork, students with different strengths have to play different roles to complete the task. The task is designed to be impossible for one student to solve alone. Through practical and well-designed collaborative learning tasks, students can appreciate their peers' contributions. (C) [What / That] they learn from these experiences will benefit them throughout the rest of their school careers and beyond.

	(A)		(B)		(C)
①	Few	……	to assign	……	What
②	Few	……	assigns	……	What
③	Few	……	to assign	……	That
④	Little	……	assigns	……	What
⑤	Little	……	assigns	……	That

1 **다음 글의 밑줄 친 부분 중, 어법상 틀린 것은?**

One practical way of predicting the future ① is to look backward to the past. English currently enjoys the status of lingua franca, as Latin did in pre-modern Europe. Latin was originally the language of the Romans. ② Having been spread by the expansion of the Roman Empire, Latin became the common language of the empire. Long after the empire ③ had fallen Classical Latin continued to thrive as a medium of writing. On the other hand, Vulgar Latin, which was used in speech, was gradually transformed into new dialects in many regions. Those dialects brought about the rise of modern Romance languages, including French, Spanish, Portuguese, and Italian. Similar evolutions have been observed today in some countries ④ which English functions as a second language. This indicates a possible future of this language—the emergence of "interlanguages," in which elements of English have merged with ⑤ those of local languages.

*lingua franca: 국제어, 공통어 **interlanguage: 중간언어

2 **(A), (B), (C)의 각 네모 안에서 어법에 맞는 표현으로 가장 적절한 것은?**

In modern culture, the pursuit of success has become a kind of religion. It creates meaning at both an intellectual and emotional level, influences the decisions we make, and (A) [containing / contains] its own morality. Furthermore, it is practiced by groups of people who share ideologies they don't fully understand. In this religion, success is not measured by self-satisfaction. Instead, it is determined by our status in the social hierarchies of the groups we belong to. The religion of success is dangerous, and few of us even realize that we are (B) [lying / laying] our lives on its altar. It has become such an integral part of our lives that we need to stop and listen (C) [close / closely] to notice the anxiety it constantly produces. Once we are aware of it, however, we have the ability to begin making decisions based on personal wisdom rather than unhealthy cultural obsessions.

	(A)		(B)		(C)
①	contains	……	lying	……	close
②	contains	……	laying	……	close
③	contains	……	laying	……	closely
④	containing	……	lying	……	close
⑤	containing	……	laying	……	closely

3

다음 글의 밑줄 친 부분 중, 어법상 틀린 것은?

Arthur Miller's play *Death of a Salesman* premiered in 1949. Miller's characterization of the main character Willy, an unstable and underperforming salesman, demonstrates Miller's argument that the ordinary man is as much a tragic figure ① as any Shakespearean king is. Willy truly believes in the American Dream, and while he considers it ② noble to be a salesman during the post-World War Two consumerism boom, he has never been successful at it. Willy starts ③ pressuring his eldest son, Biff. He wants Biff to become a businessman and ④ hopes that Biff's success will make up for his own failures. However, these are unrealistic expectations, and Biff is unwilling to live up to ⑤ it. Sadly, Willy fails to understand himself and refuses to accept that he and his son are just common people. The hopeless dreams that Willy is desperate to fulfill make him a character that is both tragic and relatable.

4

(A), (B), (C)의 각 네모 안에서 어법에 맞는 표현으로 가장 적절한 것은?

Since drones—small, unmanned aircraft—were first made available to the general public, their use (A) [expanded / has expanded] into the retail sector. Multiple businesses are currently exploring strategies of delivering packages via drones. In one trial, a drone carried an online purchase to a residence in under 15 minutes. And this may just be the beginning of a technology-driven transformation of the consumer experience. Drones (B) [have / having] the distinct advantage of being unaffected by traffic and labor strikes, while delivering packages with speed and accuracy. The main obstacle businesses face is government restrictions on the private use of airspace due to safety concerns. Apprehensions have also (C) [raised / been raised] about the number of humans in the delivery industry that could lose their job to drones, as well as the unwanted contribution drones could make to current levels of air and noise pollution in urban areas.

	(A)		(B)		(C)
①	expanded	……	have	……	raised
②	expanded	……	having	……	been raised
③	has expanded	……	have	……	raised
④	has expanded	……	have	……	been raised
⑤	has expanded	……	having	……	raised

지은이

NE능률 영어교육연구소

NE능률 영어교육연구소는 혁신적이며 효율적인 영어 교재를 개발하고
영어 학습의 질을 한 단계 높이고자 노력하는 NE능률의 연구조직입니다.

올클 수능 어법 〈완성〉

펴 낸 이 주민홍
펴 낸 곳 서울특별시 마포구 월드컵북로 396(상암동) 누리꿈스퀘어 비즈니스타워 10층
(주)NE능률 (우편번호 03925)
펴 낸 날 2018년 1월 5일 초판 제1쇄
2024년 2월 15일 제14쇄
전 화 02 2014 7114
팩 스 02 3142 0356
홈페이지 www.neungyule.com
등록번호 제1-68호
I S B N 979-11-253-1829-3 53740
정 가 12,000원

NE 능률

고객센터

교재 내용 문의 : contact.nebooks.co.kr (별도의 가입 절차 없이 작성 가능)
제품 구매, 교환, 불량, 반품 문의 : 02-2014-7114
☎ 전화문의는 본사 업무시간 중에만 가능합니다.

NE능률 교재 MAP

문법
구문

아래 교재 MAP을 참고하여 본인의 현재 혹은 목표 수준에 따라 교재를 선택하세요.
NE능률 교재들과 함께 영어실력을 쑥쑥~ 올려보세요!
MP3 등 교재 부가 학습 서비스 및 자세한 교재 정보는 www.nebooks.co.kr 에서 확인하세요.

초1-2

초3
- 그래머버디 1
- 초등영어 문법이 된다 Starter 1

초3-4
- 그래머버디 2
- 초등영어 문법이 된다 Starter 2
- 초등 Grammar Inside 1
- 초등 Grammar Inside 2

초4-5
- 그래머버디 3
- Grammar Bean 1
- Grammar Bean 2
- 초등영어 문법이 된다 1
- 초등 Grammar Inside 3
- 초등 Grammar Inside 4

초5-6
- Grammar Bean 3
- Grammar Bean 4
- 초등영어 문법이 된다 2
- 초등 Grammar Inside 5
- 초등 Grammar Inside 6

초6-예비중
- 능률중학영어 예비중
- Grammar Inside Starter
- 원리를 더한 영문법 STARTER

중1
- 능률중학영어 중1
- Grammar Zone 입문편
- Grammar Zone 워크북 입문편
- 1316 Grammar 1
- 문제로 마스터하는 중학영문법 1
- Grammar Inside 1
- 열중 16강 문법 1
- 쓰기로 마스터하는 중학서술형 1학년
- 중학 천문장 1

중1-2
- 능률중학영어 중2
- 1316 Grammar 2
- 문제로 마스터하는 중학영문법 2
- Grammar Inside 2
- 열중 16강 문법 2
- 원리를 더한 영문법 1
- 중학영문법 총정리 모의고사 1
- 중학 천문장 2

중2-3
- Grammar Zone 기초편
- Grammar Zone 워크북 기초편
- 1316 Grammar 3
- 원리를 더한 영문법 2
- 중학영문법 총정리 모의고사 2
- 쓰기로 마스터하는 중학서술형 2학년
- 중학 천문장 3

중3
- 능률중학영어 중3
- 문제로 마스터하는 중학영문법 3
- Grammar Inside 3
- 열중 16강 문법 3
- 중학영문법 총정리 모의고사 3
- 쓰기로 마스터하는 중학서술형 3학년

예비고–고1
- 문제로 마스터하는 고등영문법
- 올클 수능 어법 start
- 천문장 입문

고1
- Grammar Zone 기본편 1
- Grammar Zone 워크북 기본편 1
- Grammar Zone 기본편 2
- Grammar Zone 워크북 기본편 2
- 필히 통하는 고등 영문법 기본편
- 필히 통하는 고등 서술형 기본편
- 천문장 기본

고1-2
- 필히 통하는 고등 영문법 실력편
- 필히 통하는 고등 서술형 실전편
- TEPS BY STEP G+R Basic

고2-3
- Grammar Zone 종합편
- Grammar Zone 워크북 종합편
- 올클 수능 어법 완성
- 천문장 완성

고3

수능 이상/ 토플 80-89 · 텝스 600-699점
- TEPS BY STEP G+R 1

수능 이상/ 토플 90-99 · 텝스 700-799점
- TEPS BY STEP G+R 2

수능 이상/ 토플 100 · 텝스 800점 이상
- TEPS BY STEP G+R 3

올클 수능 어법 완성

All Clear

시험에 꼭 나오는

수능 어법 총정리

정답 및 해설

NE 능률

올클
수능
어법
완성

Chapter 01 주어 동사 파악

UNIT 01 동사의 수 일치

POINT 01 수식어구가 아닌 핵심 주어를 찾아라! p.8

대표 예문

과학자들에게 가장 중요한 외적인 보상은 동료들의 인정이다.

기출 예문 PLUS

1 지나치게 익은 과일과 마구 자란 풀로 가득한 정원은 정원사에게 즐겁지 않다.

2 우리가 이미지를 보는 맥락은 우리의 반응에 중대한 차이를 만들어낸다.

3 콘크리트와 아스팔트로 둘러싸인 가로수는 평균 7년에서 15년을 산다.

4 국방 서비스의 제공은 모두가 자유롭게 이용 가능한 것의 강력한 한 가지 예이다.

5 신선한 브로콜리 송이를 보관하는 가장 좋은 방법은 그것들을 봉하지 않은 비닐봉지에 넣어 채소 칸에서 냉장 보관하는 것이다.

기출 문장으로 PRACTICE p.9

01 (A) repel (B) have 02 fills 03 was 04 are
05 is 06 has 07 O 08 leads → lead

01 짜증을 잘 내고 우두머리 행세를 하는 지도자는 사람들의 접근을 막으며, 따르는 사람이 거의 없다.

▸ 문장의 주어는 주격 관계대명사절(who are ... bossy)의 수식을 받는 Leaders로, 주어가 복수명사이므로 복수동사 repel과 have가 오는 것이 알맞다.

02 풀이 산들바람에 춤을 출 때 야생화 향기가 대기를 채운다.

▸ 문장의 주어는 전치사구(of wildflowers)의 수식을 받는 The perfume으로, 주어가 단수명사이므로 단수동사 fills가 오는 것이 알맞다.

03 감염된 지역에서 나온 가금류의 판매와 운송을 제한하는 법이 통과되었다.

▸ 문장의 주어는 현재분사구(restricting ... area)의 수식을 받는 A law로, 주어가 단수명사이므로 단수동사 was가 오는 것이 알맞다.

04 전국적으로 판촉되는 여러 상품들의 고급 광고들은 여전히 자주 필름에 촬영된다.

▸ 문장의 주어는 전치사구(for many ... the nation)의 수식을 받는 High-end commercials로, 주어가 복수명사이므로 복수동사 are가 오는 것이 알맞다.

05 상대측이 보듯이 상황을 보는 능력은 교섭자가 가질 수 있는 가장 중요한 기술 중 하나이다.

▸ 문장의 주어는 to부정사구(to see ... it)의 수식을 받는 The ability로, 주어가 단수명사이므로 단수동사 is가 오는 것이 알맞다.

06 강 유역과 가까운 지역에 서식하는 현지의 야생동물은 농업을 위한 물줄기 방향 전환과 다양한 요인으로 인한 오염에 영향을 받아왔다.

▸ 문장의 주어는 현재분사구(inhabiting ... the basin)의 수식을 받는 The local wildlife로, 주어가 단수명사이므로 단수동사 has가 와야 한다.

07 내가 나의 어린 시절로부터 가져온 가장 유용한 것은 독서에의 자신감이었다.

▸ 문장의 주어는 목적격 관계대명사절((that) I ... my childhood)의 수식을 받는 The most useful thing으로, 주어가 단수명사이므로 단수동사 was는 어법상 바르다.

08 거주하는 예술가들 사이에 형성된 교우 관계는 흔히 마을을 넘어서는 공동 작업과 친분으로 이어진다.

▸ 문장의 주어는 과거분사구(established ... in residence)의 수식을 받는 Friendships로, 주어가 복수명사이므로 단수동사 leads를 복수동사 lead로 고쳐야 한다.

POINT 02 주어 자리에 "구"나 "절"이 오면 단수 취급하라! p.10

대표 예문

기억을 '저장소' 또는 '단계' 또는 '회로'라는 용어로 설명하는 것은 우리의 이해를 더욱 구체적으로 만든다.

기출 예문 PLUS

1 어떤 경우에도 용기를 갖는 것은 강한 결단력을 요구한다.

2 새집에 대해 내가 가장 흥미를 가지게 한 것은 뒤뜰에 있는 마구간이었다.

3 최고의 의료 서비스를 받는 것은 온라인 서점에서 무언가를 주문하는 것과는 상당히 다르다.

4 밀린 잠을 보충할 수 있는가 없는가는, 이를테면 주말에, 수면 연구가들 사이에서 뜨겁게 논의되는 주제이다.

5 어떤 종이 경쟁적으로 우위에 있느냐 하는 것은 때때로 계절적인 변화와 같은 상황에 좌우된다.

기출 문장으로 PRACTICE

p.11

01 is 02 is 03 is 04 destroys 05 is 06 are → is 07 have → has

01 우리가 누구라고 생각하는가는 우리가 누구처럼 되고 싶은가에 대해 내리는 선택의 결과이다.

▶ 문장의 주어는 의문사절(Who ... we are)로, 의문사절은 단수 취급하므로 단수동사 is가 와야 한다.

02 동물이 인간이 느끼는 외로움과 유사한 어떤 것이든 느낄 수 있는가는 말하기 어렵다.

▶ 문장의 주어는 접속사 whether절(Whether ... humans feel)로, whether절은 단수 취급하므로 단수동사 is가 오는 것이 알맞다.

03 많은 SNS 사용자들이 알아채지 못할지도 모르는 것은 그들이 게시한 모든 사진을 그 회사가 소유한다는 것이다.

▶ 문장의 주어는 관계대명사 what절(What ... realize)로, 관계대명사 what절은 단수 취급하므로 단수동사 is가 오는 것이 알맞다.

04 이미 사회적으로 고립된 이들을 투표에서 배제하는 것은, 그것이 계급제를 만들어내므로 우리 민주주의를 파괴한다.

▶ 문장의 주어는 to부정사구(To exclude ... socially isolated)로, to부정사구는 단수 취급하므로 단수동사 destroys가 와야 한다.

05 기후가 수백 만년에 걸쳐 어떻게 변화해왔는지를 이해하는 것은 현재의 지구 온난화 추세를 제대로 평가하는 데 필수적이다.

▶ 문장의 주어는 동명사구(Understanding ... millions of years)로, 동명사구는 단수 취급하므로 단수동사 is가 오는 것이 알맞다.

06 유기체를 그것들을 구성하는 물질과 다르게 만드는 것은 그것들의 조직 수준이다.

▶ 문장의 주어는 관계대명사 what절(What ... compose them)로, 관계대명사 what절은 단수 취급하므로 복수동사 are를 단수동사 is로 고쳐야 한다.

07 동물 이미지를 상업적인 목적으로 이용하는 것은 동물 권리 운동가들에게 강하게 비판을 받아왔다.

▶ 문장의 주어는 동명사구(Using ... commercial purposes)로, 동명사구는 단수 취급하므로 복수동사 have를 단수동사 has로 고쳐야 한다.

POINT 03 도치구문은 동사 뒤에 오는 주어에 동사의 수를 일치시켜라!

p.12

대표 예문

컴퓨터는 같은 문제를 처리하는 데 있어서 좀처럼 인간보다 더 민감하지도 정확하지도 않다.

기출 예문 PLUS

1 콘서트마다 유명한 음악가들을 고용할 여유가 있는 음악 단체는 드물다.

2 그의 식당 벽에는 Ernest Hemingway의 글에서 따온 인용구를 액자에 넣은 것이 있었다.

3 어느 정도의 시간과 노력이 있고 난 후에야 학습자는 통찰력과 직관력을 발달시키기 시작한다.

4 이산화탄소는 명백히 독이 없을 뿐만 아니라, 이산화탄소 수치 변화가 꼭 인간 활동을 반영하는 것은 아니다.

기출 문장으로 PRACTICE

p.13

01 are 02 were 03 do 04 was 05 has 06 do 07 do → does 08 were → was

01 제가 건강하다는 것을 입증하는 제 의료 증명서와 의사의 소견서가 첨부되어 있습니다.

▶ 보어(Attached)가 문장 앞에 나와 주어와 동사가 도치된 문장이다. 주어(my medical certificates and a doctor's note)가 복수이므로 복수동사 are가 오는 것이 알맞다.

02 탈출한 죄수들은 저 멀리 아래에서 손전등의 흔들리는 광선을 볼 수 있었다.

▶ 장소를 나타내는 부사구(In the distance below)가 문장 앞에 나와 주어와 동사가 도치된 문장이다. 주어(the escaped prisoners)가 복수이므로 복수동사 were가 와야 한다.

03 수만 명의 시리아인들은 너무 절망감을 느낀 나머지 자신의 나라에서 도망쳐 난민이 되려는 시도를 한다.

▶ 보어(So hopeless)가 문장 앞에 나와 주어와 동사가 도치된 문장이다. 주어(tens of thousands of Syrians)가 복수이므로 복수동사 do가 오는 것이 알맞다.

04 어린 범죄자가 되는 것은 더 이상 인생에서 그들의 유일한 선택권이 아니었다. 대신에 그들에게는 여러 다른 기회가 있었다.

▶ 부정어구(No longer)가 문장 앞에 나와 주어와 동사가 도치된 문장이다. 주어(being young criminals)가 동명사구로, 동명사구는 단수 취급하므로 단수동사 was가 와야 한다.

05 겨우 지난 몇십 년 안에, 식량은 지방과 관련된 건강 문제를 야기할 정도로 너무 많고 너무 얻기 쉬워졌다.

▶ 부정어 Only를 포함한 부사구(Only in the last few decades)가 문장 앞에 나와 주어와 동사가 도치된 문장이다. 주어(food)가 단수이므로 단수동사 has가 와야 한다.

06 그들은 과정에 집중하고 과정을 따르는 것에 대해 말한다. 그들은 골을 넣거나 득점하는 것에 대해서는 좀처럼 말하지 않는다.

▶ 부정어(Rarely)가 문장 앞에 나와 주어와 동사가 도치된 문장이다. 주어(they)가 복수이므로, 복수동사 do가 오는 것이 알맞다.

07 이동하는 새들의 수는 달에 따라 다를 뿐만 아니라, 종에 따라서도 다르다.

▶ 부정어(Not only)가 문장 앞에 나와 주어와 동사가 도치된 문장이다. 주어(the number of migrating birds)가 단수이므로, 복수동사 do를 단수동사 does로 고쳐야 한다.

08 인형 옆에 상아로 만든 작은 상자가 있었는데, 그것은 작은 빗과 은으로 된 거울을 담고 있었다.

▶ 장소를 나타내는 부사구(Next to the dolls)가 문장 앞에 나와 주어와 동사가 도치된 문장이다. 주어(a small box made of ivory)가 단수이므로, 복수동사 were를 단수동사 was로 고쳐야 한다.

POINT 04 「부분표현+of+명사」는 명사에 동사의 수를 일치시켜라!

p.14

대표 예문

물의 일부는 지하 수원에서 나오고, 일부는 비에서 나온다.

기출 예문 PLUS

1 마지막으로, 아이들 사이의 갈등과 싸움 대부분은 자연스러운 것이다.

2 민감한 사람들의 공통적인 문제점 중 하나는 뇌의 델타파의 과잉이다.

3 우리 모두는 행동을 계획하기 위해 자신의 사회의 구성원으로서 습득하는 문화적 지식을 이용한다.

4 미국의 주요 에너지 총생산의 2/3가 천연가스, 석탄, 그리고 석유에서 나온다.

5 대부분의 황야 지역에서, 그 지역을 방문하는 단체의 대부분은 보통 2명에서 4명 사이로 소규모이다.

기출 문장으로 PRACTICE

p.15

01 were **02** is **03** tends **04** say **05** follow
06 are **07** are → is **08** seem → seems

01 그는 Oxford에 갔는데, 그곳에서 영국 최고의 과학자 몇몇이 그 당시 연구를 하고 있었다.

▶ 관계부사절에서 some of 뒤에 복수명사(the best scientists)가 왔으므로 복수동사 were가 와야 한다.

02 많은 성공한 사람들이 하는 가장 어려운 것들 중 하나는 자신들의 생각에 이의를 제기하는 것이다.

▶ 「one of+명사」가 주어 자리에 올 경우 뒤에 단수동사가 와야 하므로 is가 알맞다.

03 미국에서, 크리스마스 준비 기간에 하는 광고의 대부분은 아이들을 겨냥하는 경향이 있다.

▶ most of 뒤에 단수명사(the advertising)가 왔으므로 단수동사 tends가 와야 한다.

04 그 결정은 바람직하지 않은 것처럼 보이지만, 거주민의 대다수가 그것을 받아들여야 한다고 말한다.

▶ the majority of 뒤에 복수명사(residents)가 왔으므로 복수동사 say가 와야 한다.

05 거의 모든 공동체 구성원이 그들의 역할에 있어 무엇이 '적절한가'에 대한 지침을 따른다.

▶ all of 뒤에 복수명사(the community members)가 왔으므로 복수동사 follow가 와야 한다.

06 SNS 게시물의 대략 절반이 '나'에 초점을 맞추고 있는데, 이는 게시물들이 사람들이 지금 하고 있는 것과 관련이 있다는 의미이다.

▶ half of 뒤에 복수동사(posts)가 왔으므로 복수동사 are가 와야 한다.

07 우리의 결정 각각은 '좋은 삶'의 본질에 대한 결정이다.

▶「each of+명사」가 주어 자리에 왔으므로 뒤에 단수동사가 와야 한다. 따라서 복수동사 are를 단수동사 is로 고쳐야 한다.

08 새의 몸의 나머지는 훨씬 더 짧은 깃털로 덮여 있었던 것처럼 보이는데, 그 깃털이 추위를 막아 주었을 것이다.

▶ The rest of 뒤에 단수명사(the bird's body)가 왔으므로 복수동사 seem을 단수동사 seems로 고쳐야 한다.

UNIT 02 동사 vs. 준동사

POINT 05 동사(v) 자리인지 준동사(to-v / v-ing) 자리인지 구분하라! pp.16-17

대표 예문 1

의사소통에서 진동을 사용하는 것은 물질이 진동하게 만드는 발신자의 능력에 달려있다.

대표 예문 2

자신의 일에서 그가 즐겼던 유일한 부분은 건물의 모형을 만드는 것이었다.

기출 예문 PLUS

1 전적으로 관객이 없는 자기 자신을 상상하는 것은 고통스럽고 어려울 것이다.

2 품질을 손상시키지 않고 비용을 억제하기 위해 우리는 할 수 있는 모든 것을 다했다.

3 당신이 체육 교사가 되기 위해 훈련을 받았다면, 체육관이 없는 것은 큰 문제가 아니다.

4 브로콜리 표면의 습기가 곰팡이의 성장을 촉진시키므로, 브로콜리를 보관하기 전에 세척하지 마라.

5 대담하게 진실에 대해 전적인 태도를 취하는 사람들은 그들의 기대를 뛰어넘는 결과를 이뤄낸다.

6 첨단 기술이나 색상을 사용하지 않고, 바위로 특정한 형태를 조각함으로써 감정을 표현하겠다는 선택을 하는 것은 예술가를 상당히 제약한다.

기출 문장으로 PRACTICE pp.18-19

01 constitute 02 keeping 03 turned 04 investing 05 living 06 lived 07 is 08 measured 09 study 10 tend 11 was developed 12 To protect 13 recalling 14 O 15 to produce → produced 16 knowing → knows

01 우리의 총체적인 가치관과 그것들이 우리에게 갖는 상대적인 중요성이 우리의 가치 체계를 구성한다.

▶ Our total set ... to us가 주어이고 our value system이 목적어로, 문장에 동사가 필요하다. 따라서 constitute가 와야 한다.

02 카메라를 보호하기 위해, 카메라를 사용하지 않을 때는 렌즈를 덮어두는 것이 권장된다.

▶ To protect your camera는 문장 전체를 수식하는 부사적 용법의 to부정사구이고, 문장 끝의 is recommended가 동사이다. 문장에 주어가 필요하므로, 주어 역할을 할 수 있는 동명사 keeping이 와야 한다.

03 Whyte에 의해 관찰된 사람들 사이의 가장 흔한 활동은 다른 사람들을 지켜보는 것임이 드러났다.

▶ 문장의 주어는 전치사구(among ... by Whyte)의 수식을 받는 The most common activity로, 문장에 동사가 필요하다. 따라서 turned가 와야 한다.

04 그런 까닭에, 배움의 기회에 정기적으로 투자하는 것은 당신이 자신에게 줄 수 있는 가장 위대한 선물 중 하나이다.

▶ 문장의 동사는 is이고 one of 이하가 주격보어로, 문장에 주어가 필요하다. 따라서 주어 역할을 할 수 있는 동명사 investing이 와야 한다.

05 다른 사람의 기대를 좇아 당신의 인생을 사는 것은 살기 어려운 방식일 수 있다는 것을 상상하기란 어렵지 않다.

▶ that 이하는 동사 imagine의 목적어 역할을 하는 명사절이다. that절의 동사는 can be이고, a difficult way 이하는 주격보어로, 절에 주어가 필요하다. 따라서 주어 역할을 할 수 있는 동명사 living이 와야 한다.

06 우리 선조들과 현대의 꼬리감는 원숭이를 포함하여 대부분의 동물들은 생존의 한계에 매우 근접하여 살았다.

▶ 문장의 주어는 Most animals이고 very close 이하는 부사구로, 문장에 동사가 필요하다. 따라서 lived가 오는 것이 알맞다.

07 사실, 사람들이 게시하는 모든 것은 전송, 배포, 혹은 공개적 게시에 대한 권한이 자동으로 E-World에 인가된다.

▶ 문장의 주어는 목적격 관계대명사절(that people post)의 수식을 받는 everything으로, 문장에 동사가 필요하다. 따라서 is가 오는 것이 알맞다.

08 안타깝게도, 내가 접한 생산성 측정 제도의 대부분은 노력 혹은 밖으로 보이는 활동을 측정했다.

▶ 문장의 주어는 목적격 관계대명사절((that) I have encountered)의 수식을 받는 most of ... schemes이고 effort 이하가 목적어로, 문장에 동사가 필요하다. 따라서 measured가 와야 한다.

09 우리에게 특정 견해를 납득시키기 위해 일하는 전문가들은 우리의 약점을 활용할 방법을 알아내기 위해 인간의 의사결정에 대한 조사를 연구한다.

▶ 주어는 주격 관계대명사절(who work ... viewpoints)의 수식을 받는 Professionals이고 research 이하가 목적어로, 문장에 동사가 필요하다. 따라서 study가 오는 것이 알맞다.

10 추운 기후에 살며 체중 대비 불리한 표면적 비율을 가지고 있어서 쉽게 열을 손실하는 많은 작은 포유동물은 수면을 많이 취하는 경향이 있다.

▶ 주어는 현재분사구(living ... climate)의 수식을 받는 Many small mammals로, 문장에 동사가 필요하다. 따라서 tend가 와야 한다. 주격 관계대명사절 who ... ratio는 선행사 Many small mammals에 대해 보충 설명을 하는 삽입절이다.

11 운하용 보트로 사람들뿐만 아니라 편지와 신문을 수송하는 체계는 17세기 네덜란드에서 발달되었다.

▶ 문장의 주어는 전치사구(of transporting ... by canal boat)의 수식을 받는 A system으로, 문장에 동사가 필요하다. 따라서 was developed가 와야 한다.

12 역사적인 건축물의 특징을 보호하기 위해, 그 도시는 간판, 현판, 그리고 포스터의 설치에 대한 세부 기준을 정했고, 도로 표지판을 개선했다.

▶ the city가 문장의 주어이고, has set과 has revised가 동사로 문장이 완전한 구조를 이루고 있다. 따라서 앞에는 문장 전체를 수식할 수 있는 부사적 용법의 to부정사 To protect가 와야 한다.

13 4월에 「Journal of Personality and Social Psychology」에 게재된 연구에 따르면, 어린 시절의 기억을 회상하는 것은 사람들이 더 윤리적으로 행동하게 할 수 있다.

▶ 문장의 동사는 can lead로, 문장에 주어가 필요하다. 따라서 주어 역할을 할 수 있는 동명사 recalling이 와야 한다.

14 물론, 가장 좋은 방법은 당신의 전화기를 가능한 한 빨리 고객 서비스 센터로 가져가는 것이다.

▶ 문장의 주어는 The best way이고 동사는 is이다. to bring은 주격보어 역할을 하는 명사적 용법의 to부정사로 어법상 바르다.

15 19세기 런던에서, 많은 비평가들에 의해 지적된 비극적인 상황은 도시를 깨끗이 하기 위한 조치들을 만들어냈다.

▶ 문장의 주어는 과거분사구(pointed out ... critics)의 수식을 받는 the tragic conditions이고 measures 이하는 목적어로, 문장에 동사가 필요하다. 따라서 to produce를 produced로 고쳐야 한다.

16 5살짜리 아이와 시간을 보내 본 사람이라면 이 나이의 아이들이 왜 모든 일이 그렇게 작동하는지에 대한 설명을 들으려고 애쓰면서 당신의 인내심의 한계를 시험할 수 있다는 것을 안다.

▶ 문장의 주어는 주격 관계대명사절(who ... a five-year-old)의 수식을 받는 Anyone이고 that 이하는 목적어 역할을 하는 명사절로, 문장에 동사가 필요하다. 따라서 knowing을 knows로 고쳐야 한다.

Chapter 01 기출 문제 공략하기

pp.20-21

1 ②

해석 20세기에, 냉장에서 정교한 오븐, 신선한 재료를 전 세계에 실어 나르는 항공 수송에 이르기까지의 기술 발전은 제과 제빵에 헤아릴 수 없을 정도로 기여했다. 21세기 초, 고급 빵과 페이스트리의 인기는 새 요리사가 훈련될 수 있는 것보다 훨씬 더 빠르게 상승하고 있다. 흥미롭게도, 제빵에 있어서의 많은 기술적 진보는 제빵사와 소비자에게 똑같이 하나의 반응을 불러일으켰다. 제빵이 더 산업화되고 구워진 제품들이 더 세련되고 표준화되고, 그리고 몇몇 사람들이 말하기로는 맛이 없어짐에 따라, 그들은 사라진 옛날 빵의 풍미 일부를 되찾기를 바라고 있다. 제빵사들은 과거의 시큼한 수제 반죽 빵을 생산하는 방법을 연구하고 있고, 풍미를 찾기 위해 특별한 밀가루로 실험하고 있다.

정답해설

② 이 문장의 핵심 주어는 전치사구(of fine ... pastries)의 수식을 받는 the popularity이다. 주어가 단수명사이므로 복수동사 are를 단수동사 is로 고쳐야 한다.

오답해설

① that은 앞의 air transportation을 선행사로 하는 주격 관계대명사로, 어법상 바르다.
③ alike는 동사구(has sparked ... and consumers)를 수식하는 부사로, 어법상 바르다.
④ were lost는 주격 관계대명사절의 동사로, 선행사인 some of the flavors가 주어 역할을 한다. 문맥상 풍미가 '사라지게 된다'라는 수동의 의미가 적절하고, 「some of+복수명사」는 복수동사를 취하므로 were lost는 어법상 바르다.
⑤ 전치사의 for의 목적어 역할을 하면서 뒤에 목적어(the handmade ... the past)를 취할 수 있는 동명사 producing은 어법상 바르다.

구문해설

4행 ..., the popularity of fine breads and pastries is growing **even** faster than new chefs can be trained.
▶ even은 '훨씬'의 의미로 비교급을 수식하는 부사이다.

6행 ... advances in bread making have sparked a reaction among bakers **and** consumers **alike**.
▶ 「A and B alike」는 'A와 B 둘 다, 똑같이'라는 의미이다.

2 ④

해석 그리스인이 두드러진 물체와 그것의 속성에 초점을 둔 것은 그들이 인과관계의 근본적인 성질을 이해하는 것을 실패하게 했다. 아리스토텔레스는 돌이 공중에서 떨어지는 것은 돌이 '중력'이라는 성질을 가지고 있기 때문이라고 설명했다. 그러나 물론 물에 던져진 나무 조각은 가라앉는 대신 뜬다. 이 현상을 아리스토텔레스는 나무가 '가벼움'이라는 성질을 가지고 있기 때문이라고 설명했다! 두 경우 모두 그 물체 밖의 어떤 힘이 관련 있을지도 모른다는 가능성에 주의를 기울이지 않고, 초점은 오로지 그 물체에 있다. 그러나 중국인들은 세계를 계속해서 상호 작용하는 물질로 구성된 것으로 여겨서, 그것을 이해하고자 하는 그들의 시도는 그들이 전체적인 '장(場)', 즉 전체로서의 맥락이나 환경의 복잡한 특징들을 지향하도록 했다. 사건은 언제나 여러 힘들의 장에서 발생한다는 개념은 중국인에게 전적으로 직관적이었을 것이다.

정답해설

④ 접속사 so 뒤에 오는 절에서, 주어는 to부정사구(to understand it)의 수식을 받는 their attempts이고 them이 목적어로, 절 안에 동사가 필요하다. 따라서 causing을 시제에 맞춰 과거동사 caused로 고쳐야 한다.

오답해설

① 복수명사 The Greeks를 지칭하는 소유격 대명사 their는 적절하다.
② 앞의 명사 a piece of wood를 수식하는 분사로, 나무 조각은 '던져지는' 대상이므로, 수동의 의미를 나타내는 과거분사 tossed는 어법상 바르다.
③ 전치사구 on the object를 수식하는 부사 exclusively는 어법상 바르다.
⑤ that은 The notion과 동격인 명사절(events always ... forces)을 이끄는 접속사로, 어법상 바르다.

구문해설

2행 Aristotle explained [**that** *a stone* {*falling* through the air} is due to *the stone* {*having* the property of "gravity}]."
▶ that은 동사 explained의 목적어 역할을 하는 명사절을 이끄는 접속사이다. falling 이하는 that절의 주어 역할을 하는 동명사구이고, having 이하는 전치사 due to의 목적어 역할을 하는 동명사구이다. a stone과 the stone은 각 동명사구의 의미상 주어이다.

4행 **This phenomenon** Aristotle explained as being due to the wood having the property of "levity"!
▶ This phenomenon은 동사 explained의 목적어로, 강조를 위해 문장 첫머리에 나왔다.

6행 In both cases the focus is exclusively on the object, **with** no attention **paid** to the possibility [*that* some force outside the object might be relevant].
▶ 「with+(대)명사+p.p.」는 '~가 …된 채로'라는 부대상황을 나타내는 분사구문으로, (대)명사와 분사가 수동의 관계임을 나타낸다. that 이하는 the possibility와 동격을 이루는 명사절이다.

Chapter 02 동사의 태

UNIT 03 능동태 vs. 수동태

POINT 06 주어와 동사의 의미 관계를 따져라! p.24

대표 예문

비록 정착민들을 위한 생필품이 지구에서 보내진다 하더라도, 목숨을 꿈과 맞바꾸는 위험을 무릅쓰는 것은 어렵다.

기출 예문 PLUS

1 대부분의 경우, 우리는 문맥을 통해 어떤 의미가 사용되고 있는지 알 수 있다.

2 콘크리트로 된 십자표들은 부주의한 어부들이 바다로 휩쓸려 간 지점을 표시하고 있었다.

3 현재 대중적인 태도는 오늘날의 환경 문제에 대해 기술을 비난하는 것이다. 우리는 이 관점이 변화되어야 한다고 믿는다.

기출 문장으로 PRACTICE p.25

01 give 02 be developed 03 been abandoned
04 were extracted 05 encouraged 06 be found
07 was held → held 08 encloses → is enclosed

01 우리는 당신이 글쓰기 과정에 대해 연설을 해줄 수 있는지 여쭤 보고 싶습니다.

▶ 당신이 연설을 '한다'라는 능동의 의미가 자연스러우므로, 능동태 give가 오는 것이 알맞다.

02 시추가 허용되기 전에 환경에 대한 위험을 줄이기 위해 새로운 기술이 개발되어야 한다.

▶ 새로운 기술이 '개발된다'라는 수동의 의미가 자연스러우므로, 수동태 be developed가 와야 한다.

03 어느 날 한 지역 신문은 죽도록 사막에 유기되었다가 구조된 말에 관한 기사를 실었다.

▶ a rescued horse를 선행사로 하는 주격 관계대명사절의 동사 부분으로, 말이 '유기된다'라는 수동의 의미가 자연스러우므로, 수동태 been abandoned가 오는 것이 알맞다.

04 하지만 이 분자들이 채소에서 추출되어 보조제로 만들어졌을 때, 그것들은 암을 줄이지 못했다.

▶ 분자들이 채소에서 '추출된다'라는 수동의 의미가 자연스러우므로, 수동태 were extracted가 알맞다.

05 수십 년 동안, 전문가들의 육아에 대한 조언은 밤 시간에 아기를 부모로부터 떼어놓을 것을 권장했다.

▶ 육아에 대한 조언이 '권장한다'라는 능동의 의미가 자연스러우므로, 능동태 encouraged가 오는 것이 알맞다.

06 Whyte는 연인들이 사적이고, 고립된 장소에서 발견될 것을 기대했으나, 주로 그들은 모든 사람들이 볼 수 있는 것들의 한가운데에 앉거나 서 있었다.

▶ 「expect+목적어+목적격보어(to-v)」 구문에서 목적어와 목적격보어 사이에는 의미상 주어와 동사 관계가 성립한다. 연인들이 '발견된다'라는 수동의 의미가 자연스러우므로, 수동태 be found가 알맞다.

07 그들은 소형 트럭 뒤 칸이 얼마나 많은 탄산음료 캔을 실었는지 맞히는 대회에 참가했다.

▶ 트럭의 뒤 칸이 탄산음료 캔을 '싣는다'라는 능동의 의미가 적절하므로, 수동태 was held를 능동태인 held로 고쳐야 한다.

08 운전자들은 직원이 돈을 받기 위한 통과 함께 유리 부스로 둘러싸여 있는 주유소에 차를 댄다.

▶ 직원이 유리 부스로 '둘러싸여 있다'라는 수동의 의미가 자연스러우므로, 능동태 encloses를 수동태 is enclosed로 고쳐야 한다.

POINT 07 수동태 뒤에 오는 명사(구)에 유의하라! p.26

대표 예문

적으로부터 자신을 보호하기 위해 그들은 오직 권총과 소총만을 지급받았다.

기출 예문 PLUS

1 18세기는 식물회화의 황금기라고 불린다.

2 무엇을 하라는 말을 듣는 것이 싫었기 때문에, 나는 기회가 있을 때마다 엄마에게 저항하려고 애썼다.

3 고국으로 돌아온 후 곧, 그는 한 신문사의 최고 경영자 자리를 제안받았다.

4 'kid'라는 단어는 한때 속어로 여겨졌는데, 왜냐하면 그것이 '어린 염소'라는 의미였고 지금도 그런 한 단어로부터 유래했기 때문이다.

기출 문장으로 PRACTICE

p.27

01 was called 02 serve 03 was awarded 04 is considered 05 given 06 O 07 offered → was offered

01 그는 약 25명의 남성들을 한 단체로 조직했는데, 이 단체는 Texas Rangers라고 불렸다.

▶ 5형식 동사 call은 뒤에 목적어와 목적격보어(명사)가 와야 하지만, 동사 뒤에 목적격보어(Taxas Rangers)만 있고, 그 단체는 '~라고 불리다'라는 수동의 의미가 자연스러우므로, 수동태 was called가 와야 한다.

02 승무원은 비행기가 순항 고도에 진입하면 승객들에게 무료 음료를 제공한다.

▶ 동사 뒤에 간접목적어(the passengers)와 직접목적어(free drinks)가 모두 있고, 승무원이 무료 음료를 '제공한다'라는 능동의 의미가 자연스러우므로, 능동태 serve가 와야 한다.

03 그의 업적은 국제적으로 인정받았다. 그의 책은 역사 부문 퓰리처상과 밴크로프트상을 받았다.

▶ award는 4형식 동사인데, 동사 뒤에 직접목적어(the Pulitzer ... the Bancroft prize)만 오고 있고, 그의 책이 '~을 수여받다'라는 수동의 의미가 자연스러우므로, 수동태 was awarded가 와야 한다.

04 최초로 FM 라디오를 개발했던 Edwin Armstrong은 라디오 역사상 가장 다작을 하고 가장 영향력이 있는 발명가로 여겨진다.

▶ consider는 5형식 동사인데, 동사 뒤에 목적격보어(the most ... inventor)만 오고 있으며, 그가 '~로 여겨진다'라는 수동의 의미가 자연스러우므로, 수동태 is considered가 오는 것이 알맞다.

05 참가자들에게는 의도적으로 그 과제에서 그들이 사용해야 하는 형태의 크기나 종이의 양에 대한 어떤 구체적인 지시 사항도 주어지지 않았다.

▶ give는 4형식 동사인데, 동사 뒤에 직접목적어(any specific ... the task)만 오고 있고, 참가자들에게 '~이 주어진다'라는 수동의 의미가 자연스러우므로 수동태가 와야 한다. 따라서 과거분사인 given이 와야 한다.

06 아들이 내가 그가 하기를 바랐던 것을 할 때마다, 나는 그에게 거의 신경을 쓰지 않았다.

▶ 4형식 동사 paid 뒤에 간접목적어(him)와 직접목적어(little attention)가 모두 오고 있으며, 내가 '~을 주다'라는 능동의 의미가 자연스러우므로 능동태 paid는 어법상 바르다.

07 Michelangelo는 1505년에 교황 Julius의 무덤을 만드는 프로젝트를 제안받았지만, 그 무덤은 1545년이 되어서야 완공되었다.

▶ 4형식 동사 offered 뒤에 직접목적어(the project ... Pope Julius)만 오고 있고, 그가 '~을 제안받았다'라는 수동의 의미가 자연스러우므로, 능동태 offered를 수동태 was offered로 고쳐야 한다.

Chapter 02 기출 문제 공략하기

pp.28-29

1 ④

해석 아이들에게 공감 능력을 길러주는 가장 간단하고 가장 효과적인 방법 중 하나는 그들이 좀 더 스스로 놀게 하는 것이다. 감독받지 않는 아이들은 서로에게 자신이 어떻게 느끼는지 말하기를 꺼리지 않는다. 게다가, 놀이를 하는 아이들은 흔히 타인의 역할을 맡아서, Walsh 교장선생님 또는 Josh의 엄마인 척하며, 기꺼이 본인들을 다른 사람이 어떻게 생각하고 느끼는지 상상하게 한다. 불행히도, 자유로운 놀이는 드물어지고 있다. Boston 대학 연구 교수인 Peter Gray는 지난 50년에 걸쳐 미국과 다른 선진국에서 아이들이 스스로 고른 방식으로 놀고 탐험할 수 있는 기회가 지속적이면서도 결국 극적으로 감소한 것을 기록해 왔다. 그는 그 영향들이 특히 공감 능력에 손상을 주고 있다고 주장한다. 그는 공감 능력의 감소와 나르시시즘의 증가가 바로 사회적으로 놀 기회가 거의 없는 아이들에게서 우리가 볼 것이라 예상하는 것이라고 결론짓는다.

정답해설

④ 영향이 공감 능력에 '손상되었다'가 아니라 '손상을 주었다'라는 능동의 의미가 자연스러우므로, 수동태 have been damaged를 능동태 have been damaging으로 고쳐야 한다.

오답해설

① 주어 자리에 「one of+복수명사」가 왔으므로, 단수동사 is는 어법상 바르다.
② 분사구문의 의미상 주어인 they(= children)가 forcing의 목적어와 동일하므로, 재귀대명사 themselves는 어법상 바르다.
③ 뒤의 형용사 dramatic을 수식하는 부사 ultimately는 어법상 바

르다.

⑤ what은 동사 concludes의 목적어 역할을 하는 that절에서 주격보어 역할을 하는 명사절을 이끄는 관계대명사로, 어법상 바르다.

구문해설

1행 One ... is [**to let** them play more on their own].

▸ to let 이하는 주격보어 역할을 하는 명사적 용법의 to부정사구이다.

2행 Unsupervised kids are not reluctant to tell one another [**how** they feel].

▸ how 이하는 tell의 직접목적어로 쓰인 의문사절이다.

3행 ..., children at play often take on other roles, [**pretending** to be Principal Walsh or Josh's mom], [**happily *forcing*** themselves *to imagine* ...].

▸ pretending 이하와 happily forcing 이하는 모두 동시동작을 나타내는 분사구문이다. 「force A to-v」는 'A를 ~하게 하다'라는 의미이다.

2 ③

해석 스포츠 분야의 승진 과정은 흔히 피라미드와 같은 모양을 하고 있다고 한다. 다시 말해서, 넓은 아래 부분에는 고등학교 운동부와 함께 많은 직업들이 있는 반면, 좁은 꼭대기에는 프로 단체와 관련된 극소수의, 매우 선망받는 직업들이 있다. 그러므로 다 합쳐 많은 스포츠 직업이 있지만, 사람이 위로 올라갈수록 경쟁은 점점 더 치열해진다. 다양한 직위의 급여가 이 피라미드 모델을 반영한다. 예를 들어, 고등학교 미식축구팀의 코치는 일반적으로 방과 후 업무로 약간 더 돈을 받는 교사들이다. 그러나 큰 대학의 같은 스포츠 코치들은 한 해에 백만 달러가 넘게 벌 수 있는데, 이는 상대적으로 대학 총장의 급여가 적어 보이게 한다. 한 등급 더 높은 곳이 프로 미식축구 연맹인데, 여기에서 수석 코치들은 최고로 보수를 받는 대학 코치들보다 몇 배 더 많이 벌 수 있다.

정답해설

③ paid는 주격 관계대명사절의 동사로, 선행사 teachers가 의미상 주어이다. 문맥상 교사들이 보수를 '지불받는'이라는 수동의 의미가 적절하므로 능동태 paid를 수동태 are[get] paid로 고쳐야 한다.

오답해설

① 주어는 전치사구(of ... sports)의 수식을 받는 The process로, 주어가 단수명사이므로 단수동사 is는 어법상 바르다.

② 뒤의 형용사 tough를 수식하는 부사 increasingly는 어법상 바르다.

④ 동사 cause는 목적격보어로 to부정사를 취하므로, to look은 어법상 바르다.

⑤ 뒤에 완전한 절이 이어지므로, the National Football League를 선행사로 하는 계속적 용법의 관계부사 where는 어법상 바르다.

구문해설

2행 ..., **at the wide base are** [**many jobs** with high school athletic teams], while **at the narrow tip are** [**the few, highly desired jobs** with professional organizations].

▸ 각각 장소를 나타내는 부사구(at the wide base / at the narrow tip)가 절의 앞으로 나와 주어(many jobs 이하 / the few, highly desired jobs 이하)와 동사(are)가 도치되었다.

8행 ... $ 1 million a year, [***causing*** the salaries of college presidents *to look* small in comparison].

▸ causing 이하는 결과를 나타내는 분사구문이다. 「cause A to-v」는 'A가 ~하게 하다'라는 의미이다.

10행 ... is the National Football League, where head coaches can earn **many times more than** their best-paid campus counterparts.

▸ 「배수사+비교급+than ~」는 '~보다 몇 배 …한'의 의미이다.

Chapter 03 문장의 구조

UNIT 04 병렬구조

POINT 08 등위접속사나 상관접속사가 연결하는 요소는 대등해야 한다! pp.32-33

대표 예문 1

나는 어떤 여자가 큰길로 진입하려고 시도하는데 끊임없는 차량 흐름 때문에 운이 별로 없는 것을 보았다.

대표 예문 2

웃음의 목적은 누군가가 명랑한 상태에 있다는 것을 전달하려는 것일 뿐만 아니라, 실제로 이런 상태를 다른 사람들에게서도 유도해내려는 것이다.

기출 예문 PLUS

1 하지만 실제로 예술의 영향력은 그렇게 확실하지도 그렇게 직접적이지도 않다.

2 그녀가 노예인지 아니면 부유한 계층 출신인지는 상당히 큰 차이를 낳았다.

3 인간은 도구를 바르게 조작하고, 그것들을 적절하고 유용한 위치에 배치하는 것을 훨씬 더 잘한다.

4 내 눈앞의 물체들은 과일 몇 개와 사발 하나를 포함하지만, 'and'라는 단어에 부합하는 물체는 세상에 혹은 내 시각적 이미지 안에 존재하지 않는다.

기출 문장으로 PRACTICE pp.34-35

01 remembered 02 running 03 use
04 determine 05 remarked 06 helping
07 to scold 08 say 09 become 10 brought
11 summarize 12 improving 13 getting → got
14 to evaluate → evaluate 15 salutes → saluting

01 Gabby는 진정하고, 그녀가 해야 하는 말을 똑똑히 기억해냈다.

▶ 등위접속사 and에 의해 동사가 병렬 연결된 구조이므로, 동사 calmed와 대등한 remembered가 알맞다.

02 다시 경기를 뛸 때 나는 무릎을 더 많이 굽히고 더 빨리 달림으로써 그의 의견에 응했다.

▶ 등위접속사 and에 의해 전치사 by의 목적어로 쓰인 동명사가 병렬 연결된 구조이므로, 동명사 bending과 대등한 running이 와야 한다.

03 당신이 감사 편지를 쓸 것이라면, 좋은 카드를 사기 위해 시간을 들이고, 품위 있는 흐름을 만들어 줄 펜을 이용해라.

▶ 등위접속사 and에 의해 명령문의 동사가 병렬 연결된 구조이므로, 동사원형 take와 대등한 use가 와야 한다.

04 그들은 급경사면의 끝으로 가서, 밑바닥까지의 하행길을 쭉 내려다보고, 그들이 시도하기에 경사면이 너무 가파르다고 결론을 내릴 것이다.

▶ 등위접속사 and에 의해 조동사 will 다음의 동사가 「A, B and C」의 구조로 병렬 연결되어 있으므로, 동사원형 go, look과 대등한 determine이 와야 한다.

05 그 사무장은 귀중품에 대한 책임을 받아들이고는 "괜찮습니다. 제가 당신을 위해 아주 기꺼이 그것들을 보관해 드리죠."라고 말했다.

▶ 등위접속사 and에 의해 동사가 병렬 연결된 구조이므로, 동사 accepted와 대등한 remarked가 와야 한다.

06 자선은 가난한 사람들에게 즉각적인 도움을 주는 것뿐만 아니라, 그들이 스스로를 부양할 수 있도록 할 방법으로 그들을 도와주는 것도 의미한다.

▶ 상관접속사 「not only A but also B」에 의해 동사 means의 목적어인 동명사구가 병렬 연결된 구조이므로, 동명사 providing과 대등한 helping이 와야 한다.

07 자녀 양육 전문가들은 항상 부모들에게 아이들이 나쁜 행동을 할 때 그들에게 나쁘다고 말하지 말고, 그보다는 나쁜 일을 한 것에 대해 그들을 꾸짖으라고 주의를 준다.

▶ 상관접속사 「not A but B」에 의해 동사 caution의 목적격보어인 to부정사구가 병렬 연결된 구조이므로, to부정사 to tell과 대등한 to scold가 와야 한다. 「caution A to-v」는 'A에게 ~하라고 경고하다[주의를 주다]'라는 의미이다.

08 연구원들은 32명의 사람들에게 흰 막대들이 검은 배경 위를 천천히 움직이는 짧은 컴퓨터 애니메이션을 보고, 그 막대들이 어느 방향으로 움직이는지 말해줄 것을 요청했다.

▶ 등위접속사 and에 의해 동사 asked의 목적격보어인 to부정사구가 병렬 연결된 구조이므로, to부정사 to watch와 대등한 (to) say가 와야 한다. say 앞의 to는 생략되었다. asked와 said가 병렬구조를 이룬다고 혼동할 수 있으나, 문맥상 보고 이야기하도록 요청 받았다는 것이 적절하다.

09 그들의 다음 목표는 화석 연료의 사용을 증가시키지 않고 도시 전체에 충분한 에너지를 제공해서, 결국 에너지 면에서 자급자족할 수 있게 되는 것이다.

▶ 등위접속사 and에 의해 주격보어인 to부정사구가 병렬 연결된 구조이므로, to부정사 to provide와 대등한 (to) become이 와야 한다. become 앞의 to는 생략되었다.

10 시간이라는 선물은 때때로 돈보다 더 만족스러울 수 있다. 당신은 노숙자 쉼터에서 자원봉사를 하거나 노인들에게 식사를 가져다주는 사람들을 보면서 이를 알 수 있다.

▶ 등위접속사 or에 의해 주격 관계대명사절의 동사가 병렬 연결된 구조이므로, have volunteered와 대등한 (have) brought가 와야 한다. brought 앞의 have는 생략되었다.

11 Tory Higgins는 대학생들에게 어떤 사람의 성격을 묘사해 놓은 것을 읽고 나서 이 사람을 좋아하거나 싫어한다고 여겨지는 다른 누군가를 위해 그것을 요약하게 했다.

▶ 등위접속사 and에 의해 사역동사 had의 목적격보어인 동사원형이 병렬 연결된 구조이므로, 동사원형 read와 대등한 summarize가 와야 한다.

12 국가는 더 고도로 숙련된 노동력을 만드는 것과, 여성과 저소득 젊은이들을 위해 노동 시장에 접근성을 향상시키는 것에 중점을 두고, 복지 국가에서 근로 복지 국가로의 이행을 시작해야 한다.

▶ 등위접속사 and에 의해 전치사 on의 목적어인 동명사구가 병렬 연결된 구조이므로, 동명사 creating과 대등한 improving이 와야 한다.

13 고등학교를 졸업한 뒤, 나는 대학에 진학하려는 꿈을 포기하고 대신 아르바이트 자리를 얻었다.

▶ 등위접속사 and에 의해 동사가 병렬 연결된 구조이므로, 과거형 동사 gave와 대등하도록 getting을 got으로 고쳐야 한다.

14 비평가로서, 당신은 책이 이야기를 기술하는 방식에 대해 그 책을 분석하고, 작문과 구조의 질을 평가한다.

▶ 등위접속사 and에 의해 동사가 병렬 연결된 구조이므로, 동사 analyze와 대등하도록 to evaluate을 evaluate로 고쳐야 한다.

15 텔레비전 위에는 Neil Armstrong이 달 표면 위에 서서 빳빳한 미국 국기에 경례를 하고 있는 큰 사진이 있다.

▶ 등위접속사 and에 의해 Neil Armstrong을 수식하는 현재분사구가 병렬 연결된 구조이므로, 현재분사 standing과 대등하도록 salutes를 saluting으로 고쳐야 한다.

POINT 09 비교 대상은 병렬구조를 이뤄야 한다! p.36

대표 예문

예를 들어, 물을 진동하게 만드는 것은 공기를 진동시키는 것보다 더 많은 에너지를 필요로 한다.

기출 예문 PLUS

1 어떤 학생들은 잠을 몇 분 더 자는 것이 오트밀 한 그릇을 먹는 것보다 더 중요하다고 말하지만, 그들은 틀렸다.

2 정해진 양의 음식은 한 번에 먹는 것보다 하루에 걸쳐 간격을 두고 먹을 때 몸에서 더 효율적으로 사용된다.

3 내성적인 사람들은 고도의 사회적 상호작용을 요하는 역할을 맡는 것보다 혼자 혹은 작은 집단에서 일하는 것을 더 선호하는 것처럼 보인다.

4 당신이 언제 먹는가는 무엇을 먹는가만큼 중요한데, 왜냐하면 같은 영양분이 다른 시간대에 섭취되었을 때 신체에 다른 효과를 낳기 때문이다.

기출 문장으로 PRACTICE p.37

01 to imitate **02** dread **03** knowing **04** eat → eating **05** O

01 전시의 스파이들에게는 적의 언어나 발음을 설득력 있게 모방하는 것보다 적의 제복을 입는 것이 훨씬 더 쉽다.

▶ 비교급이 쓰인 문장으로, 비교 대상인 to부정사 to wear와 병렬구조를 이루도록 than 다음에 to부정사 to imitate가 와야 한다.

02 미래의 상호작용에 대한 기대는 사람들이 그것을 두려워하기보다 고대할 수 있도록 다른 사람들에게서 긍정적인 특징을 찾게끔 동기를 부여한다.

▶ 「A rather than B」 구문이 쓰인 문장으로, rather than 앞의 동사원형 look과 병렬구조를 이루도록 동사원형 dread가 와야 한다.

03 학생들이 그들의 목표를 성취할 것인지를 예측하기 위해서, 성실함의 척도로 그들의 점수를 아는 것보다 과업을 향한 그들의 태

도를 보는 것이 더 유용할지도 모른다.

▸ 비교급이 쓰인 문장으로, 비교 대상인 동명사 seeing과 병렬 구조를 이루도록 동명사 knowing이 와야 한다.

04 증거는 초기 인류가 동물의 살코기를 먹는 것보다 지방과 내장육을 먹는 것을 선호했음을 시사한다.

▸「prefer A to B」 구문이 쓰인 문장으로, preferred 뒤에 오는 동명사 consuming과 병렬구조를 이루도록 to 뒤에 동명사가 와야 한다. 따라서 eat을 동명사 eating으로 고쳐야 한다.

05 구성원들은 정기 회의 도중에 자신의 생각을 공유하고, 정보와 지식은 보호되고 통제되기보다 공개되어 있다.

▸「A rather than B」 구문이 쓰인 문장으로, rather than 앞의 형용사 open과 병렬구조를 이루는 어구가 뒤에 와야 하므로, 형용사 역할을 하는 과거분사 protected와 controlled의 쓰임은 알맞다.

Chapter 03

기출 문제 공략하기

pp.38-39

1 ④

해석 건축은 일반적으로 기존 상황들에 대한 반응으로 구상되고 디자인되며 실현된다. 이러한 상황들은 근본적으로 순전히 기능적이거나, 사회적, 정치적, 경제적 풍조 역시 다양하게 반영할지도 모른다. 어떤 경우이든, 기존 상황들이 훨씬 덜 만족스럽고, 새로운 상황이 바람직할 것으로 추정된다. 모든 디자인 과정의 첫 번째 단계는 문제 상황의 인식과 그에 대한 해결책을 찾으려는 결정이다. 디자인은 무엇보다도 의도적인 노력이다. 디자이너는 우선 문제가 있는 기존 상황들을 기록하고, 분석되어야 할 관련 자료를 수집해야 한다. 이것은 디자인 과정의 대단히 중요한 단계인데, 해결책의 본질은 문제가 어떻게 정의되는가와 관련이 있기 때문이다.

정답해설

④ 등위접속사 and에 의해 조동사 must 다음의 동사가 병렬 연결된 구조이므로, 동사원형 document와 대등하도록 collecting을 동사원형 collect로 고쳐야 한다.

오답해설

① 형용사 functional을 수식하는 부사 purely는 어법상 바르다.
② much는 '훨씬'의 의미로 비교급(less)을 수식하는 부사로 어법상 바르다.
③ to find는 앞의 명사 the decision을 수식하는 형용사적 용법의 to부정사로, 어법상 바르다.
⑤ 전치사 to의 목적어 역할을 하는 의문사절(how ... defined)의 동사로, 주어가 단수명사(a problem)이므로, 단수동사 is는 어법상 바르다.

구문해설

4행 ..., it is assumed [***that*** the existing set of conditions is much less satisfactory] *and* [***that*** a new set of conditions would be desirable].

▸ it은 가주어이고, that 이하가 각각 진주어이다. 진주어 역할을 하는 명사절 두 개가 등위접속사 and에 의해 병렬 연결되어 있다.

8행 ... document the existing conditions of a problem and collect relevant data **to *be analyzed***.

▸ to be analyzed는 relevant data를 수식하는 형용사적 용법의 to부정사이다. 자료는 '분석되는' 대상이므로, to부정사의 수동태 「to be p.p.」가 쓰였다.

2 ③

해석 대부분의 벌은 꽃을 방문하여 꽃가루를 모으면서 하루를 보내지만, 몇몇 벌은 다른 벌의 고된 노동을 이용한다. 이런 도둑질하는 벌은 (숙주라 알려진) 이상한 낌새를 못 채는 '보통' 벌의 보금자리로 슬쩍 들어가서, 숙주 벌이 자기 자신의 새끼를 위해 모으고 있는 꽃가루 덩어리 근처에 알을 낳고는, 다시 슬그머니 나온다. 그 도둑의 알이 부화하면, 그것은 숙주의 새끼를 죽인 다음 희생자를 위해 마련된 꽃가루를 먹는다. 가끔 탁란(托卵) 동물로 불리는 이 벌은 뻐꾸기 벌이라고도 불리는데, 그것들이 다른 새의 둥지에 알을 낳고 그 새가 그것을 기르도록 두는 뻐꾸기와 유사하기 때문이다. 그들은 더 전문적으로는 cleptoparasite라 불린다. clepto는 그리스어로 '도둑'을 의미하여, cleptoparasite라는 용어는 구체적으로 먹이를 훔침으로써 다른 생물에 기생하는 생물을 지칭한다. 이 경우 그 cleptoparasite는 숙주가 애써서 얻은 꽃가루 비축물을 먹고 산다.

정답해설

③ cuckoo birds를 선행사로 하는 주격 관계대명사절의 동사구가 등위접속사 and로 병렬 연결된 구조이다. and 앞의 복수동사 lay와 대등하도록 단수동사 leaves를 복수동사 leave로 고쳐야 한다.

오답해설

① unsuspecting은 '이상한 낌새를 못 채는'이라는 의미이며 뒤의 명사구 "normal" bee를 수식하는 형용사로, 어법상 바르다.
② 문장의 주어 it(도둑 벌의 알에서 부화한 새끼)과 같은 대상을 지칭하므로, 소유격 대명사 its는 어법상 바르다.
④ 동사 are called를 수식하는 부사 technically는 어법상 바르다.
⑤ that은 앞의 an organism을 선행사로 하는 주격 관계대명사로, 뒤에 주어가 빠진 불완전한 절이 이어지므로 어법상 바르다.

구문해설

3행 ..., lay an egg near the pollen mass [**being** gathered by the host bee for her own offspring], ...

▸ being 이하는 앞의 명사구 the pollen mass를 수식하는 현재분사구이다.

5행 ... and then eats the pollen [**meant** for its victim].

▸ meant 이하는 앞의 명사 the pollen을 수식하는 과거분사구이다.

Chapter 04 관계사, 접속사, 전치사

UNIT 05 관계사의 쓰임

POINT 10 관계대명사의 쓰임 pp.42-43

대표 예문 1

내가 꿈꾸던 학교가 내게 전액 장학금을 제공했는데, 그것은 내가 상상할 수 있던 것보다 더 많은 돈이었다.

대표 예문 2

내가 밑에서 일했던 상사 중 한 사람은 그 당시 일반적이던 움직임에 강하게 반발했다.

기출 예문 PLUS

1 우리는 털 옷과 은신처, 그리고 우리가 가지고 사냥하고 스스로를 방어할 수 있는 무기를 만들 수 있다.

2 올해 경기 전에는 아무도 주목하지 않았던 Andrew가 결승전에 진출했다.

3 소비자들은 지역 농부들에게서 농산물과 다른 상품을 구매하고, 그 지역 농부들은 지역의 기업에서 농업자재들을 구매한다.

4 그 사람은 자신의 행동이 그 원칙을 위배할 때 죄의식을 느끼고 그들의 행동이 그 원칙과 상충하는 다른 이들을 못마땅해하는 경향이 있을 것이다.

기출 문장으로 PRACTICE pp.44-45

01 whose 02 to which 03 which 04 which 05 by which 06 whose 07 which 08 with whom 09 who 10 which 11 which 12 which → who[that] 13 it → which 14 whom → who[that] 15 which → in which[where]

01 무대 위에 있는 사람은 치아가 고르지 않은 평범한 외모의 사람이다.

▶ 절과 절을 연결하는 접속사 역할을 할 수 있고, 앞에 오는 명사 an average-looking man과 뒤에 오는 명사 teeth가 소유의 관계에 있으므로 소유격 대명사 역할을 할 수 있는 소유격 관계대명사 whose가 와야 한다.

02 연구자들은 복숭아 나무가 노출되는 일광 기간을 늘렸다.

▶ 선행사 daylight가 관계대명사절의 동사 were exposed의 직접적인 목적어가 아니라 동사에 수반되는 전치사 to의 목적어이므로 「전치사+관계대명사」인 to which가 와야 한다.

03 당신은 수없이 많은 이유로 직장을 잃을지도 모르는데, 그 중 일부는 심지어 당신의 책임이 아닐지도 모른다.

▶ 절과 절을 연결하는 접속사 역할을 하면서 앞에 오는 명사 countless reasons를 대신하는 대명사 역할도 하는 관계대명사 which가 와야 한다.

04 조랑말을 타고 있는 그 남자가 멈추지 않고 지나갔는데, 그것은 내가 눈물을 펑펑 쏟게 했다.

▶ 앞의 절 전체를 선행사로 하는 계속적 용법의 주격 관계대명사 자리이므로 which가 와야 한다. 관계대명사 that은 계속적 용법으로 쓸 수 없다.

05 필기는 그것으로 학생들이 집중을 유지하고자 시도하는 활동 중 하나이지만, 그것은 기억하는 데도 도움이 된다.

▶ 뒤에 완전한 절이 이어지고 있고, 선행사 the activities가 관계대명사절에서 '~으로'라는 의미인 전치사 by의 목적어 역할을 해야 하므로, 「전치사+관계대명사」인 by which가 와야 한다.

06 당신이 이름을 들어본 적이 있는 바이올린 연주자와 피아노 연주자는 단 한 번의 연주로 3만 달러에서 5만 달러를 정기적으로 번다.

▶ 선행사인 The violinists and pianists와 뒤의 명사 names가 소유의 관계에 있으므로, 소유격 관계대명사 whose가 와야 한다.

07 아이들이 점심 도시락 가방 쓰레기를 줄이는 것을 돕기 위해, 나는 재사용할 수 있는 점심 도시락 가방을 개발했는데, 나는 그것들은 현재 내 웹사이트에서 판매하고 있다.

▶ 선행사가 a reusable lunch bag으로 사물이며, 관계대명사절에서 목적어 역할을 하므로, 목적격 관계대명사 which가 와야 한다.

08 많은 사람들이 그들이 관계를 맺고 있는 사람과 동일하지는 않더라도 유사한 신념과 가치관을 공유하는 것이 중요하다고 믿는다.

▶ 뒤에 완전한 절이 이어지고 있고, 선행사 someone이 관계대명사절에서 전치사 with의 목적어 역할을 해야 하므로, 「전치

사+관계대명사」인 with whom이 와야 한다.

09 나는 몇 가지 특히 민감한 이슈에 대해 내가 확신하건대 거짓말을 할 한 지인의 뉴스 인터뷰를 최근에 보았다.

▸ an acquaintance를 선행사로 하며, 관계대명사절에서 주어 역할을 할 수 있는 주격 관계대명사 who가 와야 한다. 뒤의 I was certain은 삽입절이다.

10 그 기차는 내 목적지에 10분 일찍 도착했는데, 내가 오전 10시에 내 새로운 아이디어를 회사에 발표할 예정이었기 때문에, 그것은 완벽했다.

▸ 앞의 절 전체를 선행사로 하는 계속적 용법의 주격 관계대명사 자리이므로 which가 와야 한다. 관계대명사 that은 계속적 용법으로 쓸 수 없다.

11 Louisiana 주는 투표를 하여 닭싸움을 불법화했다. 이 승리는 동물 권리 운동에 있어 역사적인 성취에 해당되는데, 이 동물 권리 운동은 전국적으로 닭싸움을 금지하기 위해 오랫동안 그리고 철저히 싸워왔다.

▸ 절과 절을 연결하는 접속사 역할을 하면서, 뒤에 오는 절에서 앞의 명사구 the animal rights movement를 대신하는 대명사 역할을 할 수 있는 계속적 용법의 주격 관계대명사 which가 와야 한다.

12 숙련된 정비공은 자동차에 대해서 아무것도 알지 못하고 신경 쓰지도 않는 유니폼을 입은 십 대로 대체되었다.

▸ 선행사가 a teenager로 사람이므로, which를 주격 관계대명사 who나 that으로 고쳐야 한다.

13 협력하는 목동들은 각자의 가축 무리의 크기를 제한하는데, 이는 그들에게 지속가능한 음식 공급을 유지하게 해준다.

▸ 두 개의 절이 접속사 없이 연결되어 있고, it은 앞에 오는 절 전체를 지칭하므로, 대명사 it을 계속적 용법의 주격 관계대명사 which로 고쳐야 한다.

14 가장 성공적인 직원들은 자신의 업무를 회사와 회사의 미래에 가장 중요한 것과 일치시키는 사람들이다.

▸ those(= employees)가 선행사이고, 관계대명사절에서 주어 역할을 해야 하므로, 목적격 관계대명사 whom을 주격 관계대명사 who나 that으로 고쳐야 한다.

15 X 게임 대회는 여름마다 Rhode Island 주에서 열린다. 그 대회는 스카이서핑과 같은 스포츠를 특징으로 하는데, 이 스포츠에서 사람들은 발에 서핑보드를 부착한 채로 비행기에서 뛰어내린다.

▸ 뒤에 완전한 절이 이어지고 있고, 선행사 sky surfing이 관계대명사절에서 '~에서'라는 의미인 전치사 in의 목적어 역할을 해야 한다. 따라서 관계대명사 which를 「전치사+관계대명사」인 in which나 관계부사 where로 고쳐야 한다.

POINT 11 관계부사의 쓰임 p.46

대표 예문

Einstein이 열 살 때, 그의 가족은 그를 Luitpold Gymnasium에 입학시켰는데, 거기서 그는 권위에 대한 의심을 키워갔다.

기출 예문 PLUS

1 아리스토텔레스는 Lesbos 섬의 석공들이 자를 사용한 방식에 특히 매료되었다.

2 서기 2세기가 시작되며, 도교와 유교 학자들은 '청담(淸談)'이라고 알려진 관행에 참가했는데, 그 관행에서 그들은 정신적이며 철학적인 문제들을 토론했다.

3 삶은 롤러코스터를 타는 것과 같을 수 있다. 오르내림과, 빠르고 느린 부분, 부딪침과 흔들리는 부분, 그리고 심지어 거꾸로 매달리는 때도 있다.

4 종종 간과되는 이 효과는 유산소 운동을 하는 사람들이 새로운 신진대사와 더 마른 몸을 확립하게 되는 주된 이유이다.

기출 문장으로 PRACTICE p.47

01 when 02 where 03 when 04 where 05 why
06 where 07 there → where 08 O

01 그 수수께끼는 1970년대까지 풀리지 않았는데, 그때 심해의 틈이 발견되었다.

▸ 절과 절을 연결하는 접속사 역할을 하면서, 뒤에 오는 절에서 시간 부사 역할을 할 수 있는 관계부사 when이 와야 한다.

02 인생과 스포츠는 중대하고 어려운 결정이 내려져야만 하는 많은 상황들을 제시한다.

▸ 절과 절을 연결하는 접속사 역할을 하면서, 뒤에 오는 절에서 장소 부사 역할을 할 수 있는 관계부사 where가 와야 한다.

03 그 땅이 매물로 나왔을 때인 1887년에, 할아버지는 Granger 가(家)로부터 200 에이커의 땅을 사들였다.

▸ 절과 절을 연결하는 접속사 역할을 하면서, 뒤에 오는 절에서 시간 부사 역할을 할 수 있는 관계부사 when이 와야 한다.

04 Brown이 태어난 Candeal에서, 지역 아이들은 드럼 모임에

참가하고, 노래하고, 공연을 무대에 올리도록 권장 받았다.

▶ 절과 절을 연결하는 접속사 역할을 하면서, 이어지는 절에서 장소 부사 역할을 할 수 있는 관계부사 where가 와야 한다.

05 어떤 전자 상거래 회사도 한 제조사의 제품을 마케팅하고 판매하는 데에 스스로를 제한해야만 하는 이유는 전혀 없다.

▶ 선행사가 reason이므로, 이유를 나타내는 관계부사 why가 와야 한다.

06 우리가 요즘 해야만 하는 유일한 것은 슈퍼마켓이나 패스트푸드 식당으로 운전해 가는 것인데, 그곳에서 아주 낮은 가격에 우리는 일일 칼로리를 거의 모두 얻을 수 있다.

▶ 절과 절을 연결하는 접속사 역할을 하면서, 이어지는 절에서 장소 부사의 역할을 할 수 있는 관계부사 where가 와야 한다.

07 Paul Odland 박사와 그의 친구인 Bob은 남아메리카로 자주 여행을 가는데, 그곳에서 그들은 가난한 가정의 장애가 있는 아이들을 위한 무료 의학적 치료를 제공한다.

▶ 절과 절을 연결하는 접속사 역할을 하면서, 이어지는 절에서 부사의 역할을 할 수 있는 관계부사가 필요한 자리이다. 선행사 South America가 장소를 나타내므로, 부사 there를 관계부사 where로 고쳐야 한다.

08 현장 연구는 문화 인류학의 특징이다. 이것은 인간 문화와 개인 행동의 방대하고 세세한 복잡성에 대해 우리가 탐구하고 배우는 방법이다.

▶ 절과 절을 연결하는 자리이고, 뒤에 완전한 절이 오고 있으며, 문맥상 '~하는 방법'이라는 의미가 오는 것이 적절하므로, 관계부사 how는 어법상 바르다.

POINT 12 관계대명사 vs. 관계부사

p.48

대표 예문

긴 하루였는데, 그날은 십 대인 내 아이를 데려오는 일을 포함했다.

기출 예문 PLUS

1 때때로 우리는 되돌릴 수 없는 나쁜 결정을 내린다.

2 우리는 사람들이 자기 자신의 의학 데이터 모두와 그것을 처리할 수 있는 컴퓨터 사용 능력을 가지게 될 시대에 진입하고 있다.

3 기억에 남을 승리를 즐기고 난 후, Andrew는 곧장 요양원으로 갔는데, 그곳에는 그의 편찮으신 할아버지가 머무르고 계셨다.

4 자원봉사를 하고자 한다면, 당신을 기꺼이 환영할 많은 단체들이 있습니다. 당신이 무엇을 하든지, 그것은 거의 확실히 보람 있을 것입니다.

기출 문장으로 PRACTICE

p.49

01 which **02** which **03** why **04** whenever
05 which **06** (A) where (B) what (C) who **07** O
08 which → where

01 내년부터, 대중들이 그 집을 둘러볼 수 있는데, 그 집은 17세기에 공작이 그의 아내를 위해 지었다.

▶ 뒤에 동사 built의 목적어가 없는 불완전한 절이 이어지고 있으므로, the house를 선행사로 하는 목적격 관계대명사 which가 와야 한다.

02 그는 그의 가장 유명한 건물 중 하나인 Fallingwater를 설계했는데, 그 건물은 폭포의 꼭대기에 지어졌다.

▶ 뒤에 동사 was built의 주어가 없는 불완전한 절이 이어지고 있으므로, Fallingwater를 선행사로 하는 주격 관계대명사 which가 와야 한다.

03 두유는 무기염으로 인해 걸쭉해져서 응유를 형성한다. 그것이 두부의 다른 인기 있는 이름이 '콩 응유'인 이유이다.

▶ 뒤에 완전한 절이 이어지고 있으므로, 관계부사 why가 와야 한다. 관계부사 why 앞에 선행사 the reason이 생략되어 있다.

04 이 긴 과정 동안, 그는 위협을 느낄 때마다, 부모의 사랑과 권위라는 안전한 곳으로 되돌아온다.

▶ 뒤에 완전한 절이 이어지고 있으므로, '~할 때는 언제나'라는 의미의 복합관계부사 whenever가 와야 한다.

05 서두르는 것은 우리에게 더 적은 시간을 제공하는 것만이 아니다. 그것은 우리가 정말 가지고 있는 그 시간으로부터의 즐거움과 혜택을 빼앗아 갈 수도 있다.

▶ 뒤에 동사 have의 목적어가 없는 불완전한 절이 이어지고 있으므로, the time을 선행사로 하는 목적격 관계대명사 which가 와야 한다. 선행사만 보고 when을 고르지 않도록 한다.

06 대부분의 기록된 역사 동안, 사람들은 그들이 태어난 곳에 살았고, 그들의 부모들이 했던 일을 했고, 같은 일을 하고 있던 사람들과 사귀었다.

▶ (A) 뒤에 완전한 절이 이어지고 있으므로, 관계부사 where가 와야 한다. 관계부사 where 앞에 선행사 the place가 생략되어 있다.

(B) 뒤에 동사 had done의 목적어가 없는 불완전한 절이 이어지고 있으므로, 관계대명사 what이 와야 한다. 이때 관계대명사 what이 이끄는 명사절은 앞의 동사 did의 목적어 역할을

한다.

(C) 뒤에 동사 were doing의 주어가 없는 불완전한 절이 이어지고 있으므로, those(사람들)를 선행사로 하는 주격 관계대명사 who가 와야 한다.

07 가까운 가족 구성원을 잃은 후에는 꽤 다른 상황이 되는데, 그때는 당신의 인간성을 증명하기 위해 약간의 애도가 요구된다.

▶ 뒤에 완전한 절이 이어지고 있으므로, after the loss ... family member를 선행사로 하는 관계부사 when은 어법상 바르다.

08 이것이 상당히 중요한 한 영역은 안전하게 운전하는 능력에 잠재적으로 해로운 음악의 영향이다.

▶ 뒤에 완전한 절(this is ... significance)이 이어지고 있으며, 추상적 의미의 장소인 One domain이 선행사이므로 관계대명사 which를 관계부사 where로 고쳐야 한다.

UNIT 06 관계사, 접속사와 전치사 구분

POINT 13 what vs. which vs. that

p.50

대표 예문

인터넷은 젊은이들에게 친숙한 수단이므로, 그들이 그것으로부터 도움을 구할 것이라는 것은 논리적이다.

기출 예문 PLUS

1 당신이 딱 원하는 것을 파는 슈퍼마켓이 아마 당신의 집 근처에 있을 것이다.

2 많은 사회 과학자들은 탄생 순서가 성격과 성인생활에서의 성취 둘 다에 직접적으로 영향을 미친다고 한동안 믿어왔다.

3 전기에 대한 책 한 권과 약간의 플라스틱 파이프만 가지고, Kamkwamba는 자신의 첫 풍차를 만들었는데, 그것은 그의 방에 전등을 작동시킬 정도로 충분한 전기를 만들어냈다.

기출 문장으로 PRACTICE

p.51

01 that 02 that 03 which 04 what 05 that
06 that 07 what → that[which] 08 which → what

01 내가 배운 한 가지 교훈은 집중하는 것을 대신하는 것은 없다는 것이다.

▶ 뒤에 완전한 절이 이어지고 있으므로, 주격보어 역할을 하는 명사절을 이끄는 접속사 that이 와야 한다.

02 사실, 생명체는 무생물을 구성하는 것과 동일한 작은 분자들로 이루어져 있다.

▶ 뒤에 동사 make up의 주어가 없는 불완전한 절이 이어지고 있고, 앞의 the same tiny particles가 선행사이므로 주격 관계대명사 that이 와야 한다.

03 로봇이 방을 살펴볼 때, 그것은 직선과 곡선의 방대한 집합만을 보는데, 로봇은 이를 화소로 전환시킨다.

▶ 뒤에 동사 converts의 목적어가 없는 불완전한 절이 이어지고 있고, 앞의 a vast collection of straight and curved lines가 선행사이므로 목적격 관계대명사 which가 와야 한다.

04 최초의 지도는 기원전 7000년에 이제는 현재의 터키인 곳에 있었던 고대 도시에서 만들어진 것으로 여겨진다.

▶ 뒤에 주어가 없는 불완전한 절이 이어지고 있고, 앞에 선행사가 없으므로 선행사를 포함하는 관계대명사 what이 와야 한다.

05 자동차들이 점점 더 안전해져 가는 이유 중 하나는 우리가 시험용 인체모형으로 잘 설계된 충돌 실험을 할 수 있어서이다.

▶ 뒤에 완전한 절이 이어지고 있으므로, 주격보어 역할을 하는 명사절을 이끄는 접속사 that이 와야 한다.

06 두 남성이 길을 걸어 올라가고 있었는데, 그때 Conan Doyle은 그의 뒤에서 다른 남성이 넘어지는 소리를 들었다. 그는 그 소리로 그 넘어짐이 단순한 미끄러짐이라고 판단했다.

▶ 뒤에 완전한 절이 이어지고 있으므로, 앞의 동사 judged의 목적어 역할을 하는 명사절을 이끄는 접속사 that이 와야 한다.

07 내가 그녀에 대해 기억하는 것들이 있지만, 그것들은 꽤 최근까지 나에게 이상하다거나 흥미롭다는 인상을 주지 못했다.

▶ 이어지는 절(I remembered about her)에 동사 remembered의 목적어가 없고, 앞의 things가 선행사이므로 관계대명사 what을 목적격 관계대명사 that 혹은 which로 고쳐야 한다.

08 새 영화를 홍보하는 데 매년 십억 달러가 훨씬 더 넘게 쓰여지지만, 사람이 사람에게 이야기하는 것이 정말로 중요한 것이다.

▶ 뒤에 동사 counts의 주어가 없는 불완전한 절이 이어지고 있고, 앞에 선행사가 없으므로 관계대명사 which를 선행사를 포함하는 관계대명사 what으로 고쳐야 한다.

POINT 14 전치사 vs. 접속사 p.52

대표 예문

수면 중에 전반적인 에너지 사용이 감소되는 것은 사실이지만, 단지 조용히 휴식을 취하는 것도 거의 동일한 감소를 야기한다.

기출 예문 PLUS

1 Keith는 피아노의 결함에도 불구하고 일생일대의 연주를 하고 있었다.

2 Jessica는 밴드 교사가 여러 악기를 연주하는 동안 들었다.

3 그의 어린 시절 동안, Wright는 시골에 살았고 완만하게 경사진 풍경과 사랑에 빠졌다.

4 그는 "우리는 철학이 발달시키는 정신적 능력 때문에 철학을 공부합니다."라고 말함으로써 그의 강연을 시작했다.

5 곡식은 쉽게 도난당할 수 없으므로, 농부들은 그들의 생계수단이 밤사이 도난당할까 걱정할 필요가 없다.

기출 문장으로 PRACTICE p.53

01 during 02 because of 03 because
04 despite 05 Although 06 during → while
07 because → because of

01 참여자들에게 재료로 가득 찬 가방을 주고 나서 풀 문제를 주는 것은 창의성 세미나 중에 흔한 관행이다.

▶ 뒤에 명사구 creativity seminars가 이어지고 있으므로, 전치사 during이 와야 한다.

02 오늘날 세계에서 예술의 진정한 역할에 대해 격렬한 논쟁이 계속되는 것은 바로 그들의 의사소통 자질 때문이다.

▶ 뒤에 명사구 their communicative properties가 이어지고 있으므로 전치사 because of가 와야 한다. 이 문장은 전치사구(because of their communicative properties)를 강조하는 「It is ~ that ...」 강조 구문이다.

03 사람의 기억은 심지어 시간이 오래 경과한 후에 훨씬 더 뚜렷해진다. 이는 사람이 과거를 새로운 시각으로 보고 있기 때문이다.

▶ 뒤에 주어와 동사를 갖춘 완전한 절(one is ... fresh eyes)이 이어지고 있으므로 접속사 because가 와야 한다.

04 중형차는 1995년부터 2005년까지의 감소에도 불구하고 주어진 기간의 매해 소매 자동차 매출의 가장 높은 비율을 기록했다.

▶ 뒤에 명사구 a decrease from 1995 to 2005가 이어지고 있으므로 전치사 despite를 써야 한다.

05 로마 제국의 멸망에 대한 수많은 설명이 있지만, 더 심층적인 원인은 토양의 비옥함 감소와 농작물의 수확량 감소에 있다.

▶ 뒤에 주어와 동사를 갖춘 완전한 절(there are ... the Roman Empire)이 이어지고 있으므로 접속사 Although가 와야 한다.

06 인체 모형의 역할은 충돌이 진행되는 동안 인간을 가장하여, 차에 타고 있는 사람에게서는 얻기 불가능할 자료를 수집하는 것이다.

▶ 뒤에 주어와 동사를 갖춘 완전한 절(a crash is conducted)이 이어지고 있으므로, 전치사 during을 접속사 while로 고쳐야 한다. collecting 이하는 부대상황을 나타내는 분사구문이다.

07 노동자들은 그들이 항상 하기를 희망했던 일 중 많은 것들을 하기 위해 그들의 'golden years'를 이용할 수 있지만, 40시간이 넘는 주 노동시간 때문에 결코 그렇게 할 기회를 갖지 못했다.

▶ 뒤에 명사구 their 40-plus-hour workweeks가 이어지고 있으므로 접속사 because를 전치사 because of로 고쳐야 한다.

Chapter 04

기출 문제 공략하기 pp.54-55

1 ④

해석 Deseada는 Lesser Antilles(소 앤틸레스) 제도에 속한 작은 섬이다. 이 섬은 Christopher Columbus가 1493년에 그의 두 번째 항해에서 느꼈던 육지를 보려는 욕망으로부터 그 이름을 얻었다고 일컬어진다. 그것은 길이가 12마일이고, 폭은 6마일이다. 북쪽을 바라보고 있는 부분이 남쪽을 바라보고 있는 부분보다 더 낮다. 섬에는 이구아나와 fragata라 불리는 종의 새들이 대단히 많다. 섬에는 인디언들의 뼈와 무기가 들어있는 깊은 동굴이 있는데, 그 인디언들은 그곳에 매장된 것으로 추정된다. 1762년에 이 섬은 영국인들에 의해 점령되었는데, 그들은 그다음 해에 파리 조약에 의해 그것을 프랑스인들에게 반환했으며, 그 이후로 그것은 후자의 소유가 되었다.

정답해설

(A) 앞의 The part를 가리키며 뒤에 오는 주격 관계대명사절의 수식을 받고 있으므로, 지시대명사 that이 와야 한다. 대명사 it은 관계사절 등의 형용사절의 수식을 받을 수 없다.

(B) 복수명사 the Indians를 선행사로 하는 주격 관계대명사 who에 이어지는 동사이므로, 복수동사 were가 알맞다.

(C) 뒤에 동사 restored의 주어가 없는 불완전한 절이 이어지고 있

고, 선행사가 사람인 the English(영국 사람들)이므로, 주격 관계대명사 who가 와야 한다.

구문해설

1행 This island is said to have obtained its name from **the desire** (*that*) Christopher Columbus felt [**of seeing land on his second voyage in 1493**].

▸ the desire와 of 이하는 의미상 동격 관계이다. Christopher Columbus 앞에 the desire를 선행사로 하는 목적격 관계대명사 that이 생략되었다.

5행 The island abounds greatly in iguanas, and in a species of birds [**called** *fragatas*].

▸ called *fragatas*는 a species of birds를 수식하는 과거분사구이다.

6행 There is a deep cavern on the island, containing the bones and arms of the Indians, [**who**, {*it is supposed*}, were buried there].

▸ who는 the Indians를 선행사로 하는 계속적 용법의 주격 관계대명사이다. it is supposed는 삽입절이다.

2 ①

해석 Leonardo da Vinci는 지금껏 살았던 사람 가운데 가장 박식하고 다재다능한 사람 중 한 명이었다. 잠자리의 날개부터 지구의 탄생까지 전 우주가 그의 호기심 많은 지성의 놀이터였다. 그러나 Leonardo는 통찰력과 독창성에 있어서 어떤 신비롭거나 타고난 재능을 가지고 있었던 것일까, 아니면 그의 탁월함은 학습되고 획득된 것일까? 분명 그는 흔치 않은 지성과 다른 사람들이 보지 않는 것을 보는 예리한 능력을 가지고 있었다. 하지만, 육천 페이지의 상세한 메모와 그림은 근면하고 호기심 많은 학생, 즉 부지런히 지식을 좇아, 끊임없이 탐구하고, 질문하고, 시험하는 영원한 학습자라는 명백한 증거를 제시한다. 당신의 지성을 확장하는 것은 창의적으로 되는 것에 필수적이다. 그러므로 학습 기회에 자주 투자하는 것은 당신이 스스로에게 줄 수 있는 가장 훌륭한 선물 중 하나이다.

정답해설

(A) 문장의 주어는 전치사구(from the wing ... the earth)의 수식을 받는 The entire universe로, 주어가 단수명사이므로 단수동사 was가 와야 한다.

(B) 뒤에 동사 see의 목적어가 없는 불완전한 절이 이어지고 있고, 앞에 선행사가 없으므로, 선행사를 포함하는 관계대명사 what이 와야 한다.

(C) 주어 자리이므로 주어 역할을 할 수 있는 동명사 investing이 와야 한다.

구문해설

5행 Certainly he had an unusual mind and an uncanny ability [**to see** what others didn't see].

▸ to see는 앞의 명사 an uncanny ability를 수식하는 형용사적 용법의 to부정사이다.

7행 ... clear evidence of a diligent, curious student — a perpetual learner in laborious pursuit of wisdom [**who** was constantly *exploring, questioning, and testing*].

▸ who 이하는 앞의 a perpetual learner를 선행사로 하는 주격 관계대명사절이다. 현재분사 exploring, questioning, testing은 등위접속사 and에 의해 「A, B, and C」의 구조로 병렬 연결되어 있다.

9행 Therefore, [**investing** regularly in learning opportunities] **is** one of the greatest gifts [(*that*) you can give yourself].

▸ investing 이하는 문장의 주어 역할을 하는 동명사구로, 동명사구 주어는 단수 취급하므로 뒤에 단수동사 is가 쓰였다. you 앞에 명사 the greatest gifts를 선행사로 하는 목적격 관계대명사 that이 생략되어 있다.

Chapter 05 준동사

UNIT 07 분사와 분사구문

POINT 15 의미가 '~하는'이면 현재분사를, '~되는'이면 과거분사를 써라!

pp.58-59

대표 예문

농구 코치인 John Wooden은 흔히 그의 팀을 정교하게 조율된 자동차라고 묘사했다.

기출 예문 PLUS

1 그는 불쾌하고 차가운 땀이 그의 등을 따라 흘러내리는 것을 느꼈다.

2 그는 일생의 너무나 많은 부분을 예술에 몰입되어 보낸 나머지 자신의 공적인 임무를 간과했다.

3 그들이 읽었던 것을 떠올려보라고 요청받았을 때, 그들은 그 묘사를 실제보다 더 긍정적인 것으로 기억했다.

4 사람들은 자신의 견해를 뒷받침하는 정보에는 관심을 가지는 반면, 그와 반대인 증거는 무시한다.

5 청소년들은 대부분이 의사소통하기 위해 인터넷을 사용하면서, 빠르게 과학기술에 몰두해 왔다.

6 두 명의 프로그래머가 나란히 일하고 있는 모습을 상상해보아라. 한 명은 눈이 감기고 발이 책상에 올려진 채 의자에 기대어 앉아 있다.

7 법원 서기는 보통 배심원이 특정 재판에 선정되면 하루 종일 어떤 일이 일어나는지에 대한 개요를 설명하는 영화를 보여준다.

기출 문장으로 PRACTICE

pp.60-61

01 acting **02** hidden **03** installed **04** observing
05 folded **06** armed **07** held **08** Assumed
09 experiencing **10** accepting **11** brought
12 knowing **13** Situating → Situated
14 followed → following **15** spending → spent

01 Bob이 그의 통역자 역할을 하며, Paul은 300달러를 제안했고, 상대측은 450달러를 제안했다.

▸「with+(대)명사+분사」 구문으로, Bob이 '역할을 하는'으로 명사와 분사가 능동의 의미 관계이므로 현재분사 acting을 써야 한다.

02 그것은 당신이 기회를 볼 수 있게 하고, 그렇지 않았을 경우에는 숨겨져 있었을지도 모르는 자원을 이용할 수 있게 해줄 것이다.

▸ resources를 선행사로 하는 주격 관계대명사절의 주격보어이며, 자원이 '숨겨지는'으로 주어와 분사가 수동의 의미 관계이므로 과거분사 hidden이 알맞다.

03 창틀에 설치될 때, 유리는 안정성을 위해 더 두꺼운 쪽이 아래로 가게 설치되곤 했다.

▸ 접속사 When이 생략되지 않은, 때를 나타내는 분사구문으로, 분사구문의 의미상 주어는 the glass이다. 유리가 '설치되는'으로 의미상 주어와 분사가 수동의 의미 관계이므로 과거분사 installed가 오는 것이 알맞다.

04 그는 가족생활의 개인적인 세세한 모습을 관찰하며 마을을 거니는 자신의 일과를 묘사했다.

▸ 부대상황을 나타내는 분사구문으로, 분사구문의 의미상 주어는 He이다. 그가 '관찰하는'으로 의미상 주어와 분사가 능동의 의미 관계이므로 현재분사 observing을 써야 한다.

05 전문 서퍼의 전화번호가 그녀의 호주머니 안에 접혀 넣어진 채, 그녀는 흥미로운 새 삶에 대한 밝은 징조를 느꼈다.

▸「with+(대)명사+분사」 구문으로, 전화번호가 '접혀진'으로 명사와 분사가 수동의 의미 관계이므로, 과거분사 folded가 오는 것이 적절하다.

06 구석기 시대에, 원시 무기만으로 무장된 사냥꾼들은 성난 매머드에 진정한 상대가 되지 못했다.

▸ 앞의 명사 the hunters를 수식하는 분사로, 사냥꾼들이 무기로 '무장되는'으로 명사와 분사가 수동의 의미 관계이므로 과거분사 armed가 와야 한다.

07 영향을 받은 부분 위에 20분 정도까지 진공청소기가 들려진 채로, 모든 남아있는 습기를 끌어내어 제거하라.

▸「with+(대)명사+분사」 구문으로, 진공청소기가 '들려지는'으로 명사와 분사가 수동의 의미 관계이므로, 과거분사 held를 써야 한다.

08 상당한 양의 물을 가지고 있다고 추정되기 때문에, 화성은 우리 태양계의 모든 행성 중 아마 가장 거주에 적합할 것이다.

▶ 이유를 나타내는 분사구문으로, 의미상 주어는 Mars이다. 화성이 물을 가지고 있다고 '추정되는'으로 의미상 주어와 분사가 수동의 의미 관계이므로, 과거분사 Assumed가 와야 한다.

09 아기가 엄마가 슬픈 감정을 느끼는 것을 볼 때 그들은 본능적으로 그것을 인지한다고 한다.

▶ 동사 watch의 목적격보어로 쓰인 분사로, 엄마가 슬픈 감정을 '느끼는'으로 목적어와 분사가 능동의 의미 관계이므로 현재분사 experiencing이 와야 한다.

10 태어난 순서는 가족 안에서 당신의 역할을 정의할지도 모르지만, 당신이 다른 사회적 역할을 받아들이며 어른이 되어감에 따라, 태어난 순서는 중요하지 않게 된다.

▶ 부대상황을 나타내는 분사구문으로, 분사구문의 의미상 주어는 you이다. 당신이 '받아들이는'으로 의미상 주어와 분사가 능동의 의미 관계이므로 현재분사 accepting을 써야 한다.

11 정복 후, 이탈리아로 다시 들여진 어마어마한 부가 중산층과 상류층 여성들이 더 많은 독립성과 힘을 가지고 상황을 운영할 수 있게 했다.

▶ 앞의 명사 the enormous wealth를 수식하는 분사로, 엄청난 부가 '들여진'으로 명사와 분사가 수동의 의미 관계이므로, 과거분사 brought를 써야 한다.

12 우리는 당신이 저희 기금에 관대하게 기부하는 것을 고려해 주시기를 희망합니다. 당신이 전문 직종에서의 미래 지도자 육성을 지원하는 데 도움이 되고 있다는 것을 알면 기분이 좋을 것입니다.

▶ 때를 나타내는 분사구문으로, 분사구문의 의미상 주어는 You이다. 당신이 '알면'으로 의미상 주어와 분사가 능동의 의미 관계이므로, 현재분사 knowing을 써야 한다.

13 해발 1,350 미터 높이에 위치되어 있어서, Kathmandu 시는 연중 따뜻한 기후를 누린다.

▶ 부대상황을 나타내는 분사구문으로, 분사구문의 의미상 주어는 the city of Kathmandu이다. 도시가 '위치되는'으로 의미상 주어와 분사가 수동의 의미 관계이므로 현재분사 Situating을 과거분사 Situated로 고쳐야 한다.

14 그 규정은 합리적인 것 같았고 빠르게 유행하여, 몇 년 안에 백 개가 넘는 다른 지방 의회에서 그것을 따랐다.

▶ 「with+(대)명사+분사」 구문으로, 다른 지방 의회들이 '따르는'으로 명사와 분사가 능동의 의미 관계이므로, 과거분사 followed를 현재분사 following으로 고쳐야 한다.

15 신문을 읽는 습관은 줄어들고 있고, 이전에 신문 광고에 쓰였던 돈의 일부는 인터넷으로 이동해갔다.

▶ 앞의 명사 the dollars를 수식하는 분사로, 돈이 '쓰여진'으로 명사와 분사가 수동의 의미 관계이므로 현재분사 spending을 과거분사 spent로 고쳐야 한다.

POINT 16 감정을 나타내는 분사: v-ing vs. p.p. p.62

대표 예문

그러므로 애완동물은 우울감을 느끼거나 만성적인 질병이 있는 환자들의 치료에 중요하다.

기출 예문 PLUS

1 학생들이 협력할 때 더 잘 배우는 것은 놀라운 일이 아닐 것이다.

2 발표는 기대보다 더 잘 진행되었고, 우리 팀장님이 특히 기뻐하시는 것처럼 보였다.

3 여느 다른 날처럼 시작했다. 나는 내 생애 가장 무시무시한 경험 중 하나를 겪게 될 것을 전혀 몰랐다.

4 한 무리의 겁먹은 아이들이 Amy Brown 뒤에 가까이 서 있었는데, 그녀는 침입자에게 막 맞서려 하고 있었다.

기출 문장으로 PRACTICE p.63

01 delighted **02** interested **03** satisfying **04** overwhelmed **05** frustrated **06** frightening → frightened **07** amazed → amazing

01 Andrew는 할아버지가 회복하고 있다는 사실에 매우 기뻤다.

▶ 주격보어로 쓰인 분사로, Andrew가 '기쁜 감정을 느끼는' 것이므로, 과거분사 delighted를 써야 한다.

02 보고서와 신문을 읽는 대부분의 독자들은 그 주제에 흥미를 느끼기 때문에 그 문서를 읽고 있다.

▶ 주격보어로 쓰인 분사로, 독자들이 '흥미를 느끼는' 것이므로, 과거분사 interested를 써야 한다.

03 음악가가 되어 단체로 함께 연주하는 것이 더 재미있어 보였고, 범죄자가 되는 것보다 더 만족스러웠다.

▶ 주격보어로 쓰인 분사로, 음악가가 되어 함께 연주하는 것이 '만족스러운 감정을 유발하는' 것이므로, 현재분사 satisfying이 와야 한다.

04 발표, 보고서 마감, 혹은 시험으로 압도되는 기분을 느끼고 있다면, 당신은 그 압박감을 처리하는 데 당신의 모든 시간을 쓰게 될

것이다.

▶ 주격보어로 쓰인 분사로, 당신이 '압도되는 감정을 느끼는' 것이므로, 과거분사 overwhelmed가 와야 한다.

05 한 연구에서, 침팬지들은 다른 수의 간식을 담고 있는 두 접시 사이에서 선택해야 했다. 만약 침팬지가 더 많은 간식이 든 접시를 가리키면, 그 접시는 다른 침팬지에게 가게 되고, 낙담한 실험대상은 더 적은 양을 받게 된다.

▶ the subject를 수식하는 분사로, 실험대상이 '낙담한 감정을 느끼는' 것이므로 과거분사 frustrated가 와야 한다.

06 좋든 나쁘든 네 기분을 인정해라. 단순히 스스로, 혹은 다른 누군가에게 "나는 겁을 먹었다"라고 말하는 것은 좋은 출발이다.

▶ 주격보어로 쓰인 분사로, 내가 '겁먹은 감정을 느끼는'의 의미가 되어야 하므로 현재분사 frightening을 과거분사 frightened로 고쳐야 한다.

07 스노클링을 하러 가본 적이 있다면, 물고기 떼 전체가 한 단일체로 갑자기 방향을 바꾸는 놀라운 광경을 본 적이 있을지도 모른다.

▶ sight를 수식하는 분사로, 광경이 '놀라운 감정을 유발하는'의 의미가 되어야 하므로 과거분사 amazed를 현재분사 amazing으로 고쳐야 한다.

UNIT 08 to부정사와 동명사

POINT 17 동사의 목적어로 쓰이는 to부정사 vs. 동명사

p.64

대표 예문

전설에 따르면 한 가난한 관리는 아주 정직해서 뇌물을 받기를 거부했다고 한다.

기출 예문 PLUS

1 오래지 않아, 그는 Los Angeles의 화창한 날씨와 흥미로운 생활 방식을 떠나온 것을 후회했다.

2 이 이동식 주택들은 이동될 수 있고, 많은 사람들이 그것들을 가지고 이곳저곳을 여행하기를 즐긴다.

3 Paul은 그들의 문제를 무시하려고 애썼지만, 곧 그들을 돌보고 자신의 집을 그들과 공유하는 자기 자신을 발견했다.

4 그는 다섯 살 때 주머니 나침반을 보고는 바늘이 항상 북쪽을 향한다는 것에 경탄했던 것을 기억했다.

기출 문장으로 PRACTICE

p.65

01 (A) to stay (B) sinking **02** to oil **03** (A) to do (B) taking **04** to let **05** (A) to congratulate (B) being **06** to fight → fighting **07** O

01 당신이 어느 때고 유사에 빠진다면, 침착할 것과 가라앉는 것이 멈출 때까지 움직이지 말 것을 기억하라.

▶ (A) 아직 일어나지 않은 일이므로 remember의 목적어로 to부정사인 to stay가 와야 한다.

(B) 문맥상 '가라앉는 것이 멈추다'라는 의미가 되어야 하므로, stopped의 목적어가 와야 한다. 동사 stop은 목적어로 동명사를 취하므로 sinking이 적절하다.

02 그녀의 몇몇 높은 음은 누군가가 기름칠하는 것을 잊은 문 (소리) 같이 들리는 경향이 있었지만, 그녀는 아주 좋은 목소리를 가지고 있었다.

▶ 문맥상 '기름칠하는 것을 잊었다'는 의미가 되어야 하므로, had forgotten의 목적어로 to부정사인 to oil이 와야 한다.

03 그는 지니고 있던 빠지지 않는 초과 체중에 대해 무언가를 하기로 결심했기 때문에, 다양한 운동을 시작하는 것을 고려했다.

▶ (A) 동사 decide는 목적어로 to부정사를 취하므로 to do가 오는 것이 알맞다.

(B) 동사 consider는 목적어로 동명사를 취하므로 taking이 알맞다.

04 두 개 블록을 지나서, 그녀가 몇 대의 차를 더 차선으로 끼워주기 위해 멈춰서 우리 둘 다 다음 신호를 놓치게 했을 때까지 나는 기분이 꽤 좋았다.

▶ 문맥상 '끼워주기 위해 멈추었다'라는 의미가 되어야 하므로, stopped 뒤에는 목적을 나타내는 부사적 용법의 to부정사 to let이 와야 한다.

05 그 이야기를 들은 모든 이들이 그 남자에게 축하를 하고 싶어했지만, 그는 언론을 피했고 촬영되기를 피했다.

▶ (A) 동사 want는 목적어로 to부정사를 취하므로 to congratulate가 알맞다.

(B) 동사 avoid는 목적어로 동명사를 취하므로 being이 알맞다.

06 다음날, 그는 가장 친한 친구와 싸운 것을 후회했지만, 그가 Paul에게 먼저 전화를 해야 하는지에 대해서는 망설였다.

▶ '싸운 것을 후회한다'라는 의미가 되어야 하므로, 동사 regretted의 목적어 자리에 있는 to fight를 동명사 fighting

으로 고쳐야 한다.

07 물에 빠진 전화기 내부 부품에서 액체를 빨아내고 싶다면, 진공 청소기를 사용해봐라.

▶ 문맥상 '(시험 삼아) ~해보다'의 의미가 되어야 하므로, try의 목적어로 쓰인 동명사 using은 어법상 바르다.

POINT 18 명사 vs. 동명사 p.66

대표 예문

전통적으로, 지적 재산은 기초 과학 발달을 증진시키는 데 오직 작은 역할만을 해왔다.

기출 예문 PLUS

1 영상기법인 초음파는 음파가 신체 내부 기관에 부딪혀 되돌아오게 함으로써 이미지를 만들어낸다.

2 하지만, 광고의 빈도를 증가시키는 것은 더 많은 돈이 들고, 광고는 가장 효과적인 곳에서 가장 비싸다.

3 갈색 나무 뱀은 괌의 토종 새 대부분을 멸종에 이르게 한 것으로 악명 높다.

4 바다 상황이 동해 연안을 따라 거칠어질 것이므로, 기상청은 모든 어로 작업의 보류를 제안했다.

기출 문장으로 PRACTICE p.67

01 approving 02 creating 03 performing
04 transmitting 05 recognizing 06 evaluation
07 avoiding

01 회사에서 제 대학 등록금 지불 요청을 승낙해 주셔서 감사드리고 싶습니다.

▶ 앞의 전치사 for의 목적어 역할을 하면서, 목적어(my request)를 취할 수 있는 동명사 approving이 와야 한다.

02 브라질의 산불이 결국 러시아 위를 떠가는 거대한 먼지 구름을 만듦으로써 모스크바의 날씨에 영향을 미칠 수 있다.

▶ 전치사 by의 목적어 역할을 하면서, 목적어(huge dust clouds)를 취할 수 있는 동명사 creating이 와야 한다.

03 대학 생활을 바쁘다. 활동들, 친구들, 그리고 오락거리가 당신이 당면한 진짜 과제를 수행하는 데 약간의 어려움을 일으킬지도 모른다.

▶ 전치사 in의 목적어 역할을 하면서, 목적어(the real job)를 취할 수 있는 동명사 performing이 와야 한다.

04 사실에 입각한 구체적인 정보를 전송하는 체계로써, 꿀벌의 신호 체계는 인간의 그것보다 우월할지도 모른다.

▶ 전치사 for의 목적어 역할을 하면서, 목적어(specific factual information)를 취할 수 있는 동명사 transmitting이 와야 한다.

05 15세기 이후, 이 전통은 개인의 성취를 인정하는 것과 관련이 있었다.

▶ 전치사 with의 목적어 역할을 하면서, 목적어(individual achievements)를 취할 수 있는 동명사 recognizing이 와야 한다.

06 대조적으로, 체조나 피겨 스케이팅과 같은 종목에서의 연기 평가는 정교한 채점 규칙이 그것이 더 객관적일 수 있게 돕는다고 하더라도 보다 주관적이다.

▶ 동명사와 명사 모두 주어로 쓰일 수 있지만, 뒤에 「전치사+명사」가 이어지므로, 명사 evaluation이 적절하다.

07 서로서로 피하고, 위장과 활동 정지를 통해 포식자에게서 숨는 것 대신에, 이집트 땅메뚜기는 방대한 무리를 지어서 단순히 수로 포식자들을 압도한다.

▶ 전치사 of의 목적어 역할을 하면서, 목적어(one another)를 취할 수 있는 동명사 avoiding이 와야 한다.

POINT 19 to부정사와 「전치사 to+동명사」를 구분하라! p.68

대표 예문

인도에서, 토론은 종교적 논란을 해결하는 데 사용되었으며 매우 인기 있는 오락의 한 형태였다.

기출 예문 PLUS

1 당신에게서 곧 소식을 듣기를 고대합니다.

2 현대 세계에서, 사람들은 불편하게 사는 것에 익숙하지 않다.

3 죄책감이 동기가 되어, 그들은 자신의 행동에 대해 보상을 하고 싶어 한다.

4 그는 자신의 명성에 대한 심지어 아주 작은 도전에도 반응해 기꺼이 싸우고자 했다.

기출 문장으로 PRACTICE

p.69

01 describe 02 photographing 03 use
04 upload 05 hearing 06 experience
07 planning

01 '멀티태스킹'이라는 용어는 1960년대까지는 존재하지 않았다. 처음에 그것은 사람이 아니라 컴퓨터를 묘사하는 데 사용되었다.

▸ 문맥상 '~하는 데 사용되다'라는 의미가 적절하므로, 「be used to-v」를 써야 한다. 따라서 to 뒤에는 동사원형 describe가 와야 한다.

02 나는 그의 첫째이자 유일한 아이의 탄생 사진을 찍는 것에 진정으로 헌신했던 한 아버지를 안다.

▸ '~하는 것에 헌신하다'라는 의미인 「devote oneself to v-ing」가 와야 하므로, to 뒤에는 동명사 photographing이 알맞다.

03 코끼리와 같은 큰 동물들은 작은 동물들보다 의사소통을 위해 토양의 진동을 이용할 가능성이 더 높다.

▸ 문맥상 '~할 것 같다'라는 의미가 적절하므로, 「be likely to-v」를 써야 한다. 따라서 to 뒤에는 동사원형 use를 쓴다.

04 많은 사진을 찍은 후 호텔 방으로 돌아왔을 때, 나는 내 블로그에 그 사진들을 올리고 싶었다.

▸ 문맥상 '~하고 싶어 하다'라는 의미가 적절하므로, 「be eager to-v」가 와야 한다. 따라서 to 뒤에는 동사원형 upload가 알맞다.

05 어떤 사람들은 그들 내면의 비평가들의 이야기를 듣는 것에 너무 익숙해서, 그들이 스스로를 비하할 때 심지어 알아차리지도 못한다.

▸ 문맥상 '~하는 것에 익숙하다'라는 의미가 적절하므로, 「be used to v-ing」가 와야 한다. 따라서 to 뒤에는 동명사 hearing이 알맞다.

06 사람들이 근본적으로 통제 불가능한 상황들을 통제하려고 애쓸 때, 그들은 높은 수준의 스트레스를 경험하는 경향이 있다.

▸ '~하는 경향이 있다'의 의미인 「be inclined to-v」가 와야 하므로, to 뒤에는 동사원형 experience가 알맞다.

07 여러분이 다른 사람들과 하려고 생각하는 대화를 계획하는 것에 관해서는, 신중하게 단어를 고르는 것은 훨씬 더 중요해진다.

▸ '~하는 것에 관한 한'이라는 의미의 「when it comes to v-ing」가 와야 하므로, to 뒤에는 동명사 planning이 알맞다.

Chapter 05

기출 문제 공략하기

pp.70-71

1 ④

해석 Jack Welch는 미국 최고 경영주 중 한 사람으로 여겨진다. 상징적이면서 실제적인 표현으로 Welch는 GE사의 구식 Blue Books를 불태우는 의식을 지시했다. Blue Books는 GE 관리자들이 조직 내에서 어떻게 업무를 수행해야 하는지를 알려주는 일련의 경영 훈련 매뉴얼이었다. 이 훈련 교재들이 15년 정도 쓰이지 않았다는 사실에도 불구하고, 그것들은 여전히 GE 관리자들의 행동에 막대한 영향을 미치고 있었다. 매일 매일의 경영 문제들에 대해 관리자들이 스스로의 해답을 작성해야 하는 필요성을 언급하며, Welch는 조직 문화에서 Blue Books를 없애버림으로써, 구식 체제를 없애버렸다. 현재, GE 관리자들은 먼지 쌓인 옛 책에서 해결책을 찾기보다는 그들 스스로의 해결책을 찾도록 지도되고 있다.

정답해설

④ 분사구문의 의미상 주어는 Welch로, 그가 '언급하는'으로 주어와 분사가 능동의 의미 관계이다. 따라서 과거분사 Cited를 현재분사 Citing으로 고쳐야 한다.

오답해설

① that은 a gesture를 선행사로 하는 주격 관계대명사로 어법상 바르다.

② 동사 get의 목적격보어로, 업무가 '수행되는'으로 목적어(tasks)와 목적격보어가 수동의 의미 관계이므로 과거분사 done은 어법상 바르다.

③ 주절의 과거시제(had great influence)보다 먼저 시작된 일이 과거 기준 시점까지 계속되고 있음을 나타내고 있고, 책은 '사용되지 않은' 대상이므로 과거완료 수동태인 had not been used는 어법상 바르다.

⑤ 「동사+부사」 형태의 구동사의 목적어로 대명사가 올 경우, 「동사+대명사+부사」의 어순으로 쓰이므로 look them up은 어법상 바르다.

구문해설

3행 The Blue Books were a series of management training manuals [**that** told {*how* GE managers were to get tasks done in the organization}].

▸ that 이하는 management training manuals를 선행사로 하는 주격 관계대명사절이다. how 이하는 동사 told의 목적어 역할을 하는 의문사절이다. 「be to-v」는 '~해야 한다'라는 의미로 의무를 나타낸다.

7행 Citing the need **for managers** [**to write** their own answers to day-to-day management challenges], Welch swept away the old order ....

▸ to write 이하는 the need를 수식하는 형용사적 용법의 to부정사이며, for managers는 to 부정사의 의미상 주어이다.

2 ⑤

<u>해석</u> Double Dutch는 두 명의 참가자가 두 개의 줄을 돌리는 동안 한 명 또는 두 명의 참가자가 그 줄 사이로 통과해 뛰는 줄넘기의 한 방식이다. Double Dutch는 아이들이 정말로 사랑하는 역동적인 형태의 줄넘기이다. 유익한 심장 혈관 운동인 것 외에도, Double Dutch는 조정능력과 민첩함도 향상시킨다. 게다가, 이것은 세 명에서 네 명의 참가자들이 긴밀하게 함께 움직이는 것을 요하기 때문에, 아이들의 협동 능력을 발달시키는 데도 좋다. 최상급의 수준에서, Double Dutch는 아이들 무리가 강한 에너지의 진정으로 멋있는 춤 동작을 하는 격렬한 스포츠 경기로도 행해지고 있다.

<u>정답해설</u>

(A) 전치사 to의 목적어 역할을 하는 동명사 being이 와야 한다. its는 동명사의 의미상 주어이다.

(B) 전치사 for의 목적어 역할을 하면서 뒤에 목적어(cooperative skills)를 취할 수 있는 동명사 developing이 와야 한다.

(C) an extreme competition sport를 선행사로 하는 관계사 자리로, 뒤에 완전한 절이 이어지고 있으므로 관계부사인 where가 와야 한다.

<u>구문해설</u>

1행 Double Dutch is a style of jumping rope [**in which** there are two participants turning two ropes while *either* one *or* two participants jump through the ropes].

▸ which는 a style of jumping rope를 선행사로 하며, 관계대명사절에서 전치사 in의 목적어 역할을 하는 목적격 관계대명사이다. 「either A or B」는 'A이거나 B'라는 의미이다.

7행 ..., Double Dutch **is** also **being done** as an extreme competition sport where groups of kids are doing high-energy dancing routines [*that* are truly amazing]

▸ 「be being p.p.」는 '~되고 있다'라는 의미의 진행형 수동태이다. that은 high-energy dancing routines를 선행사로 하는 주격 관계대명사이다.

Chapter 06 동사 I

UNIT 09 시제

POINT 20 단순 과거 시제 vs. 완료 시제 p.74

대표 예문

2000년에 첫 등장한 이후, 범죄 현장 수사를 다루는 한 미국 드라마가 매우 인기 있게 되었다.

기출 예문 PLUS

1 2만 년 전에, 해수면이 너무 낮아서 육지가 현재는 분리된 대륙인 땅들과 연결돼 있었다.

2 3개월 동안 서로 보지 못했던 Kate와 Joan은 Joan의 아파트에서 신나게 담소를 나누고 있었다.

3 자동차 충돌 실험의 도입 이래로, 자동차에 의한 사상자의 수는 많은 국가에서 감소해왔다.

기출 문장으로 PRACTICE p.75

01 had rained 02 have been 03 have strived
04 discovered 05 has been → was 06 O

01 그 주 초반에 비가 내려, 강은 탁해지고 불어나 있었다.

▶ 강이 탁해지고 불어난 과거 시점(was)보다 이전에 일어난 일을 나타내므로, 과거완료 시제인 had rained가 와야 한다.

02 James, 당신은 이제 6년째 저희와 함께 했습니다. 제가 당신에게 런던에 있는 판매부장 자리를 제안한다면 기분이 어떠시겠습니까?

▶ 「for+기간」이 쓰여 6년 전 과거 시점부터 지금까지 계속되는 일을 나타내므로, 현재완료 시제인 have been을 써야 한다.

03 1980년대 이래로, 동물원은 콘크리트 바닥과 강철봉을 풀, 바위, 그리고 물웅덩이로 대체하면서, 동물들을 위한 자연 서식지를 재현해내려고 애써 왔다.

▶ 「since+과거 시점」이 쓰여 1980년대부터 지금까지 계속되는 일을 나타내므로, 현재완료 시제인 have strived가 알맞다.

04 인간들은 수천 년 전에 섬유를 꼬아서 실을 만드는 방법을 발견했고, 그것을 더 쉽고 더 빠르게 하기 위한 여러 장비들을 개발해 왔다.

▶ 과거의 특정 시점(thousands of years ago)에 일어난 일을 나타내므로, 과거 시제인 discovered가 와야 한다.

05 운송과 메시지 통신 사이의 전통적인 관계가 깨진 것은 바로 1837년에 전기 전신의 발명으로 인해서였다.

▶ 과거의 특정 시점(in 1837)에 일어난 일을 나타내므로, 완료 시제 has been을 과거 시제인 was로 고쳐야 한다.

06 2000년 1월에, J. K. Rowling은 그녀가 소식을 들었던 암으로 고통 받고 있던 8세 소녀, Catie Hoch에게 이메일을 보냈다.

▶ J. K. Rowling이 편지를 보낸 과거 시점(sent)보다 더 이전에 일어난 일을 나타내므로 과거완료 시제 had heard는 어법상 바르다.

POINT 21 「조동사+동사원형」 vs. 「조동사+have p.p.」 p.76

대표 예문

Rust Belt의 짙은 안개는, 특히 그것이 가장 짙었을 때 기후 변화의 영향을 늦추는 데 도움이 되었을지도 모른다.

기출 예문 PLUS

1 책상 위에 발을 올려놓은 그 노동자는 생각을 하고 있는 것일 수 있고, 다른 한 명은 타자를 치느라 너무 바빠서 집중하지 못하는 것일지도 모른다.

2 석기 시대의 어떤 10살짜리도 현대의 감자 칩, 햄버거, 그리고 파스타와 같은 부드러운 음식을 먹고 살지 않았을 것이다.

3 입 냄새를 방지하는 것에 대한 여러 이야기가 있다. 여기 당신이 들어봤을지도 모르는, 사실이 아닌 입 냄새에 대한 두 가지가 있다.

기출 문장으로 PRACTICE

p.77

01 have left 02 have been 03 arrive
04 have been 05 spend → have spent
06 be → have been

01 쇼핑을 마쳤을 때, 특히 다른 누군가가 그 주차 공간을 기다리고 있었다면, 당신은 약간 망설이면서 그 자리를 떠났을지도 모른다.

▶ '~했을지도 모른다'의 의미로 과거의 일에 대한 약한 추측을 나타내므로, 조동사 may 뒤에 have left가 오는 것이 알맞다.

02 소규모 마을 정착지의 작은 움막에 살았던 고대 부족에서, 한 엄마는 밤에 어떤 아기가 우는 소리라도 들을 수 있었을 것이다.

▶ '~했을 것이다'의 의미로 과거의 일에 대한 확실한 추측을 나타내므로, 조동사 would 뒤에 have been이 오는 것은 알맞다.

03 우선, 배심원 자격으로 출석하라고 소환된 모든 이들은 아침 9시까지 도착해 배심원실에 모여야 한다.

▶ '~해야 한다'의 의미로 미래의 일에 대한 의무를 나타내므로, 조동사 must 뒤에는 동사원형 arrive가 와야 한다.

04 조랑말을 탄 남자가 "나는 계속 너의 집을 찾아 곳곳을 살폈단다. 나는 여기에 7시에 왔어야 했다. 너희 아버지가 나에게 여기로 조랑말을 데려와 너에게 그 녀석을 넘겨주라고 말씀하셨지."라고 말했다.

▶ '~했어야 했다'의 의미로, 과거의 일에 대한 후회를 나타내므로, 조동사 should 뒤에 have been이 와야 한다.

05 대부분의 부모들처럼, 당신은 당신의 아이가 별로 가지고 놀지 않은 장난감에 돈을 썼을지도 모른다.

▶ '~했을지도 모른다'의 의미로 과거의 일에 대한 약한 추측을 나타내므로, 조동사 might 뒤에 오는 동사원형 spend를 have spent로 고쳐야 한다.

06 호주는 아프리카로부터 동쪽으로 퍼져나간 개척자들에 의해 4만 5천 년 전에 식민지화되었다. 그러한 이주의 선발대는 틀림없이 수가 적었을 것이다.

▶ '~했음이 틀림없다'의 의미로, 과거의 일에 대한 강한 추측을 나타내므로, 조동사 must 뒤에 오는 동사원형 be를 have been으로 고쳐야 한다.

UNIT 10 가정법

POINT 22 가정법 과거 vs. 가정법 과거완료

p.78

대표 예문

도망치던 나치 병사들이 Ponte Vecchio 다리를 파괴했더라면, 그녀는 절대 그것을 볼 수 없었을 것이다.

기출 예문 PLUS

1 어떤 사람이 당신에게 중국 진시황제가 잔인한 통치자였다고 말한다면, 당신은 단순히 이것을 진실로 받아들이겠습니까?

2 당신의 친구가 중요한 축구 시합 도중 결승 골을 넣을 때, 당신은 연상에 의해 마치 그것이 당신의 승리이기도 한 것처럼 그녀의 승리 축하에 기쁨을 느낀다.

3 그는 넘어진 그 사람이 예민하고 쉽게 당황한다는 것을 알고 있어서, 그는 돌아서지 않았고, 대신에 그는 아무것도 듣지 못한 것처럼 성큼성큼 걸었다.

기출 문장으로 PRACTICE

p.79

01 knew 02 pay 03 had been 04 have been
05 were

01 사람들은 자신들이 테스트받고 있다는 것을 안다면, 모든 이들은 즉시 그 낯선 사람을 도우러 올 것이다.

▶ 현재 사실과 반대되는 일을 가정하는 가정법 과거이므로, if절에는 동사의 과거형 knew가 와야 한다.

02 당신이 거대한 시끄러운 사람들 무리에서 여기저기로 밀리고 있다 하더라도, 누군가가 당신의 이름을 부르는 것을 듣는다면, 당신은 주의를 기울여 들을 것이다.

▶ 현재 사실과 반대되는 일을 가정하는 가정법 과거이므로, 주절에는 「조동사의 과거형+동사원형」이 와야 한다. 따라서 pay가 알맞다.

03 그 화재는 교외에 있는 한 블록의 집들 전체를 파괴했다. 우리 소방관들이 현장에 제시간에 도착할 수 있었더라면, 화재는 그렇게 멀리 그리고 그렇게 빠르게 퍼지지 않았을 것이다.

▶ 과거 사실과 반대되는 일을 가정하는 가정법 과거완료이므로, if절의 동사로는 had p.p.의 형태인 had been이 와야 한다.

04 우리 조상들이 손실에 대해 괴로워하지 않고, 대신 큰 이득을 좇

아서 지나치게 많은 위험을 무릅썼더라면, 그들은 멸망해서 결코 그 누구의 조상도 되지 못했을 가능성이 더 크다.

▶ 과거 사실과 반대되는 일을 가정하는 가정법 과거완료이므로, 주절의 동사로는 「조동사의 과거형+have p.p.」가 와야 한다. 따라서, have been이 적절하다.

05 두 개의 서로 다른 종이 같은 자원을 이용하고, 그 자원이 희박하다면, 그 두 개의 종은 마치 그들이 같은 개체군의 구성원인 것처럼 서로를 상대로 경쟁해야 한다.

▶ 「as if 가정법」으로 주절과 같은 시점의 일을 가정하고 있으므로 as if절에는 가정법 과거가 와야 한다. 따라서, 동사의 과거형 were가 알맞다.

Chapter 06 기출 문제 공략하기

pp.80-81

1 ⑤

해석 고고학자 Mark Aldenderfer는 작년 히말라야 높은 곳의 고대 정착지 근처에서 인간 유해를 찾는 것을 목표로 하여 네팔의 Mustang 지역의 외진 절벽 면에 있는 동굴을 탐사하기 위해 떠났다. 거의 바로, 그는 자신이 찾고 있던 것과 맞닥뜨렸다. 바위에서 툭 튀어나와, 한 해골이 그가 그것을 보는 동안 그를 똑바로 응시하고 있었다. 아마 2천5백 년까지 거슬러 올라가는 그 해골은 여러 매장굴 안에 쌓여있는 많은 인간 뼈 사이에 있었다. Aldenderfer와 그의 팀은 DNA 분석이 이 고립된 지역 거주자들의 기원을 정확히 찾아줄 것을 희망하고 있는데, 그들은 아마도 티베트 고원이나 남쪽 지역에서 이주해왔을지도 모른다.

정답해설

⑤ 문맥상 고립 지역 거주자들이 이주해왔을지도 모른다는 내용이 되어야 하므로, 과거의 일에 대한 추측을 나타내는 「may have p.p.」가 와야 한다. 따라서 may 뒤의 동사원형 migrate를 「have p.p.」 형태의 have migrated로 고쳐야 한다.

오답해설

① high는 '높은'의 의미로 앞에 오는 명사구 an ancient settlement를 수식하는 형용사로 어법상 바르다.
② 전치사 with의 목적어 역할을 하는 명사절을 이끄는 선행사를 포함하는 관계대명사 what은 어법상 바르다.
③ as는 때를 나타내는 접속사로 뒤에 주어와 동사를 갖춘 완전한 절이 이어지고 있으므로, 어법상 바르다.
④ 앞의 명사구 many human bones를 수식하는 분사로, 뼈가 '쌓여진'이라는 수동의 의미를 나타내므로 과거분사 piled는 어법상 바르다.

구문해설

1행 Archaeologist Mark Aldenderfer set out last year [**to explore** remote cliffside caves in Nepal's Mustang district], [*aiming* to find human remains …].
▶ to explore 이하는 목적을 나타내는 부사적 용법의 to부정사구이다. aiming 이하는 부대상황을 나타내는 분사구문이다.

5행 **The skull**, [*dating* back perhaps 2,500 years], **was** among many human bones piled inside several burial caves.
▶ The skull이 주어이고, was가 동사이다. dating 이하는 The skull에 대해 부연 설명하는 현재분사구이다.

6행 Aldenderfer and his team hope [**that** DNA analysis will pinpoint the origins of this isolated region's inhabitants, {*who* may have migrated from the Tibetan Plateau or southern points}].
▶ that 이하는 동사 hope의 목적어 역할을 하는 명사절이다. who 이하는 this isolated region's inhabitants를 선행사로 하는 계속적 용법의 주격 관계대명사절이다.

2 ②

해석 Washington, D.C의 혼잡한 지하철 역의 추운 겨울날 아침이었다. 청바지와 티셔츠를 입고 바이올린을 아주 열정적으로 연주하는 한 젊은 남자가 있었다. 그는 거의 한 시간 동안 연주를 했는데, 그 시간 동안 적어도 천 명의 사람들이 지나쳐갔음에 틀림없다. 그를 알아보는 사람은 거의 아무도 없는 것 같았다. 대부분의 사람들은 바쁘게 지나가고 있었고, 아마 그가 돈을 벌고자 하는 그저 또 한 명의 음악가라고 생각했을 것이다. 대부분의 행인들이 직장으로 서둘러 가고 있었겠지만, 만약 그들이 그 젊은 음악가가 세계적으로 유명한 바이올린 연주자인 Tony Adamson이라는 것을 알았더라면 그 장면은 상당히 달랐을지도 모른다. 하지만, 놀라움이나 그들의 행운에 대한 이해를 보인 사람들은 거의 없어서 한 손으로 셀 수 있었을 것이다.

정답해설

(A) 앞의 명사 a young man을 수식하는 분사로, 한 젊은 남자가 바이올린을 '연주하는'으로 명사와 분사가 능동의 의미 관계이므로 현재분사 playing이 와야 한다.
(B) 과거 사실에 대한 반대를 나타내는 가정법 과거완료 구문이므로, 주절의 동사 형태는 「조동사의 과거형+have p.p.」가 와야 한다. 따라서, have been이 알맞다.
(C) 주어는 주격 관계대명사절(who ... good fortune)의 수식을 받는 복수명사 those이므로, 복수동사 were를 써야 한다.

구문해설

1행 There, [**clothed** in jeans and a T-shirt], was a young man playing his violin with great passion.
▶ clothed 이하는 주어 a young man에 대해 부연 설명하는 과거분사구이다.

3행 He played for almost an hour, [during **which** time at least a thousand people *must have passed* by].

▶ which는 an hour를 선행사로 하는 관계형용사이다. 「must have p.p.」는 '~했음에 틀림없다'라는 의미로 과거 사실에 대한 강한 추측을 나타낸다.

5행 Most people were busily hurrying along and probably thought [(**that**) he was just another musician {*trying* to make money}].

▶ he was 앞에 동사 thought의 목적어 역할을 하는 명사절을 이끄는 접속사 that이 생략되어 있다. trying 이하는 앞의 another musician을 수식하는 현재분사구이다.

10행 ... were **so** few **that** you *could have counted* them on one hand.

▶ 「so+형용사+that ~」은 '너무 …해서 ~하다'라는 의미이다. 「could have p.p.」는 '~했을 수도 있다'라는 의미로 과거 사실에 대한 불확실한 추측을 나타낸다.

Chapter 07 동사 Ⅱ

UNIT 11 목적격보어의 형태

POINT 23 목적격보어의 형태는 동사가 결정한다! p.84

대표 예문

Meredith 씨는 이따금 그를 쓰러지게 하는 희귀한 질병을 앓고 있었다.

기출 예문 PLUS

1 적절한 제도, 지식, 협의 방법 혹은 참여 기제가 의견 충돌을 사라지게 할 수 있다고 생각하는 것은 잘못되었다.

2 상점의 계산대에서 일하면서, 한 젊은 대학생은 노부부가 휠체어에 탄 손녀와 함께 들어오는 것을 보았다.

3 과거의 경험은 그가 명백히 옳은 것을 하는 것에 대해 칭찬을 받는 것은 적절하지 않으리라는 신념을 키우는 데 도움이 되었다.

기출 문장으로 PRACTICE p.85

01 come 02 feel 03 to step 04 to try
05 to come 06 know 07 did → do[doing]
08 understanding → understand[to understand]

01 그때, 그녀는 운전자의 얼굴에 갑자기 불안한 표정이 드리우는 것을 알아챘다.

▸ 지각동사 notice는 목적격보어로 동사원형을 취하므로 come이 와야 한다.

02 그저 당신을 기분 좋게 해주는 피드백은 장기적으로 당신이 테니스 기술을 발전시키는 데 도움이 되지 않을 것이다.

▸ 사역동사 make는 목적격보어로 동사원형을 취하므로 feel이 와야 한다.

03 게다가, 사적인 대화를 나누는 사람들은 인도 한가운데 서서, 사람들이 그들 주위를 걸어가도록 했다.

▸ 동사 force는 목적격보어로 to부정사를 취하므로 to step이 알맞다.

04 단지 즐거움만 주는 책도 학생들의 자신감을 키워줄 것이고, 그들이 학교에서 더 전문적인 자료를 읽으려고 노력하도록 장려할 것이다.

▸ 동사 encourage는 목적격보어로 to부정사를 취하므로 to try가 와야 한다.

05 관광은 각기 다른 지역과 문화권에서 온 사람들이 함께 모이도록 해주는데, 이는 관광객들과 관광지의 지역사회가 서로에 대해 배울 수 있게 해준다.

▸ 동사 allow는 목적격보어로 to부정사를 취하므로 to come이 와야 한다.

06 종이 한 장이든 제품이든, 청중이 당신이 들고 있는 것이 중요하다는 것을 알게 하고 싶다면, 그것을 정중하고 주의 깊게 다루어라.

▸ 사역동사 let은 목적격보어로 동사원형을 취하므로 know가 알맞다.

07 병원에서, Tom은 친구가 마술을 하는 것을 보는 동안 자신은 아이스크림을 제공했다.

▸ 지각동사 watch는 목적격보어로 동사원형이나 현재분사를 취하므로, did를 do나 doing으로 고쳐야 한다.

08 작은 카메라를 동물에게 부착함으로써 동물에 대해 더 많이 배우는 것은 사람들이 동물의 행동과 서식지에 대해 더 많이 이해하도록 돕는다.

▸ 동사 help는 목적격보어로 동사원형이나 to부정사를 취하므로, understanding을 understand나 to understand로 고쳐야 한다.

POINT 24 목적어와 목적격보어의 능동/수동 관계를 따져라! p.86

대표 예문

당신의 생각을 점검해봐라, 그러면 당신은 그것들이 완전히 과거나 미래에 사로잡혀 있는 것을 알게 될 것이다.

기출 예문 PLUS

1 그 방은 밝은 빨간색으로 칠해졌는데, 이는 그 사람들이 흥분하거나 심지어 격앙되게 했다.

2 마이크 쪽으로 다가섰을 때, Gabby는 얼굴과 목에 땀이 흘러내리는 것을 느낄 수 있었다.

3 포유류와 조류는 보통 소리로 그들의 존재를 인식시키는데, 새들이 그것에 훨씬 능하다.

기출 문장으로 PRACTICE

p.87

01 unlocked 02 sunbathing 03 motivated
04 satisfied 05 exposed 06 rendered
07 shaken → shake[shaking] 08 to remove → removed

01 지난 여름 어느 날, 화장실 문의 자물쇠가 꼼짝하지 않았다. 내가 아무리 애를 써도 그것을 열 수 없었다.

▶ 동사 get의 목적어인 it(= the lock)과 목적격보어가 '그것이 열리는'이라는 수동의 관계이므로 목적격보어로 과거분사 unlocked가 알맞다.

02 나는 조련사들이 점심시간에 바다사자들과 포개어져 일광욕을 하는 것을 보고 놀랐다.

▶ 지각동사 see의 목적어(trainers)와 목적격보어가 '조련사들이 일광욕을 하는'이라는 능동의 관계이므로 목적격보어로 현재분사 sunbathing을 써야 한다.

03 이런 칭찬하는 편지와 같은 고객 반응은 저희가 동기를 부여받게 하고, 저희 서비스를 개선하도록 이끕니다.

▶ 동사 keep의 목적어(us)와 목적격보어가 '저희가 동기를 부여받는'이라는 수동의 관계이므로, 목적격보어로 과거분사 motivated가 와야 한다.

04 한 연구원에 따르면, 뇌는 돌이킬 수 없는 선택에 대해 우리가 만족감을 느끼게 하기 위해 작동하는 일종의 타고난 방어기제를 가지고 있다.

▶ make의 목적어(us)와 목적격보어가 '우리가 만족감을 느끼는'이라는 수동의 관계이므로, 목적격보어로 과거분사 satisfied가 알맞다.

05 로마 통치 말기에, 이탈리아의 삼림층이 베어졌다. 안타깝게도, 삼림 벌채는 토양이 혹독한 날씨에 노출되게 했다.

▶ 동사 left의 목적어(the soil)와 목적격보어가 '토양이 노출되는'이라는 수동의 관계이므로, 목적격보어로 과거분사 exposed가 알맞다.

06 대중들은 자신들을 기쁘게 해주는 방식으로 그들에게 서비스가 제공되기를 원한다. 그들은 효율성뿐만 아니라, 정중함과 배려도 원한다.

▶ 동사 have의 목적어(the service)와 목적격보어가 '서비스가 제공되는'이라는 수동의 관계이므로, 목적격보어로 과거분사 rendered가 와야 한다.

07 그는 그의 대사를 할 수 있는 한 최선으로 잘 전달하려고 애썼지만, 그는 자신의 목소리가 떨리는 것을 느낄 수 있었다.

▶ 지각동사 feel의 목적어(his voice)와 목적격보어가 '목소리가 떨리는'이라는 능동의 관계이므로, 목적격보어로 동사원형이나 현재분사를 써야 한다. 따라서 shaken을 shake나 shaking으로 고쳐야 한다.

08 그가 못을 제거하기 위해 몇 분만 들였더라면, 그는 아마 바로 그 날 바퀴가 펑크 나지는 않았을 것이다.

▶ 동사 get의 목적어(the nail)와 목적격보어가 '못이 제거되는'이라는 수동의 관계이므로, 목적격보어로 과거분사를 써야 한다. 따라서 to remove를 removed로 고쳐야 한다.

UNIT 12 주의해야 할 동사

POINT 25 「동사+it+목적격보어+to-v」 형태에 주의하라!

p.88

대표 예문

현대 의학은 우리가 더 오래 살게 해주지만, 정부는 늘어나는 고령인구를 보살피는 것에 어려움을 겪고 있다.

기출 예문 PLUS

1 충분히 이상하게도, 얼룩말의 줄무늬는 다른 동물들에게 각각의 얼룩말이 구분되지 않게 하는 반면, 사실 얼룩말들이 서로서로를 분간하는 것은 더 쉽게 해준다.

2 그들은 더 젊고 더 생산적인 세대에게 그들의 제한된 자원을 쓰는 것이 더 낫다고 생각했는데, 이는 그 종족이 어떻게 혹독한 환경에서 살아남았는지를 설명해준다.

3 한 35세 여성은 쓰라리고 감염이 될 때까지 손으로 눈을 비비곤 했다. 그녀는 화장을 하는 것이 눈을 비비고 싶을 때 도움이 된다는 것을 발견했다.

기출 문장으로 PRACTICE

p.89

01 to call 02 it 03 to talk 04 it 05 recognize → to recognize 06 find very difficult → find it very difficult

01 어떤 사람들은 그들이 친밀한 사이가 아닐 때 이름으로 다른 이들을 부르는 것이 매우 무례하다고 생각한다.

▶ 동사 consider 뒤에 가목적어 it과 목적격보어(extremely rude)가 있으므로 진목적어 역할을 할 수 있는 to부정사 to call이 와야 한다.

02 인플레이션은 대부분의 사람들에게 삶의 주요한 걱정거리일 수 있다. 그것은 가정들이 장래의 계획을 세우는 것을 어렵게 한다.

▶ 동사 makes의 목적격보어(difficult) 뒤에 진목적어(to plan ahead)가 왔으므로 가목적어 it이 와야 한다. for households는 to부정사의 의미상 주어이다.

03 대화를 조성하는 가정에서 자란 아이들은 장래에 그들의 실망감, 두려움, 좌절, 그리고 다른 감정을 다른 이들에게 이야기하는 것을 더 쉽게 여긴다.

▶ 동사 find 뒤에 가목적어 it과 목적격보어(easier)가 왔으므로 진목적어 역할을 할 수 있는 to부정사 to talk가 와야 한다.

04 그의 의심하는 습관은 그가 오랫동안 지속된 여러 과학적 가정들에 의문을 제기하는 것을 쉽게 해주었다.

▶ 동사 made의 목적격보어(easy)와 진목적어(to question)가 뒤에 왔으므로, 가목적어 it이 와야 한다.

05 어떤 야생화 책은 모든 흰 꽃 종들이나 모든 노란 꽃 종들을 한데 배열해 놓는다. 하지만, 그러한 분류는 자연적인 관계성을 반영하지 않으며, 식물군의 특징을 구분하는 것을 어렵게 만든다.

▶ 동사 make 뒤에 가목적어 it과 목적격보어(difficult)가 왔으므로, 진목적어 역할을 할 수 있는 to부정사가 와야 한다. 따라서 recognize를 to recognize로 고쳐야 한다.

06 모든 현재 쓰이고 있는 언어는 변하지만, 변화의 정도는 시기에 따라, 그리고 언어에 따라 다르다. 예를 들어, 현대의 아이슬란드인들은 중세의 아이슬란드 영웅 전설을 읽는 것이 아주 어렵다고 여기지 않는다.

▶ 동사 find 뒤의 very difficult가 목적격보어이고, 그 뒤의 to read 이하가 진목적어이다. 동사 find 뒤에 진목적어를 대신하는 가목적어 it이 와야 하므로 find very difficult를 find it very difficult로 고쳐야 한다.

POINT 26 형태가 유사한 자동사와 타동사를 구분하라!

p.90

대표 예문

Namibia, Botswana, 그리고 Zimbabwe는 남아프리카공화국의 북쪽에 놓여 있다.

기출 예문 PLUS

1 그는 즉시 일어나서 병원 복도를 따라 내려가 그녀의 방으로 갔다.

2 회사가 새 제품을 출시하면, 그 회사는 기존 제품의 가격을 올린다.

3 이집트 가정들은 고양이의 죽음을 애도했고, 고양이들이 마지막으로 매장되기 전에 그것들의 사체를 천으로 감쌌다.

기출 문장으로 PRACTICE

p.91

01 lay 02 raised 03 lies 04 (A) rise (B) reached 05 laid 06 arouses

01 어떤 물고기는 해류 속이나 근처에 알을 낳는데, 그러면 해류가 알을 성장에 유리한 환경으로 실어 나를지도 모른다.

▶ 뒤에 목적어(their eggs)가 이어지고 있고, '(알을) 낳다'라는 의미가 되어야 하므로, 타동사인 lay가 와야 한다.

02 원래 양과 염소들은 주로 고기를 위해 길러졌다. 이 동물들은 후에 우유와 털을 위해서도 가치 있게 되었다.

▶ 수동태로 쓰였으며, 문맥상 '길러지다'의 의미이므로 타동사 raise의 과거분사 형태인 raised가 알맞다.

03 왜 뜨거운 수프 한 솥이 수프 한 스푼보다 더 큰 피해를 입히는가? 그 문제에 대한 정답은 온도와 열 사이의 차이에 있다.

▶ 뒤에 목적어가 없고, 문맥상 '~에 놓여있다'라는 의미가 되어야 하므로, 자동사인 lies가 알맞다.

04 청소부가 "준비됐다"라고 외치자, 대형 쓰레기통이 땅에서 올라가기 시작했다. 그것은 곧 꼭대기에 다다랐고, 쓰레기가 트럭 속으로 떨어졌다.

▶ (A) 뒤에 목적어가 없고, 문맥상 '오르다'의 의미가 되어야 하므로, 자동사인 rise가 알맞다.
(B) 뒤에 전치사 없이 바로 목적어(its peak)가 왔으므로, '~에 이르다'라는 의미의 타동사 reached가 와야 한다.

05 현대 서양사상의 기원은 고대 그리스의 황금기로 거슬러 올라갈 수 있는데, 이때 그리스 사상가들은 현대 서구 정치, 철학, 과학,

그리고 법을 위한 토대를 놓았다.

▶ 뒤에 목적어(the foundations)가 이어지고 있고, 문맥상 '~을 놓다'의 의미가 되어야 하므로, 타동사 lay의 과거형인 laid가 알맞다.

06 'uncanny valley'는 로봇과 컴퓨터 애니메이션 같은 인조인간이 아주 똑같지는 않지만 거의 진짜 인간같이 보일 때, 이 인간과의 유사함이 어느 정도의 불쾌한 느낌을 불러일으킨다는 개념이다.

▶ 뒤에 목적어(certain unpleasant feelings)가 이어지고 있고, 문맥상 '~을 불러일으키다'라는 의미가 되어야 하므로 타동사 arouses가 와야 한다.

POINT 27 do동사의 쓰임

p.92

대표 예문

당신은 짐 쌀 물건이 실제로 그런 것만큼 많지 않다는 잘못된 생각을 가지고 있다.

기출 예문 PLUS

1 그리스인들은 페르시아인이나, 그리스인이 아닌 다른 이들과 했던 것보다 서로 간에 훨씬 더 자주 거래했다.

2 집단의 단 한 명의 구성원도 그 노래를 안다고 할 수는 없지만, 그 집단 자체는 그 노래를 아는 일종의 집단의식이 생겨난다.

3 연구는 운전자들이 표시가 안 된 횡단보도에서보다 표시가 된 횡단보도에서 보행자에게 더 양보할 가능성이 있다는 것을 정말로 보여준다.

기출 문장으로 PRACTICE

p.93

01 do **02** did **03** (A) do (B) do **04** does **05** did
06 are → do **07** does → did

01 많은 사용자들이 아마 차에서보다 인터넷상에서 더 많은 시간을 보낼 것이다.

▶ 앞에 오는 일반동사구 spend time을 대신하는 대동사 do가 와야 한다.

02 더 비싼 도시에서 이사 온 사람들은 과거에 그랬던 것처럼 그들의 새로운 주거환경에 같은 액수의 돈을 투자한다.

▶ 앞에 오는 일반동사구 sink the money를 대신하는 대동사가 와야 하는데, 뒤에 과거를 나타내는 부사구(in the past)가 쓰였으므로 과거형 did가 알맞다.

03 대부분의 아마추어 연설가들은 일대일 상황에서 그러는 것보다 무대 위에서 더 힘있게 말해야 한다는 생각을 가지고 있다.

▶ (A) 뒤에 오는 일반동사 have를 강조하는 동사로, 주어(Most amateur speakers)가 3인칭 복수이므로, 복수동사 do가 오는 것이 알맞다.

(B) 앞에 오는 일반동사구 speak with power를 대신하는 대동사 do가 와야 한다.

04 '예술은 문제를 해결하지는 않지만, 우리로 하여금 그것들의 존재를 인지하게 한다'라고 한 조각가가 한때 말했다. 반면에 예술교육은 문제를 정말로 해결한다.

▶ 뒤에 오는 일반동사 solve를 강조하는 동사로, 주어(Art education)가 3인칭 단수이므로, 단수동사 does가 적절하다.

05 당신은 아마도 한두 번 Luciano Pavarotti가 그 노래를 부르는 것을 들어봤을 것이다. 하지만, 그것은 Paul Potts라는 이름의 휴대전화 판매원에 의해 불렸을 때 영국의 한 무대에서 그랬던 만큼의 큰 의미를 결코 갖지 못한다.

▶ 앞에 오는 일반동사구 have meaning을 대신하는 대동사가 와야 하는데, 과거의 일을 나타내고 있으므로 과거형 did가 적절하다.

06 유기농 방식의 농부들은 전통적 방식의 농부들의 농작물에 못지않게 해충에 시달리는 농작물을 재배한다. 벌레들은 일반적으로 우리가 그러는 것처럼 유기농 농작물과 전통적인 농작물을 구분하지 않는다.

▶ 앞에 오는 일반동사구 discriminate ... crops를 대신하는 대동사가 와야 하는데, 주어가 1인칭 복수형이므로 are를 do로 고쳐야 한다.

07 에베레스트 산 정상에 도달하는 것은 한때 놀라운 업적으로 여겨졌다. 하지만 거의 4,000명의 사람들이 그곳의 정상에 도달했기 때문에, 그 업적은 반세기 전에 그랬던 것보다 의미가 덜하다.

▶ 앞에 오는 일반동사 mean을 대신하는 대동사가 와야 하는데, 뒤에 과거를 나타내는 부사구(half a century ago)가 이어지고 있으므로 현재형 does를 과거형 did로 고쳐야 한다.

POINT 28 당위성을 내포한 that절의 동사는 「(should+) 동사원형」으로 쓴다!

p.94

대표 예문

보답의 규칙은 한 사람이 다른 사람이 제공한 것에 대해 동일하게 보답하도록 노력해야 함을 요구한다.

기출 예문 PLUS

1 소비자가 잘 알고 결정을 내리기 위한 적절한 정보가 부족할 때, 정부는 회사가 정보를 제공해야 한다고 요구하기 위해 개입할지도 모른다.

2 제 직업 때문에 이제 저는 대부분의 주에 여행을 하고, 저는 정말로 일간 신문을 받아볼 수 없습니다. 그래서 저는 당신이 신문을 저희 집에 배달하는 것을 중단해달라고 요청하고 싶습니다.

3 최근의 증거는 네안데르탈인과 현대인의 공통 조상이 아마도 약 40만 년 전에 꽤 정교한 언어를 사용했음을 시사한다.

기출 문장으로 PRACTICE p.95

01 is 02 be 03 retire 04 be 05 be → is
06 (A) were → (should) be (B) O

01 새로운 연구는, 운전 중에 문자 메시지를 보내는 사람들의 수가 이를 막기 위한 다양한 캠페인에도 불구하고 사실상 늘어나고 있음을 시사한다.

▶ 동사 suggest가 이끄는 that절이 당위성을 내포하지 않고 객관적 사실을 나타낸다. 따라서 동사는 직설법인 is로 써야 한다. 이때 suggest는 '시사하다'의 의미이다.

02 제 발의 문제로, 저는 트럭에 짐을 싣고 내리는 제 직무를 계속하는 것 대신에 창고에서의 사무직 업무를 받아야 한다고 요청해왔습니다.

▶ 요청을 나타내는 동사 ask가 이끄는 that절이 당위성을 나타내므로, 동사를 「(should+) 동사원형」 형태로 써야 한다. 따라서 be가 알맞다.

03 William의 아버지는 그의 아들이 밤늦게 책을 읽는 것이 다음 날 학업을 위한 에너지를 줄일 것이라는 느낌을 받았다. 그는 다른 가족들이 잠자리에 들 때 William도 그래야 한다고 주장했다.

▶ 주장을 나타내는 동사 insist가 이끄는 that절이 당위성을 나타내므로, 동사를 「(should+) 동사원형」 형태로 써야 한다. 따라서 retire가 알맞다.

04 한 연구는 생후 3개월 즈음에 아기가 자기 방으로 옮겨져야 한다고 권장한다. "자주 부모의 방에서 자는 아이들은 이러한 채비에 의존하게 되기 쉽다."라고 그 연구는 보고한다.

▶ 권유를 나타내는 동사 recommend가 이끄는 that절이 당위성을 나타내므로, 동사를 「(should+) 동사원형」 형태로 써야 한다. 따라서 be가 적절하다.

05 우리는 일찍 그리고 자주 실패에 노출되기를 희망해야 한다. 사회학자 Glen Elder는 10대 후반에서 30대 초반에 이르는 실패가 가장 유익한 성장에 민감한 시기가 있다고 제시했다.

▶ 동사 proposed가 이끄는 that절이 당위성을 내포하지 않고 객관적인 사실을 나타내므로 직설법으로 써야 한다. 따라서 be를 is로 고쳐야 한다.

06 미국 전문가들은 약간의 혈압 상승이 있는 환자들이 약을 복용하도록 권장되어야 한다고 제안하는 지침을 작성했다. 하지만, 유럽에서, 전문가들은 같은 증상을 가진 사람들이 약을 복용하는 것을 피해야 한다고 조언했다.

▶ (A) 제안을 나타내는 동사 suggest가 이끄는 that절이 당위성을 나타내므로, 동사를 「(should+) 동사원형」 형태로 써야 한다. 따라서 were를 be나 should be로 고쳐야 한다.
(B) 충고를 나타내는 동사 advise가 이끄는 that절이 당위성을 나타내므로, 동사를 「(should+) 동사원형」 형태로 써야 한다. 따라서 avoid는 어법상 바르다.

Chapter 07
기출 문제 공략하기 pp.96-97

1 ②

해석 공감은 거울 뉴런이라 불리는 특수한 신경 세포 그룹에 의해 가능해진다. 이 특별한 세포들은 우리가 감정을 '반영할' 수 있게 한다. 거울 뉴런은, 원숭이의 뇌 안의 개별 신경 세포 활동을 관찰하는 도중, 그 동물들이 특정 행동을 하든지 단순히 또 다른 원숭이가 같은 행동을 하는 것을 관찰하든지, 뇌의 같은 영역의 뉴런이 활성화된다는 것을 알아챈 이탈리아의 과학자들에 의해 최초로 발견되었다. 그것은 마치 관찰자의 뇌 안의 세포들이 행위자의 뇌의 활동을 '반영하는' 것처럼 보였다. 우리가 누군가가 어떤 감정을 느끼는 것을 보고 그에 반응해 같은 감정을 느낄 때 비슷한 현상이 발생한다. 동일한 신경 체계가 거울 뉴런 체계의 일부인 뇌섬엽의 한 영역과, 관찰된 감정과 관련된 감정적인 뇌의 영역에서 활성화된다.

정답해설

(A) Italian scientists를 선행사로 하는 주격 관계대명사절에서 동사가 필요하므로 noticed가 와야 한다.
(B) 지각동사 watch의 목적어(someone)과 목적격보어가 '누군가가 감정을 느끼는'이라는 능동의 관계이므로, 목적격보어로 현재분사 experiencing이 와야 한다.
(C) 절과 절을 연결하는 접속사 역할을 하면서 앞의 명사 the insula를 선행사로 하는 주격 관계대명사 which가 와야 한다.

구문해설

2행 These special cells **enable** us **to** **"mirror"** emotions.

▸「enable A to-v」는 'A가 ~하는 것을 가능하게 하다'라는 의미이다.

3행 ... Italian scientists who, [**while** looking at the activity of individual nerve cells inside the brains of monkeys], noticed [*that* neurons in the same area of the brain were activated {whether the animals were ... or simply **observing** another monkey **perform** the same action}].

▸ while ... monkeys는 접속사를 생략하지 않은 분사구문이다. that 이하는 동사 noticed의 목적어 역할을 하는 명사절이다. 「whether ~ or ...」는 '~이든 …이든'의 의미로 부사절을 이끄는 접속사이다. 지각동사 observe의 목적격보어로 동사원형 perform이 쓰였다.

11행 ..., and in the emotional brain areas [**associated** with the observed emotion].

▸ associated 이하는 the emotional brain areas를 수식하는 과거분사구이다.

2 ②

해석 물은 칼로리가 없지만, 위에서 공간을 차지하는데, 이는 포만감을 만들어낸다. 최근, 한 연구는 식사 전에 물 두 잔을 마신 사람은 더 빨리 배가 부르게 되었고, 더 적은 칼로리를 섭취하게 되었으며, 더 많은 체중을 감량했다는 것을 발견했다. 당신은 수분이 더 적은 것보다 수분 함량이 더 높은 음식을 선택함으로써 같은 전략이 작용하게 할 수 있다. 예를 들어, 포도와 건포도의 유일한 차이점은 포도가 약 6배 더 많은 수분을 가지고 있다는 것이다. 그 수분은 그것들이 얼마만큼 당신을 배부르게 하느냐에 있어 큰 차이를 만든다. 당신은 100칼로리 상당의 건포도를 먹은 후보다 100칼로리 상당의 포도를 먹은 후에 훨씬 더 만족감을 느낄 것이다. 상추, 오이, 그리고 토마토와 같은 샐러드 채소 역시 묽은 수프가 그러하듯 수분 함량이 아주 높다.

정답해설

(A) 뒤에 완전한 절이 이어지므로, 동사 found의 목적어 역할을 하는 명사절을 이끄는 접속사 that이 와야 한다.

(B) 문장의 주어는 전치사구(between ... raisins)의 수식을 받는 단수명사구 the only difference이므로, 단수동사 is가 오는 것이 알맞다.

(C) 앞의 일반동사구 have a very high water content를 대신하므로 대동사 do가 알맞다. 이때, 동사(do)와 주어(broth-based soups)가 도치를 이루고 있다

구문해설

1행 Water has no calories, but it takes up a space in your stomach, [**which** creates a feeling of fullness].

▸ which 이하는 앞 절 전체(it ... stomach)를 선행사로 하는 계속적 용법의 주격 관계대명사절이다.

4행 ... by choosing foods [**that** have a higher water content over *those* with less water].

▸ that 이하는 앞의 foods를 선행사로 하는 주격 관계대명사절이다. those는 앞의 foods를 대신하는 대명사이다.

7행 That water makes a big difference in [**how much** they *fill you up*].

▸ how much 이하는 앞의 전치사 in의 목적어 역할을 하는 의문사절이다. 「동사+부사」의 목적어로 대명사가 올 때는 「동사+대명사+부사」의 어순으로 쓴다.

Chapter 08 형용사와 부사

UNIT 13 형용사와 부사

POINT 29 형용사 자리와 부사 자리를 구분하라!

pp.100-101

대표 예문

심리학자들은 왜 사람들이 자기 자신의 불완전함에 대해 듣는 것에 그렇게 민감한지에 대한 많은 이론을 가지고 있다.

기출 예문 PLUS

1 우리는 미래가 너무 천천히 오고 있다는 것을 발견하고 그것을 재촉하려 애쓰는 것처럼 미래를 기대한다.

2 물고기가 지느러미와 강력한 꼬리와 함께 유선형이고 매끄러운 몸통을 가지고 있는 것은 우연이 아니다.

3 요즘, 젊은이들은 휴대전화나 다른 디지털 기기를 이용해서 점점 더 소셜 네트워킹 웹사이트에 접속한다.

4 이번 학기 강좌는 학생들이 어느 강좌를 듣고 싶은지 선택할 수 있도록 각 학과별로 알파벳 순으로 배열되어 있다.

5 누군가가 거짓말을 할 때 평상시 패턴에서 벗어남을 알아채기 위해서는 그 사람의 평상시 패턴에 세심한 주의를 기울여야 한다. 때로 그 변화는 말을 잠깐 쉬는 것만큼 미묘하다.

기출 문장으로 PRACTICE

pp.102-103

01 frequently 02 easy 03 increasingly
04 well 05 legal 06 (A) relatively (B) quickly
07 extremely 08 close 09 inherent 10 objective
11 (A) positively (B) accessible 12 (A) happily
(B) casually 13 appropriate 14 effective → effectively 15 defenselessly → defenseless

01 광고가 텔레비전에 나온다면, 광고가 자주 방영되면 될수록, 그것은 더 많은 사람들에게 닿을 것이다.

▶ 동사(is run)를 수식하는 부사 frequently가 와야 한다.

02 우울증을 겪는 사람들은 큰 이미지나 장면을 해석하는 것이 쉽다고 생각하지만, 미세한 세부 사항에 있어 '차이를 발견하는' 것은 힘들어한다.

▶ 「동사+it(가목적어)+목적격보어+to-v(진목적어)」 구문으로, find it 뒤에 목적격보어 역할을 할 수 있는 형용사 easy가 와야 한다.

03 점점 세계화되는 세계에서, 번역된 문학 작품은 문화 사이의 가교로서 특히 중요한 역할을 한다.

▶ 형용사처럼 쓰이는 과거분사(globalized)를 수식하는 부사 increasingly가 와야 한다.

04 가면은 무한정으로 지탱하기에는 너무 무겁고, 당신이 아무리 자신을 잘 감추고 있다고 믿어도, 다른 사람들은 항상 알게 된다.

▶ 동사(are disguising)를 수식하는 부사 well이 와야 한다.

05 Louisiana 주는 닭싸움이 합법으로 남아있던 유일한 주였는데, 왜냐하면 닭들은 주의 법에 따르면 동물로 정의되지 않았기 때문이다.

▶ 관계부사절의 주어(cockfighting)를 설명하는 주격보어 자리이므로, 형용사인 legal이 와야 한다.

06 금은 상대적으로 무른 금속인데, 매우 물러서, 쉽게 긁히기 때문에 반지는 순금으로는 거의 만들어지지 않는다.

▶ (A) 형용사(soft)를 수식하는 부사 relatively가 와야 한다.
(B) 동사(get scratched)를 수식하는 부사 quickly가 와야 한다.

07 그 어느 때보다도 더 많은 정보가 현재 텍스트를 통해 교환되는데, 이는 당신이 글 형식으로 효과적으로 의사소통할 수 있다는 것을 매우 중요하게 만든다.

▶ 「동사+it(가목적어)+목적격보어+that절(진목적어)」 구문으로, 목적격보어로 쓰인 형용사(important)를 수식하는 부사 extremely가 와야 한다.

08 양식장에 인접한 지역에 서식하고 있는 현지 야생동물에 미치는 부정적인 영향이 계속해서 그 산업의 지속적인 대민관계의 문제가 되고 있다.

▶ 앞의 명사(areas)를 수식하는 형용사 close가 와야 한다.

09 지식은 도덕 관념이 없는데, 비도덕적인 것이 아니라 도덕 중립적인 것이다. 지식에는 어떤 특정 사회적 혹은 도덕적인 적용을 좌우하는 내재적인 것은 존재하지 않는다.

▶ 앞의 대명사(nothing)을 수식하는 형용사 inherent가 와야 한다.

10 운동행동을 연구하는 관점에서, 채점이 가능한 한 객관적일 수 있는 실험실에서의 행동을 이용하는 것이 중요하다.

▶ 관계대명사절의 주어(the scoring)를 설명하는 주격보어 자리이므로, 형용사 objective가 와야 한다.

11 관광지 유인 효과는 관광지를 더 접근하기 용이하게 만드는 관광 호의적인 정책의 도입과 강화에 의해 긍정적으로 영향을 받을 수 있다.

▶ (A) 동사(be influenced)를 수식하는 부사 positively가 와야 한다.
(B) 관계대명사절에서 목적어(the destination)를 설명하는 목적격보어 자리이므로, 형용사 accessible이 와야 한다.

12 그녀는 야자나무와, 달리기하거나 스케이트보드를 타거나 친구들과 편히 시간을 보내는 건강한 모습의 사람들로 가득 찬 인도를 바라보며, 창밖을 행복하게 응시했다.

▶ (A) 동사(gazed)를 수식하는 부사 happily가 와야 한다.
(B) 현재분사구(hanging out with friends)를 수식하는 부사 casually가 와야 한다.

13 죽은 애완동물을 애도하는 것은 아이들에게 인간 가족 구성원의 죽음에 대한 유용한 '예행연습'을 제공하지만, 이는 성인들에게는 적합한 것으로 여겨지지 않는데, 다 자란 사람이 그러한 슬픔을 겪는 것에 대해 사회적인 지지가 부족하기 때문이다.

▶ 주어 it(= Mourning a dead pet)을 설명하는 주격보어 자리이므로, 형용사 appropriate이 와야 한다.

14 우리가 잘 쉬었을 때 그러는 것만큼 우리의 면역체계는 효과적으로 작동하지 않아서, 우리는 아프게 된다.

▶ as와 as 사이에 동사(are functioning)를 수식하는 부사가 와야 하므로, 형용사 effective를 부사 effectively로 고쳐야 한다.

15 농부들은 토양을 갈아엎어, 농사짓기에 가장 좋은 상태로 만들어 둔다. 그러나, 이 과정은 흙 입자를 제자리에 붙잡아 두는 중요한 표층 식물들을 제거해서, 토양을 바람과 물에 의한 침식에 무방비하게 만든다.

▶ 분사구문의 목적어(soil)를 설명하는 목적격보어이므로 부사 defenselessly를 형용사 defenseless로 고쳐야 한다.

POINT 30 수량형용사 뒤에 오는 명사의 수에 주목하라!

p.104

대표 예문

당신은 짧은 거리를 이사하는 것이 너무 쉬워서 거의 노력을 들이지 않고 할 수 있다고 생각할지도 모른다.

기출 예문 PLUS

1 오두막 주변의 황량하고 바위로 된 지형에는 식물이 별로 없었다.

2 걸러어는 수백 년 동안 말해졌지만, 최근까지 그것을 적으려는 시도는 거의 없었다.

3 나무에는 실제로 깊은 곳으로 파고드는 작은 뿌리가 약간 있지만, 대부분의 뿌리는 토양의 위에서 0.5미터 이내에 있다.

4 날씬해지겠다는 모든 열망으로, 많은 사람들이 심지어 몸에 있는 약간의 지방조차도 제거해야 할 어떤 것으로 보는 것은 놀라운 일이 아니다.

기출 문장으로 PRACTICE

p.105

01 little **02** much **03** a few **04** (A) much (B) little **05** less → fewer **06** few → little

01 몇 년간의 조각 후에, 그는 무덤의 가장 유명한 조각상 중 하나인 '모세'를 완성했다. 하지만, 다음 교황인 Leo 10세는 그 프로젝트를 계속하는 것에 거의 관심이 없었다.

▶ 뒤에 셀 수 없는 명사인 interest가 이어지고 있으므로, 수량형용사 little이 와야 한다.

02 아무리 많은 일이 있더라도, 항상 하루 저녁 내내 휴식을 취하겠다고 스스로에게 약속해라. 휴식을 위해 시간을 내면 당신은 일을 더 잘하게 될 것이다.

▶ 뒤에 셀 수 없는 명사인 work가 이어지고 있으므로, 수량형용사 much를 쓰는 것이 적절하다.

03 초기에, 사람들은 그들이 필요로 하는 상품을 대가로 그들이 만든 작물이나 물건을 거래했다. 최초의 상점들은 고기와 빵과 같은 약간의 제품만을 팔았다.

▶ 뒤에 셀 수 있는 명사의 복수형인 products가 이어지고 있으므로, 수량형용사 a few가 오는 것이 알맞다.

04 사람들은 비축하기 위한 더 많은 농작물을 생산하도록 특별히 동기를 부여 받지 않았는데, 왜냐하면 약탈로부터의 보호가 거의 없는 곳에서 그렇게 할 유인책이 별로 없었기 때문이었다.

▶ (A) 뒤에 셀 수 없는 명사인 incentive가 이어지고 있으므로 수량형용사 much가 와야 한다.
(B) 뒤에 셀 수 없는 명사인 security가 이어지고 있으므로, 수량형용사 little이 알맞다.

05 광고가 유동인구가 많은 곳에 설치되면, 더 많은 사람들이 그것을 볼 것이다. 그것이 유동인구가 적은 곳에 설치되면, 더 적은 사람들이 그것을 볼 것이다.

▶ 뒤에 셀 수 있는 명사의 복수형인 people이 이어지고 있으므로, 수량형용사 little의 비교급인 less를 few의 비교급인 fewer로 고쳐야 한다.

06 전략적 비전은 그것이 효과적으로 하층의 관리자와 직원들에게 완전하게 전달되지 않으면, 조직에서 거의 가치를 지니지 못한다.

▶ 뒤에 셀 수 없는 명사인 value가 이어지고 있으므로, 수량형용사 few를 little로 고쳐야 한다.

POINT 31 형태가 유사한 형용사, 부사, 전치사를 구분하라!

p.106

대표 예문

연구원들은 리더나 통제하는 세력이 없다는 결론을 내렸다. 대신 각개의 새들은 무리 안의 이웃의 움직임에 거의 즉각적으로 반응하고 있다.

기출 예문 PLUS

1 Pompeii 시는 현대의 Naples 근처에 있는 부분적으로 파묻힌 로마의 도시이다.

2 당신이 어떤 상황을 다루고 있든 간에, 지금으로부터 1년 후에는 당신이 신경 쓰고 있지 않을 가능성이 매우 크다.

3 당신은 이삿짐 운송 회사의 서비스 대신 자신의 차를 사용하기로 결정할지도 모른다. 하지만 당신의 차가 당신이 가능할 것이라고 생각했던 것만큼 많이 옮길 수 없다는 것을 너무 늦게 발견할지도 모른다.

기출 문장으로 PRACTICE

p.107

01 lately 02 alike 03 near 04 highly 05 hardly

01 나는 당신이 최근에 힘든 시간을 보내고 있었고 당신의 삶에 대해 긍정적으로 느끼고 있지 않다는 것을 안다.

▶ 앞의 동사구(have been having a hard time)를 수식하는 부사로, '최근에'라는 의미의 lately가 적절하다. late는 '늦은; 늦게'의 의미이다.

02 지구상의 모든 장소는 서로 다르다. 마치 사람들처럼, 어떤 두 장소도 똑같을 수 없다.

▶ 주어를 설명하는 주격보어 자리로 '비슷한'이라는 의미인 형용사 alike가 와야 한다. like는 '~와 같이, ~처럼'이라는 의미의 전치사이다.

03 나는 뒤쪽 벽의 작은 창문을 기억해냈다. 창문 근처의 대야가 올라가기 쉬운 발판을 제공해 주었다.

▶ 뒤에 오는 명사(the window)를 목적어로 취하며 '~ 가까이에'라는 의미인 전치사 near가 와야 한다. nearly는 '거의'라는 의미의 부사이다.

04 일부 코치들은 정신 능력 훈련이 고도로 숙련된 선수들의 성과를 완벽하게 하는 데만 도움이 될 수 있다고 잘못 믿고 있다.

▶ 형용사처럼 쓰이는 과거분사(skilled)를 수식하며 '몹시'라는 의미인 부사 highly가 와야 한다. high는 '높은; 높게'라는 의미이다.

05 내 친구와 그의 아내는 하와이에 있었고, 해변에 서서 아름다운 석양을 바라보고 있었는데, 그 광경이 얼마나 멋진지 거의 믿을 수 없었다.

▶ 동사구(were able to believe)를 수식하며 문맥상 '거의 ~ 않다'라는 의미인 부사 hardly가 와야 한다. hard는 '단단한; 어려운; 열심히'라는 의미이다.

UNIT 14 비교구문

POINT 32 비교구문의 형태와 의미를 파악하라!

p.108

대표 예문

오늘날 젊은 운동선수들은 위험과 자극을 원하는데, 극한에 가까우면 가까울수록 더 좋다.

기출 예문 PLUS

1 모호함을 피하는 유일한 방법은 가능한 한 명시적으로 사항들을 자세히 설명하는 것이다.

2 우리는 점점 더 적은 시간 안에 점점 더 많은 활동들을 밀어 넣으려고 애쓰느라 너무 바쁘다.

3 꽃으로든 열매로든, coral bean은 미국 남서부 지역에서 가장 눈에 띄는 식물 중 하나이다.

기출 문장으로 PRACTICE

p.109

01 deeper 02 as 03 faster 04 than
05 hierarchical → more hierarchical
06 poisonous → poisonous as 07 O

01 유사에서는, 네가 몸부림을 치면 칠수록, 너는 더 깊이 빠질 것이다. 하지만 네가 가만히 있으면, 너는 떠오르기 시작할 것이다.

▶ 앞에 the more가 쓰인 것으로 보아 「the+비교급, the+비교급」 구문이므로, 비교급 형태인 deeper가 와야 한다.

02 지구상의 어떤 동물도 아프리카 코끼리만큼 많은 무게를 들어 올릴 수 없는데, 아프리카 코끼리는 등에 자기 무게의 25퍼센트까지 나를 수 있다.

▶ 앞에 as much weight가 있는 것으로 보아 「as+원급+as」 구문이므로, 비교대상 the African elephant 앞에는 as가 와야 한다.

03 가끔씩, 바람은 경작된 밭에서 흙을 날려 보낸다. 많은 지역에서 토양 침식은 자연적인 풍화작용이 대체할 수 있는 것보다 더 빠른 속도로 발생한다.

▶ 뒤에 than이 있는 것으로 보아 「비교급+than」 구문이 와야 한다. 따라서 비교급 형태인 faster가 와야 한다.

04 집단의 규모가 야영지에 미치는 영향은 공식적으로는 연구된 적이 전혀 없지만, 큰 집단이 작은 집단보다 훼손되지 않은 곳에 더 빠르게 충격을 야기할 수 있다는 것은 타당하다.

▶ 앞에 비교급 more rapidly가 있는 것으로 보아 「비교급+than」 구문이 와야 한다. 따라서 비교대상인 a small group 앞에 than이 와야 한다.

05 권력 차이에 있어서, 당신의 문화나 배경이 더 계층적일수록, 권력 차이는 더 큰 경향이 있다.

▶ 뒤에 the greater가 쓰인 것으로 보아 「the+비교급, the+비교급」 구문이므로, 원급 hierarchical을 비교급 more hierarchical로 고쳐야 한다.

06 Gila monster는 세계에서 독이 있는 단 두 종류의 도마뱀 중 하나이다. 그들의 독은 방울뱀의 독만큼이나 독성이 있다.

▶ 앞에 as가 있고, Gila monster의 독과 방울뱀의 독을 동등하게 비교하고 있으므로, 「as+원급+as」 구문을 써야 한다. 따라서 poisonous를 poisonous as로 고쳐야 한다.

07 우리의 식습관을 바꾸는 것은 우리가 할 수 있는 가장 힘든 일 중 하나인데, 왜냐하면 우리의 기호를 지배하려는 욕구가 심지어 우리 자신으로부터도 보통 숨어있기 때문이다.

▶ 「one of the+최상급+복수명사」 구문으로, 최상급 형태인 hardest는 어법상 바르다.

POINT 33 비교급을 수식하는 부사와 수식할 수 없는 부사를 구분하라!

p.110

대표 예문

사실, 로봇은 인간보다 훨씬 더 잘 볼 수 있지만, 그것들은 보고 있는 것을 이해하지 못한다.

기출 예문 PLUS

1 그림을 그리는 올바른 방식이란 없다. 이를 명심한다면, 당신은 당신에게서 나오는 독특한 그림을 그리며 훨씬 더 재미있을 것이다.

2 어떻게 당신은 통화하고 있는 상대방이 특별하다고 느끼게 만들 수 있을까? 그저 직접 만나서 하는 것보다 통화하는 사람의 이름을 훨씬 더 자주 불러라.

3 당신의 인생에는 당신이 전적으로 즐기기를 기다리는 좋은 일들이 많이 있다. 당신이 그렇게 한다면, 이 긍정적인 것들은 훨씬 더 강해질 것이다.

기출 문장으로 PRACTICE

p.111

01 much **02** (A) much (B) far **03** still
04 much **05** O **06** very 삭제, 또는 very → much[even/far/a lot]

01 빠른 근섬유는 느린 근섬유보다 더 빠르고 강력하게 수축될 수 있지만 훨씬 더 쉽게 피로해질 수 있는 세포이다.

▶ 비교급 more easily를 수식하는 비교급 강조 부사 much가 와야 한다. very는 비교급을 수식할 수 없다.

02 나는 이메일보다 실물 카드를 보내는 것이 훨씬 더 낫다고 생각한다. 당신의 손으로 직접 쓴 메모는 화면 위에 타자로 친 몇 줄보다 훨씬 더 중요하다.

▶ (A) 비교급 nicer를 수식하는 비교급 강조 부사 much가 와야 한다.
(B) 비교급 more를 수식하는 비교급 강조 부사 far가 와야 한다.

03 그것을 34명의 사람들에게 적용해본 후, 연구원들은 본래의 연구 결과를 확인했고 남성들이 여성들보다 간지럼을 더 잘 탄다는 것을 보여줌으로써 그 지식의 경계를 훨씬 더 넓혔다.

▶ 비교급 further를 수식하는 비교급 강조 부사 still이 와야 한다.

04 토마토를 재배하는 것은 농부에게 비용이 거의 들지 않아서, 농부는 그것을 슈퍼마켓에서의 값보다 훨씬 더 저렴하게 당신에게

판매하면서도, 여전히 괜찮은 수익을 거둘 수 있을지도 모른다.

▶ 비교급 less를 수식하는 비교급 강조 부사 much가 와야 한다.

05 별로 유명하지 않은 음악가 중 몇몇은 재능과 에너지로 가득 차 있고, 그들은 유명한 음악가 중 몇몇보다 연주를 훨씬 더 잘한다.

▶ 비교급 better를 수식하는 비교급 강조 부사 a lot은 어법상 바르다.

06 Conan Doyle은 나중에 "그는 지독하게 자부심이 높은 노인이었고, 제 직감에 따르면 도움을 받아 일으켜질 때의 그의 창피함이 제가 그에게 줄 수 있는 어떠한 위안보다도 훨씬 더 클 것 같았습니다."라고 설명했다.

▶ 부사 very는 비교급을 수식할 수 없다. 따라서 very를 삭제하거나, very를 비교급 강조 부사인 much, even, far, a lot 등으로 고쳐야 한다.

Chapter 08 기출 문제 공략하기

pp.112-113

1 ②

해석 우리가 눈으로 듣는 것은 아니지만, 때로는 마치 우리가 거의 그러는 것처럼 보인다. 한 환경부 공무원은 혼잡한 주 고속도로에 가까운 아파트에 살던 몇몇 사람들에 대한 놀라운 사건을 이야기해준다. 그 가구들은 소음 때문에 괴로워졌고, 그들은 시청에 항의했다. 시 공무원들은 고속도로 소음을 줄이는 것에 대한 어떤 조치가 이루어져야 한다고 요청하기 위해 반복하여 주 의회에 갔다. 그들은 반복해서 회피를 당했다. 마침내 시 공무원들은 한 가지 아이디어를 떠올렸다. 그들은 아파트 건물 앞에 한 줄의 나무를 심었다. 그 나무는 소음의 양에는 거의 어떤 차이도 만들지 못했지만, 그것들은 고속도로의 모습을 정말 가로막았다. 그 이후, 그 건물의 사람들로부터 거의 불평이 없었다.

정답해설

② 주어를 설명하는 주격보어 자리이므로 부사 miserably를 형용사 miserable로 고쳐야 한다. 이 문장은 5형식 문장(The noise made the families miserable)이 수동태로 전환된 문장으로, 5형식 문장의 목적격보어는 수동태 문장에서 주격보어가 된다.

오답해설

① 뒤에 주어가 없는 불완전한 절이 이어지고 있으므로 some people을 선행사로 하는 주격 관계대명사 who는 어법상 바르다.
③ 요구를 나타내는 동사 ask가 이끄는 that절이 당위성을 나타내므로 동사는 「(should+)동사원형」 형태로 써야 한다. 따라서 be는 어법상 바르다.
④ 뒤의 일반동사 block을 강조하는 동사로, 과거의 일을 말하고 있으므로 과거형인 did는 어법상 바르다.
⑤ few는 셀 수 있는 명사의 복수형과 쓰이는 수량형용사로, few 뒤에 복수명사 complaints가 왔으므로 어법상 바르다.

구문해설

2행 ... some people who lived in an apartment building [**close** to a busy state highway].
▶ close 이하는 앞의 명사구 an apartment building을 수식하는 형용사구이다.

4행 City officials went to the state capital again and again [**to ask** that something (should) be done about {*quieting* the highway noise}].
▶ to ask 이하는 목적을 나타내는 부사적 용법의 to부정사구이다. quieting은 전치사 about의 목적어로 쓰인 동명사이다.

2 ④

해석 1992년 1월 10일, 거친 바다를 항해하던 배 한 척이 12개의 화물 컨테이너를 잃어버렸는데, 그중 하나는 28,800개의 물에 뜨는 목욕용 장난감을 싣고 있었다. 밝은 색깔의 오리, 개구리, 그리고 거북이들이 태평양 한가운데에 떠다니게 되었다. 7개월 뒤, 첫 번째 장난감들은 그것들이 분실되었던 장소에서 3,540킬로미터 떨어진 Alaska의 Sitka 인근 해변에 도달했다. 다른 장난감들은 Alaska 해안을 따라 그리고 Bering 해를 건너서 북쪽과 서쪽으로 떠갔다. 어떤 장난감 동물들은 바다에 훨씬 더 오래 남아 있었다. 그것들은 완전히 북태평양 해류를 따라 떠다녔고, 결국 Sitka로 되돌아갔다.

정답해설

(A) 앞의 명사 a ship을 수식하는 분사이다. 배가 '항해하는'이라는 능동의 관계이므로, 현재분사 traveling이 오는 것이 알맞다.
(B) 뒤에 완전한 절이 이어지고 있으므로 관계부사 where가 오는 것이 알맞다. 관계부사 where 앞에 선행사 the place가 생략돼 있다.
(C) 비교급 longer를 수식하는 부사 even이 오는 것이 알맞다. very는 비교급을 수식할 수 없다.

구문해설

1행 ... through rough seas lost 12 cargo containers, [one of **which** held 28,800 floating bath toys].
▶ which는 12 cargo containers를 선행사로 하며 관계대명사절에서 전치사 of의 목적어 역할을 하는 계속적 용법의 목적격 관계대명사이다.

7행 They floated completely along the North Pacific currents, [**ending** up back in Sitka].
▶ ending 이하는 결과를 나타내는 분사구문이다.

Chapter 09 대명사

UNIT 15 대명사의 쓰임

POINT 34 대명사는 그것이 대신하는 명사와 수·격이 일치해야 한다!

p.116

대표 예문

당신이 죽은 새나 모기를 발견한다면, 그것의 날개를 보고서 비행이 그것의 보편적인 이동 방식이었다는 것을 추측할 수 있을 것이다.

기출 예문 PLUS

1 생명체들은 생명이 없는 우주 안에 존재하며, 많은 면에서 그것에 의존한다.

2 그는 많은 흥미로운 발견을 했고, 그는 그것들을 뒷받침할 증거를 가지고 있었다.

3 Sissi는 그녀가 축구를 하도록 두지 않는 소년들로 인해 낙담하지 않았다. 결국, 그녀는 Brazil의 Salvador 거리에서 자기 뜻대로 하게 되었는데, 왜냐하면 소년들이 가지고 놀고 싶어했던 그 축구공은 그녀의 것이었기 때문이다.

기출 문장으로 PRACTICE

p.117

01 their 02 that 03 yours 04 it 05 him 06 O
07 their → its

01 냉담한 개인들은 심지어 그것이 그들 자신의 행복에 연관되어 있을 때조차 좀처럼 용기를 보여주지 않는다.

▶ 앞의 복수명사 halfhearted individuals를 지칭하는 대명사이므로, 복수형 소유격 대명사인 their를 써야 한다.

02 2011년에 브라질은 멕시코보다 더 많은 입증된 석유 매장량을 보유했지만, 2010년에 브라질의 일일 석유 생산량은 멕시코의 그것보다 더 적었다.

▶ 앞의 단수명사 the daily oil production을 지칭하는 대명사이므로, 단수형 지시대명사인 that이 와야 한다.

03 당신이 설정한 기준이 당신의 것이 아니라면, 스스로 당신 개인의 기대를 정의하고, 자기 실현을 당신의 목표로 삼을 때일지도 모른다.

▶ '당신의 것'이라는 의미로 「소유격 대명사+명사」인 your standards를 대신하는 소유대명사가 와야 하므로, yours가 적절하다.

04 첨단 기술이나 색상을 사용하지 않고 바위로 특정 형태를 조각함으로써 감정을 표현하겠다는 선택을 하는 것은 예술가를 상당히 제약한다. 그러한 선택은 창의력을 제한하기 위해 만들어지는 것이 아니라, 외려 그것을 기르기 위해 만들어진다.

▶ 앞의 단수명사 creativity를 지칭하는 대명사이므로, 단수형 대명사인 it을 써야 한다.

05 부상 때문에, Jim은 그해 나머지 기간 동안 농구팀에서 경기를 할 수 없었지만, 감독은 그가 와서 연습할 수 있도록 그를 장비 관리자로 만들었다.

▶ Jim을 지칭하는 대명사가 와야 하는데 동사 did make의 목적어 자리이므로 목적격 대명사인 him이 와야 한다. 뒤의 equipment manager는 목적격보어로 쓰였다.

06 사실, 모든 복잡한 생물들, 특히 뇌를 가진 것들은 정보 과부하에 시달린다.

▶ 앞의 복수명사 complex organisms를 지칭하는 대명사이므로, 복수형 지시대명사인 those는 어법상 바르다.

07 좋은 회사가 대중에게 기여하기 위해서는, 그 회사의 사람들이 대중에게 효과적으로 그리고 만족스러운 방식으로 기여한다는 것을 보장해 줄 경영 철학이 반드시 있어야 한다.

▶ 앞의 단수명사 a great company를 지칭하는 대명사이므로, 복수형 소유격 대명사 their를 단수형 소유격 대명사인 its로 고쳐야 한다.

POINT 35 인칭대명사 vs. 재귀대명사

p.118

대표 예문

당신은 셰익스피어가 될 필요는 없지만, 글쓰기 형태로 자신을 적절하게 표현하는 방법을 정말 알 필요가 있다.

기출 예문 PLUS

1 나는 지나치게 심각하게 여기곤 했던 것들에 대해 내 자신이 웃어넘기고 있는 것을 발견한다.

2 불이 Glenn의 다리에 심하게 화상을 입혔다. 참을 수 없는 고통 속에서도, 그는 매일 자신이 운동하게 했고 마침내 고통스러운 몇 걸음을 떼었다.

3 만약 항상 계획을 세우는 것을 고집한다면, 당신은 직관적인 자아와 그것이 제공하는 내적인 기쁨에서 자신을 단절시키게 된다. 계획 세우기 중독을 깨기 위해서, 자신에게 한 번의 자유를 허락하라.

기출 문장으로 PRACTICE

p.119

01 himself 02 myself 03 yourself 04 herself
05 them 06 myself → me 07 them → themselves

01 Jake는 자기소개를 해야 했으나, 그가 입을 열자마자 모든 사람들이 웃기 시작했다.

▶ 동사 introduce의 의미상 주어와 목적어가 동일한 대상이므로 재귀대명사 himself를 써야 한다.

02 나는 육체적으로 그리고 감정적으로 피곤해서 나 자신을 편안하게 하려고 하며, 차가운 음료를 마시기 위해 앉는다.

▶ 동사 make의 의미상 주어와 목적어가 동일한 대상이므로, 재귀대명사 myself를 써야 한다.

03 스스로에게 너는 이것을 할 수 없다 혹은 저것을 할 수 없다고 계속해서 말하지 마라. 당신이 할 수 있다고 생각한다면 당신은 그 무엇이든 할 수 있다!

▶ 명령문의 동사 Don't keep telling의 생략된 주어(You)와 목적어가 동일한 대상이므로, 재귀대명사 yourself를 써야 한다.

04 낮 동안에 Louise Wilkinson은 사서로 일한다. 일단 해가 지면, 그녀는 흡혈귀로 변신한다.

▶ 동사 transforms의 주어와 목적어가 동일한 대상이므로, 재귀대명사 herself를 써야 한다.

05 사람들은 자기 중심적이고 그들에게 개인주의를 고취시키도록 하는 메시지와 제안에 더 관심을 보이고 더 우호적으로 반응했다.

▶ 동사 allowed의 주어는 주격 관계대명사절의 선행사인 messages and proposals이고, 목적어는 문장의 주어인 People을 대신하므로, 주어와 목적어는 대상이 서로 다르다. 따라서 목적어로 인칭대명사 them이 와야 한다.

06 어느 날 밤, 내 아내는 아이들과 저녁을 챙겨서 내 직장으로 나를 보러 와서 나를 놀라게 했다.

▶ 동사 surprised의 주어와 목적어는 서로 다른 대상이므로, 목적어로 인칭대명사가 와야 한다. 따라서 재귀대명사 myself를 인칭대명사 me로 고쳐야 한다.

07 그리스인들은 그들 자신이 속해 있음을 발견한 세상의 본질에 대해 그들의 동시대인들보다 훨씬 더 많이 사색했고, 그것의 모형을 만들어냈다.

▶ 동사 found의 주어와 목적어가 동일한 대상이므로, 인칭대명사 them을 재귀대명사 themselves로 고쳐야 한다.

POINT 36 부정대명사는 주변 명사와 동사의 수를 살펴라!

p.120

대표 예문

무수히 많은 품종의 야생화 수십 그루가 길 양쪽 땅을 덮고 있다.

기출 예문 PLUS

1 탁자 위에는 두 개의 그릇이 있었는데, 하나는 갓 구운 쿠키를 담고 있었고, 나머지 하나는 무를 담고 있었다.

2 그가 승선했을 때, 그는 다른 한 승객이 그와 선실을 공유할 것임을 알았다.

3 계획을 세우는 것은 논리적 사고를 조절하는 뇌의 반쪽만을 관여하게 한다. 뇌의 나머지 반쪽은 이러한 계획을 세우는 과정에서 배제된다.

기출 문장으로 PRACTICE

p.121

01 either 02 both 03 others 04 (A) other
(B) another 05 O 06 Other → Another

01 앞쪽 창문의 양쪽 벽에 그녀의 아버지 직장에서 찍은 사진이 일렬로 걸려 있다.

▶ 뒤에 단수명사(side)가 이어지고 있으므로, 부정형용사 either가 와야 한다.

02 렌즈를 직접 해 방향으로 향하게 하는 것은 카메라에 손상을 줄지도 모른다. 렌즈는 인간의 눈과 비슷하다. 둘 다 빛을 직접 응시하면 손상을 입는다.

▶ 뒤에 복수동사(are)가 이어지고 있으므로, 부정대명사 both가 와야 한다.

03 강사가 새로운 개념을 잇따라 제시하면, 학생들의 얼굴은 좌절감의 징조를 드러내기 시작한다. 일부는 맹렬하게 공책에 기록을 하는 반면, 다른 일부는 완전히 단념하고 적는 것을 포기한다.

▶ 여러 대상 중 일부는 some 다른 막연한 일부는 others로 나타내므로, others가 와야 한다.

04 문학은 문화들 사이의, 특히 서양과 아랍 사회 사이의 가교로서 역할을 하기 때문에, 커가는 관심이 번역에 있어 호황을 일으키고 있다. 하지만, 대부분의 번역은 영어에서 다른 언어들로 이루어지지, 아랍어와 같은 다른 언어에서 영어로 이루어지지 않는다.

▶ (A) 뒤에 복수명사(languages)가 이어지고 있으므로, 부정형용사 other가 와야 한다.
(B) 뒤에 단수명사(language)가 이어지고 있으므로, 부정형용사 another가 와야 한다.

05 우리 도시의 시장님이시니, 우리 지역에 새 소방서를 설립해주시겠습니까? 우리는 그것이 긴급히 필요합니다.

▶ 앞에 언급된 단수명사(a new fire station)를 받아 같은 종류의 불특정한 것을 나타내는 부정대명사 one은 어법상 바르다.

06 관광은 다른 장소와 문화에서 온 사람들이 새로운 사고방식을 배울 수 있게 해준다. 관광의 다른 긍정적 효과는 그것이 다른 문화의 생존을 지원해준다는 것이다.

▶ 뒤에 단수명사(positive effect)와 단수동사(is)가 이어지고 있으므로 부정형용사 Other를 Another로 고쳐야 한다.

Chapter 09 기출 문제 공략하기

pp.122-123

1 ⑤

해석 우리가 일의 정해진 순서를 만들어두면, 우리는 매일 모든 일의 우선순위를 정하는 데 귀중한 에너지를 소비할 필요가 없다. 우리는 정해진 순서를 만드는 데 그저 적은 양의 최초 에너지만 들이면 되고, 그런 다음 남겨진 모든 일은 그것을 따르는 것뿐이다. 메커니즘에 의해 정해진 순서가 어려운 일들이 쉬워지게 한다고 그 메커니즘을 설명하는 많은 과학적 연구가 있다. 한 간단한 설명은 우리가 반복적으로 특정한 일을 할 때, 뉴런 즉 신경세포가 '시냅스'라고 불리는 전달 관문을 통해 새로운 연결들을 만든다. 반복을 통해 그 연결들은 강해지고, 뇌가 그것들을 활성화시키는 것이 더 쉬워진다. 예를 들어, 당신이 새로운 단어를 배울 때, 그 단어가 숙달되기 위해서는 다양한 간격으로 여러 번 반복하는 것이 필요하다. 추후에 그 단어를 떠올리기 위해서, 의식적으로 그 단어를 생각하지 않고 결국 그 단어를 알게 될 때까지 당신은 동일한 뉴런을 활성화시킬 필요가 있을 것이다.

정답해설

(A) 뒤에 완전한 절이 이어지고 있고, 선행사 the mechanism이 관계대명사절에서 '~로, ~에 의해(수단)'라는 의미의 전치사의 목적어 역할을 하므로, 「전치사+관계대명사」인 by which가 와야 한다.
(B) 문장의 주격보어 역할을 하는 that절에서 주어 the neurons에 대한 동사가 필요하므로 make가 오는 것이 알맞다. that 뒤의 as는 '~할 때'라는 의미의 접속사로 명사절 안에서 부사절(as ... a certain task)을 이끌고 있다.
(C) 앞에 나온 단수명사 the word를 가리키는 대명사이므로 단수형 대명사 it이 와야 한다.

구문해설

2행 We must simply expend a small amount of initial energy [**to create** the routine], and then all [*that* is left to do] is (to) follow it.

▶ to create 이하는 목적을 나타내는 부사적 용법의 to부정사구이다. that 이하는 앞의 대명사 all을 선행사로 하는 주격 관계대명사절이다. follow는 주격보어로 쓰인 원형부정사이다. be동사 앞의 주어에 do가 포함되는 경우, 주격보어로 to부정사의 to가 생략된 원형부정사가 올 수 있다.

7행 With repetition, the connections strengthen and **it** becomes easier *for the brain* [**to activate** them].

▶ it은 가주어이고, to activate 이하가 진주어이다. for the brain은 to부정사의 의미상 주어이다. them은 앞에 나온 the connections를 가리킨다.

2 ②

해석 노화는 신체의 세포와 기관들이 점차적으로 스스로를 교체하고 회복시키지 못하는 결과로 생긴다. 이것은 각각의 세포가 분열할 수 있는 횟수에 한계가 있기 때문이다. 신체의 세포가 이 한계에 근접하기 시작함에 따라, 그것들이 분열하는 속도가 느려진다. 때때로 생성되는 새로운 세포는 결함을 가지고 있거나 평소 하던 일을 효과적으로 이행하지 못한다. 그렇게 되면 신체 기관이 제대로 작동하지 못하기 시작하고, 조직들은 구조의 변화를 일으키며, 신체에 활력을 공급하는 화학반응이 덜 효율적이게 된다. 때로는 뇌로의 혈액 공급이 원활하지 않다. 뇌세포는 산소와 영양분이 부족하게 되어, 건망증으로 이어지게 된다.

정답해설

(A) 앞의 동사 replace and repair의 의미상 주어와 목적어가 the body's cells and organs로 동일한 대상이므로, 재귀대명사 themselves가 오는 것이 알맞다.
(B) 동사구(do not carry out ... task)를 수식할 수 있는 부사 effectively가 오는 것이 알맞다.
(C) 주격 관계대명사절(that power the body)의 수식을 받는 주어 the chemical reactions에 대한 동사가 필요하므로, become이 오는 것이 알맞다.

구문해설

1행 Aging is a result of the gradual failure of the body's cells and organs [**to replace** and (**to**) **repair** themselves].

▸ to replace and (to) repair 이하는 the gradual failure를 설명하는 형용사적 용법의 to부정사구이다.

3행 **As** the body's cells begin to near this limit, the rate [*at which* they divide] slows down.

▸ As는 '~하면서, ~함에 따라'라는 의미의 접속사이다. which는 the rate를 선행사로 하며, 관계대명사절에서 전치사 at의 목적어 역할을 하는 목적격 관계대명사이다.

8행 The brain cells become short of oxygen and nutrients, [**leading** to forgetfulness].

▸ leading 이하는 결과를 나타내는 분사구문이다.

Actual TEST 01

pp.126-127

1 ③ 2 ④ 3 ② 4 ③

1 ③

해석 최저 임금은 고용주가 그들의 고용인에게 지불하도록 법적으로 허용된 시간당 가장 낮은 임금이다. 그것은 고용인들이 빈곤선은 넘어서 살아가도록 보장하기 위해 만들어진 것이다. 최근 몇 년간 최저 임금 인상에 대한 가능성이 사회적인 논란거리가 되어왔다. 찬성하는 사람들은 최저 임금이 물가상승률을 따라가지 못해 근로자와 그들의 가족이 빈곤해지게 된다고 주장한다. 고용인에게 더 많은 돈을 지불하는 것은 그들의 삶의 질을 향상시킬 것이다. 더 넓은 규모로는, 그것이 그들로 하여금 더 많은 소비를 하게 할 것이고, 이는 경제를 강화시킬 것이다. 반면, 최저 임금 인상을 반대하는 사람들은 이러한 인상이 추가 비용을 발생시켜 기업에 부담을 줄 것이고, 수익 저하로 이어진다고 주장한다. 게다가, 더 높은 최저 임금에 의해 고용률 또한 감소할 수 있으며, 기업들은 제품의 가격을 높이는 것으로 상쇄할 필요성을 느낄지도 모른다.

어휘 **minimum wage** 최저 임금 **employer** 고용주 **legally** 법적으로 **employee** 고용인, 종업원 **formulate** 만들어내다 **poverty line** 빈곤선 **prospect** 가능성, 가망 **proponent** 지지자 **inflation** 인플레이션, 물가 상승률 **impoverish** 빈곤하게 하다 **scale** 규모 **opponent** 반대자 **burden** 부담을 지우다 **expense** 돈, 비용 **employment** 취업, 고용 **compensate** 보상하다; *상쇄하다

정답해설

③ 주어는 전치사구(of an increase in the minimum wage)의 수식을 받는 복수명사 opponents이므로 단수동사 claims를 복수동사 claim으로 고쳐야 한다.

오답해설

① in recent years가 쓰여 현재까지 최근 몇 년간 계속되는 일을 나타내므로 현재완료 시제는 어법상 바르다.
② 현재분사 leaving의 목적격보어 역할을 하는 분사로, 목적어(workers and their families)와 분사가 '빈곤해지게 되는'이라는 수동의 관계이므로 과거분사 impoverished는 어법상 바르다.
④ leading 이하는 결과를 나타내는 분사구문으로 어법상 바르다.
⑤ 전치사 by의 목적어 역할을 하면서 뒤에 오는 the prices를 목적어로 취할 수 있는 동명사 increasing은 어법상 바르다.

구문해설

1행 The minimum wage is the lowest hourly wage [**that** employers are legally allowed to pay their employees].
▶ that은 앞의 the lowest hourly wage를 선행사로 하는 목적격 관계대명사이다.

4행 Proponents argue [**that** the minimum wage has not kept up with inflation], [*leaving* workers and their families impoverished].
▶ that 이하는 동사 argue의 목적어로 쓰인 명사절이다. leaving 이하는 결과를 나타내는 분사구문이다.

2 ④

해석 'tone과 'mood'는 둘 다 문학 작품을 이해하고 분석하는 데 중요하지만, 많은 사람들이 그 두 용어 사이의 차이를 모른다. 작품의 tone은 그것이 냉소적이건, 낙관적이건, 반어적이건 또는 유머러스하건, 쓰여지고 있는 것에 대한 작가의 태도를 전달한다. 작가가 고르는 단어가 tone을 결정하고, 이것이 독자의 mood에 영향을 미친다. 공포, 짜증, 행복, 그리고 안도감이 독자의 mood로 가능한 예들이다. tone을 형성함으로써 작가는 독자가 작품의 맥락을 이해하도록 돕는 것을 목적으로 한다. 그러나 tone은 등장인물들의 성장뿐만 아니라 소설의 구성에 따라서도 바뀔 수 있다. 어떤 경우에 tone은 등장인물들이 나이가 들거나 굉장히 충격적인 사건을 겪는 책 한 권이나 책 시리즈에 걸쳐 점차 더 진지해진다.

어휘 **tone** 어조 **mood** 기분 **literary** 문학의 **sarcastic** 냉소적인, 빈정대는 **optimistic** 낙관적인 **ironic** 반어적인 **convey** 전달하다 **irritation** 짜증 **context** 문맥, 맥락 **plot** 줄거리, 구성 **progressively** 점진적으로 **throughout** ~동안 내내 **age** 나이가 들다 **traumatic** 대단히 충격적인

정답해설

(A) 주어가 전치사구(of a work)의 수식을 받는 단수명사 The tone이므로 단수동사 conveys가 오는 것이 알맞다. whether ... humorous는 삽입절이다.
(B) 절과 절을 연결하는 접속사 역할을 하면서, 앞의 선행사 the tone을 대신하여 관계사절 안에서 주어 역할을 할 수 있는 관계대명사 which가 와야 한다. 대명사 it은 접속사 역할을 할 수 없다.
(C) 동사 help는 동사원형 또는 to부정사를 목적격보어로 취하므로, 동사원형 understand가 오는 것이 알맞다.

구문해설

2행 The tone of a work, ..., conveys the writer's attitude toward [**what** is being written about].
▶ 선행사를 포함하는 관계대명사 what이 이끄는 관계대명사절이

전치사 toward의 목적어로 쓰였다.

8행 The tone, however, may change depending on the plot of the novel **as well as** the characters' development.

▶ 「B as well as A」는 'A뿐만 아니라 B도'라는 의미이다.

9행 ... the tone becomes progressively more serious throughout a book or a book series [**where** the characters age or experience traumatic events].

▶ where 이하는 a book or a book series를 선행사로 하는 관계부사절이다. where는 추상적 의미의 장소를 나타내는 명사도 선행사로 취할 수 있다.

3 ②

해석 폴리카보네이트는 병, 안경 렌즈, 그리고 다양한 제품의 코팅을 만드는 데 쓰이는 내구성 있고, 흠집에 강한 소재이다. 현재 폴리카보네이트를 제조하는 데 쓰이는 과정은 비스페놀 A(BPA)로 알려진 합성물을 필요로 한다. 불행히도, 연구는 BPA가 인간의 뇌와 생식기관의 발달에 부정적인 영향을 미친다는 것을 증명했다. 이러한 연구 결과에 대한 대응으로, 과학자들은 설탕과 이산화탄소로 만들어진 훨씬 안전한 대체 폴리카보네이트를 개발했다. 그것의 물리적 성질은 석유 화학물에서 추출되는 폴리카보네이트의 그것들과 유사하다. 다른 점은 그것은 특수 효소의 이용으로 다시 원재료로 분해될 수 있다는 것이다. 이 새로운 소재는 결국 젖병과 식품 용기의 전통적인 폴리카보네이트를 대체할 것으로 예상된다.

어휘 **durable** 내구성 있는 **resistant** (~에) 잘 견디는, 저항력이 있는 **employ** (기술 등을) 쓰다 **manufacture** 제조하다 **synthetic compound** 합성물 **adverse** 부정적인 **reproductive** 생식의 **in response to** ~에 대응하여 **alternative** 대체의 **carbon dioxide** 이산화탄소 **property** 재산; *특성 **derive** 이끌어 내다, 얻다 **petrochemical** 석유 화학 (제품) **degrade** 비하하다; *(화학적으로) 분해하다 **enzyme** 효소

정답해설

② 과거분사구(currently employed ... polycarbonate)의 수식을 받는 The process가 주어이고 a synthetic compound가 목적어로, 문장에 동사가 없다. 따라서 현재분사 requiring을 동사 requires로 고쳐야 한다.

오답해설

① 문맥상 '~하는 데 사용되다'의 의미이므로 「be used to-v」의 to 부정사는 어법상 바르다

③ '훨씬'의 의미로 비교급(safer)을 수식하는 부사 much는 어법상 바르다.

④ 앞의 명사(polycarbonates)를 수식하는 분사로, 폴리카보네이트가 '추출되는'으로 수동의 의미가 적절하므로 과거분사 derived는 어법상 알맞다.

⑤ that은 주격보어 역할을 하는 명사절을 이끄는 접속사로 어법상 바르다.

구문해설

6행 ..., scientists have developed an alternative polycarbonate [**made** with sugar and carbon dioxide] [*that* is much safer].

▶ made 이하는 앞의 an alternative polycarbonate를 수식하는 과거분사구이다. that 이하는 an alternative polycarbonate를 선행사로 하는 주격 관계대명사절이다.

7행 Its physical properties are similar to **those** of polycarbonates ....

▶ those는 앞의 physical properties를 가리키는 대명사이다.

8행 [**What** is different] is that it can be degraded back into its original ingredients ....

▶ What은 선행사를 포함하는 관계대명사로, 문장의 주어 역할을 하는 명사절을 이끌고 있다.

4 ③

해석 가장 잘 알려진 공상 과학 시리즈 중 하나인 '스타트렉'은 '스타워즈'가 그러하듯 그 시대의 정서와 신념을 명확히 보여준다. 이들 시리즈는 둘 다 당대 사회를 반영하는 우주를 만들어냈고, 이는 그 영화들을 그 사회의 모습을 이해하는 데 아주 유용한 도구로 만든다. '스타트렉'의 세계는 1966년에 처음 방송된 TV 시리즈로 시작됐다. 이때는 유럽과 북미의 경제가 현대사의 어느 경제만큼이나 강했던 시기이다. 그에 알맞게, '스타트렉'은 미래의 기술뿐만 아니라 이상적이고 합법적인 유토피아 사회를 특징으로 하는데, 그곳에는 인종 차별과 성차별이 현저히 부재한다. 반면에 '스타워즈'는 사람들이 점차 경제 성장이 환경에 미친 피해를 인식하게 되던 때인 1970년대 후반에 개봉했다. '스타트렉'의 밝은 색상과 낙관주의와는 대조적으로, '스타워즈'는 미래에 대한 더 어두운 관점을 제시한다.

어휘 **illustrate** 설명하다, 분명히 보여주다 **sentiment** 정서, 감정 **contemporary** 현대의, 당대의 **air** 방송되다 **feature** 특징으로 삼다 **futuristic** 미래의, 미래에 관한 **idealism** 이상주의 **lawfulness** 합법 **racism** 인종 차별(주의) **sexism** 성차별(주의) **noticeably** 두드러지게, 현저히 **premiere** (영화가) 개봉되다 **take a toll** 큰 피해를 입히다

정답해설

(A) 앞의 일반동사 illustrates를 대신하는 대동사가 와야 하므로 does가 알맞다.

(B) as와 as 사이에 관계부사절의 주어(the economies)를 설명하는 주격보어가 와야 하므로 형용사 strong이 오는 것이 알맞다. 부사는 보어 역할을 할 수 없다.

(C) 앞에 선행사(the toll)가 있고, 뒤에 동사 had taken의 목적어가 빠진 불완전한 절이 이어지고 있으므로, 관계대명사 that이 와야 한다. what은 선행사를 포함하는 관계대명사로, 앞에 선행사를 취할

수 없다.

구문해설

2행 Both of these series created universes [**that** reflect contemporary society], [*which* makes them such useful tools ...].

▶ that은 앞의 universes를 선행사로 하는 주격 관계대명사이다. which는 앞의 절 전체를 선행사로 하는 계속적 용법의 주격 관계대명사이다.

5행 This was (a time) [**when** the economies of Europe and North America were as strong as ...].

▶ when 이하는 앞에 선행사 a time이 생략된 관계부사절이다.

6행 Accordingly, Star Trek features **not only** futuristic technology **but also** a utopian society ..., *where* racism and sexism are noticeably absent.

▶ 「not only A but also B」는 'A뿐만 아니라 B도'라는 의미이다. where 이하는 a utopian society를 선행사로 하는 계속적 용법의 관계부사절이다.

Actual TEST 02

pp.128-129

1 ③ 2 ④ 3 ⑤ 4 ③

1 ③

해석 어린 시절의 괴롭힘에 대한 설명은 종종 반 친구들에게 신체적으로 학대를 받거나 여러 가지 조롱과 모욕에 시달려야 하는 아이들을 묘사한다. 이 두 가지 유형의 괴롭힘에 더하여, 세 번째이면서 똑같이 교활한 형태인 지적인 괴롭힘이 있다. 그것은 학생들이 그들의 성적으로 결정되는 지적 계층 구조 안에 놓일 때 시작된다. 그러나 진짜 문제는 그들의 또래들보다 더 똑똑하다고 인정받는, 지적으로 괴롭히는 사람들이 자신들보다 더 낮은 성적과 더 적은 상을 받은 사람들에게 굴욕감을 주는 것이 부당하게 허용될 때 시작된다. 다시 말해서, 학생들은 소위 우월한 또래로부터 부과된 감정적인 괴롭힘에 시달린다. 지적인 괴롭힘은 다른 형태의 괴롭힘들보다 일반적으로 훨씬 더 적은 주목을 받는 반면, 이것은 비슷하게 지속적인 영향을 미친다. 누군가가 이 학대를 받는 쪽에 있으면, 그것은 성인기까지 계속될 수 있는 열등감과 자존감의 부족을 야기할 수 있다.

어휘 **account** 설명 **bully** (약자를) 괴롭히다; 괴롭히는 사람 **abuse** 학대하다 **taunt** 조롱 **insult** 모욕 **insidious** 교활한, 음흉한 **intellectual** 지적인 **hierarchical** 계급[계층]에 따른 **humiliate** 굴욕감을 주다 **harassment** 괴롭힘 **impose** 부과하다 **receiving end** (불쾌한 일을) 받는 쪽, 당하는 쪽 **inferiority** 열등함 **self-esteem** 자존감, 자존심 **adulthood** 성인(임), 성년

정답해설

③ 앞의 명사 intellectual bullies를 설명하는 분사로, 괴롭히는 사람들이 똑똑하다고 '인정되는'으로 명사와 분사 사이에 수동의 의미 관계가 성립한다. 따라서 현재분사 recognizing을 과거분사 recognized로 고쳐야 한다.

오답해설

① 등위접속사 or에 의해 명사 children을 수식하는 현재분사구가 병렬 연결된 구조로, 앞의 being과 대등한 having은 어법상 바르다.

② which는 앞의 an intellectual hierarchical structure를 선행사로 하는 주격 관계대명사로 어법상 바르다.

④ 앞의 복수명사 students를 지칭하는 복수형 소유격 대명사 their은 어법상 바르다.

⑤ '훨씬'의 의미로 비교급 less를 수식하는 부사 much는 어법상 바르다.

구문해설

8행 ..., students suffer emotional harassment [**imposed** by their supposedly superior peers].

▶ imposed 이하는 앞의 emotional harassment를 수식하는 과거분사구이다.

11행 ..., it can cause feelings of inferiority and a lack of self-esteem [**that** may continue well into adulthood].

▶ that 이하는 앞의 feelings of inferiority and a lack of self-esteem을 선행사로 하는 주격 관계대명사절이다.

2 ④

해석 비트코인은 자체적 가치를 갖도록 설계된 가상 화폐의 한 형태이다. 각각의 비트코인은 블록체인이라 불리는 디지털 장부를 가지고 있다. 그것은 개개의 코인이 포함되는 모든 거래를 기록한다. 이는 블록체인으로 하여금 거래가 중복되는 것을 방지하고 사람들이 비트코인을 위조하는 것을 막도록 돕는다. 비록 물리적인 표상이 없지만, 비트코인은 마치 당신의 주머니에 있는 실제 동전인 것처럼 사용될 수 있다. 비트코인은 투자자들에게 인기가 있으며 온라인으로 상품과 서비스를 구매하는 데 흔히 사용된다. 하지만 많은 오프라인 시설에서도 이제 비트코인을 받는다. 비트코인 하나의 가치는 매일 변동되며 온라인으로 추적될 수 있다. 코인이 총 2100만 개에 이르면 새 비트코인은 생산이 중단될 것이다. 이것은 2040년경의 언젠가 일어날 것으로 예상된다.

어휘 **virtual** 사실상의; *가상의 **currency** 통화, 화폐 **self-contained** 자급자족의, 독립의 **ledger** 장부 **transaction** 거래, 매매 **duplicate** 복제하다 **counterfeit** 위조하다 **representation** 묘사; *형상, 표상 **investor** 투자자 **establishment** 기관, 시설 **fluctuate** 변동을 거듭하다 **on a daily basis** 매일

정답해설

(A) 앞의 명사 a form of virtual currency를 수식하는 분사로, 화

폐가 '설계된'이라는 수동의 의미를 나타내므로 과거분사 designed가 오는 것이 알맞다.
(B) 주절과 같은 시점의 일을 가정하고 있으므로 as if 가정법 과거인 「as if+주어+동사의 과거형」을 써야 한다. 따라서 동사의 과거형 were가 오는 것이 알맞다.
(C) 문맥상 '생산되는 것'을 멈춘다는 의미가 되어야 하므로 동사 stop의 목적어인 동명사 being이 오는 것이 알맞다. 「stop to-v」는 '~하기 위해 멈추다'라는 의미이다.

구문해설

2행 Each bitcoin contains a digital ledger [**called** a blockchain].
▶ called 이하는 앞의 a digital ledger를 수식하는 과거분사구이다.

3행 This **helps** blockchains ***prevent*** transactions *from being* duplicated and ***stop*** people *from counterfeiting* bitcoins.
▶ 동사 help의 목적격보어로 쓰인 동사원형 prevent와 stop이 등위접속사 and에 의해 병렬 연결되어 있다. 「prevent A from v-ing」와 「stop A from v-ing」는 둘 다 'A가 ~하는 것을 막다'라는 의미이다.

3 ⑤

해석 흔히 BaP로 칭해지는 벤조피렌은 섭씨 300도에서 600도 사이의 온도에서 불완전 연소가 일어나는 동안 형성되는 일종의 탄화수소이다. BaP 분자가 오래전 지구상에 생명체에게 적합한 환경을 만들었을지도 모른다고 여겨진다. 불행히도, BaP는 인간에게 심각한 건강상의 위협을 가한다. 바비큐용 그릴에 스테이크를 굽는 것과 같이 연소가 발생하는 일상적인 상황은 BaP가 우리의 공기, 흙, 음식으로 들어가도록 한다. 그러나 그 어떤 것도 담배보다 인간에게 더한 BaP 위협을 만들어내지는 않는다. 독성 탄화수소가 우리 몸에 들어오면, 그것들은 더 작은 분자로 분해된다. 이 과정은 우리의 DNA와 단단히 결합하는 화합물을 만들어내는데, 이는 DNA가 제대로 복제되지 못하고 돌연변이를 일으킨다는 것을 의미한다. 이것은 잠재적으로 암의 발생으로 이어질 수 있다.

어휘 **refer to A as B** A를 B라고 부르다 **hydrocarbon** 탄화수소 **incomplete** 불완전한 **combustion** 연소 **molecule** 분자 **pose** (위협 · 문제 등을) 가하다, 제기하다 **toxic** 유독성의 **break down** 분해하다 **compound** 화합물 **bond** 결합되다 **mutation** 돌연변이 **occurrence** 발생

정답해설
⑤ 앞 절의 내용을 선행사로 하는 계속적 용법의 주격 관계대명사가 와야 하므로, what을 which로 고쳐야 한다. 관계대명사 what은 계속적 용법으로 쓸 수 없다.

오답해설
① during은 '~동안'의 의미를 나타내는 전치사로 뒤에 목적어 역할을 하는 명사구가 이어지므로 어법상 바르다.
② '~했을지도 모른다'라는 의미로 과거의 일에 대한 추측을 나타내고 있으므로 「may have p.p.」는 어법상 바르다.
③ 주어(Everyday situations)가 복수명사이므로 복수동사 cause는 어법상 바르다.
④ they는 앞의 복수명사 toxic hydrocarbons를 지칭하는 복수형 대명사로 어법상 바르다.

구문해설

1행 Benzo[α]pyrene, [**commonly referred** to as BaP], is a type of hydrocarbon [*that* is formed during incomplete combustion ...].
▶ commonly referred 이하는 삽입된 분사구로, 벤조피렌이 '칭해지는'이라는 수동의 의미이므로 과거분사가 쓰였다. that 이하는 a type of hydrocarbon을 선행사로 하는 주격 관계대명사절이다.

2행 **It is believed that** BaP molecules may have created the conditions for life on Earth long ago.
▶ 「It is believed that ...」은 '~라고 여겨진다'라는 의미이다.

4행 Everyday situations [**in which** combustion occurs], ... , *cause* BaP *to enter* our air, soil and food.
▶ which는 앞의 Everyday situations를 선행사로 하며 관계대명사 절에서 전치사 in의 목적어 역할을 하는 목적격 관계대명사이다. in which는 관계부사 where로 바꿔 쓸 수 있다. 「cause A to-v」는 'A가 ~하게 하다'라는 의미이다.

4 ③

해석 1차 산업혁명 동안 증기력이 생산 과정을 기계화하는 데 사용되었다. 2차 산업혁명에서는 산업에서의 대량 생산이 가능하도록 한 것은 바로 전력이었다. 정보기술은 3차 산업혁명의 핵심이었고, 기업들이 생산 과정을 완전히 자동화할 수 있도록 했다. 그리고 이제 4차 산업혁명이 3차를 기반으로 하여 진행 중이다. 그것은 디지털, 물리적, 생물학적 요소 사이의 경계를 흐리게 하는 새로운 형태의 기술로 특징지어진다. 이전 것들과 비교해서, 4차 산업혁명은 제조 영역에서뿐만 아니라 경영과 관리 영역에서도 시스템을 광범위하게 변형시키며 맹렬한 속도로 일어나고 있다. 공유 지식과 처리 능력으로 연결된 수십억 명의 사람들의 가능성은 무한하다. 4차 산업혁명은 결국 인공지능과 나노기술, 그리고 양자컴퓨팅에서의 획기적인 발전으로 이어질 것으로 기대된다.

어휘 **mechanize** 기계화하다 **mass production** 대량 생산 **automate** 자동화하다 **underway** 진행 중인 **characterize** 특징짓다 **blur** 흐리게 하다 **boundary** 경계 **biological** 생물학의 **component** 요소 **predecessor** 이전 것 **at breakneck speed** 무서운 속도로 **extensively** 광범위하게 **management** 경영 **governance** 관리, 통치 **limitless** 무한한 **breakthrough** 획기적인 발전 **quantum** 양자

정답해설

(A) 문맥상 '~하는 데 사용되다'라는 의미가 적절하므로 「be used to-v」가 되어야 한다. 따라서 to 뒤에 동사원형 mechanize가 오는 것이 알맞다. 「be used to v-ing」는 '~하는 데 익숙하다'라는 의미이다.

(B) 분사구문의 생략된 주어는 the Fourth Industrial Revolution으로, 4차 산업 혁명이 '비교되는'이라는 수동의 관계가 성립하므로 과거분사 Compared가 오는 것이 알맞다.

(C) 주어가 전치사구(of billions of people ... processing power)의 수식을 받는 복수명사 The possibilities이므로 복수동사 are가 오는 것이 알맞다.

구문해설

2행 ..., **it was** electrical power **that** enabled mass production in industry.

▶ 「it is[was] ~ that」 강조 구문으로, electrical power를 강조한다.

3행 Information technology was the key to the Third Industrial Revolution, [***allowing*** companies *to fully automate* the production process].

▶ allowing 이하는 부대상황을 나타내는 분사구문이다. 「allow A to-v」는 'A가 ~하는 것을 허용하다'라는 의미이다.

6행 It is characterized by a new form of technology [**that** blurs the boundaries ...].

▶ that 이하는 a new form of technology를 선행사로 하는 주격 관계대명사절이다.

Actual TEST 03

pp.130-131

1 ② 2 ④ 3 ⑤ 4 ③

1 ②

해석 어떤 사람들은 자신의 신체를 수치스럽게 생각한다. 그들은 끊임없이 스스로를 남들과 비교하고서 자기 자신의 외모를 비판한다. 때때로 수치스러움을 느끼는 것이 비만인 사람들에게 더 건강한 생활 방식으로 살도록 동기를 부여한다고는 하지만, 이를 뒷받침하는 그 어떤 증거도 없다. 그들이 더 나은 결정을 하도록 격려하는 대신에, 수치심은 사람들이 대인 관계를 끊고 사회 활동을 피하고 싶게 만든다. 사실, 자신의 신체를 수치스러워하는 사람들이 의도적으로 운동을 피한다는 것을 인정할 가능성이 더 크다는 것이 밝혀졌다. 이것은 수치심이 사실은 체중 문제를 극복하는 것을 더 어렵게 만든다는 것을 의미한다. 그러므로, 사람들은 자신의 신체를 그들이 아끼는 사람들을 보는 것과 같은 방식으로, 즉 불완전하지만 본질적으로 존중 받을 자격이 있다고 보도록 격려 받아야 한다.

어휘 **ashamed** 수치스러운, 부끄러운 **constantly** 끊임없이 **criticize** 비판하다 **appearance** 외모 **overweight** 비만의, 과체중의 **cut off** 자르다 **interpersonal** 대인관계에 관련된 **deliberately** 고의로, 의도적으로 **imperfect** 불완전한 **inherently** 본질적으로

정답해설

② 사역동사 make는 동사원형을 목적격보어로 취하므로 to want를 동사원형 want로 고쳐야 한다.

오답해설

① 동사(compare)의 목적어가 주어(they)와 동일한 대상이므로 재귀대명사 themselves는 어법상 바르다.

③ 동사의 성질을 가지는 동명사 avoiding을 수식하는 부사 deliberately는 어법상 바르다.

④ 「make+it(가목적어)+목적격보어+to-v(진목적어)」 구문으로, 진목적어 to overcome weight issues에 대한 가목적어 it은 어법상 바르다.

⑤ 전치사 of의 목적어로 쓰인 동명사로, 문맥상 '대우받는'이라는 수동의 의미이므로 동명사의 수동태 being treated는 어법상 바르다.

구문해설

2행 Although **it is** sometimes **said that** [*feeling ashamed*] can motivate overweight people to live a healthier lifestyle, ...

▶ 「It is said that ~」은 '~이라고 한다'의 의미이다. feeling ashamed는 that절의 주어 역할을 하는 동명사구이다. to live는 동사 motivate의 목적격보어 역할을 하는 to부정사이다.

6행 In fact, **it** has been shown [**that** people {*who* are ashamed of their bodies} are more likely to admit to deliberately avoiding exercise].

▶ it은 가주어이고, that 이하의 명사절이 진주어이다. who 이하는 people을 선행사로 하는 주격 관계대명사절이다. avoiding은 동사 admit에 수반하는 전치사 to의 목적어 역할을 하는 동명사이다.

2 ④

해석 두뇌-컴퓨터 인터페이스(BCI)는 인간의 뇌와 전자 장치 사이의 직접적인 통신 연결 수단이다. 지금까지, BCI 연구의 주요 관심사는 시력, 청력, 근육 운동과 같이 인간의 손상된 신체 기능을 회복시키는 데 있었다. 그러나 BCI는 게임 산업의 관심도 끌어왔다. 뉴로게이밍으로 알려진 최첨단 분야는 플레이어가 조종 장치를 사용하지 않고 게임과 상호 작용하도록 하기 위해 현재 BCI 기술을 이용하고 있다. 특수하게 설계된 소프트웨어가 게임 내에서 무슨 일이 일어날지 결정하기 위해 플레이어의 뇌파와 얼굴 표정, 그리고 심장 박동수를 추적 관찰한다. 심지어 각 플레이어의 기분을 감지하고 그에 따라 게임의 음악과 이미지를 조정하는 BCI 기술도 있다. 이것은 사용자의 반응이 실시간으로 바로 게임의 가상 환경에 반영되도록 한다. 몇 안 되는 기본적

인 뉴로게임만 현재 이용할 수 있지만, 그것들은 가까운 미래에 개선되고 수가 늘어날 것으로 예상된다.

어휘 **to date** 지금까지 **restore** 회복시키다 **function** 기능 **vision** 시력 **cutting-edge** 최첨단의 **utilize** 이용하다, 활용하다 **interact** 상호 작용을 하다 **monitor** 추적 관찰하다 **brainwave** 뇌파 **adjust** 조정하다 **accordingly** 그에 맞춰, 부응해서 **virtual** 가상의

정답해설

(A) 앞의 전치사(on)의 목적어 역할을 하면서 목적어(human bodily functions)를 취할 수 있는 동명사 restoring이 오는 것이 알맞다.
(B) 앞의 명사 BCI technology가 선행사이므로 주격 관계대명사 that이 오는 것이 알맞다. what은 선행사를 포함하는 관계대명사로, 앞에 선행사가 오지 않는다.
(C) 뒤에 셀 수 있는 명사의 복수형인 basic neurogames가 이어지고 있으므로 수량형용사 a few가 오는 것이 알맞다. a little은 셀 수 없는 명사와 쓰인다.

구문해설

2행 ... on restoring human bodily functions— ... —[**that** have been damaged].
▶ that 이하는 human bodily functions를 선행사로 하는 주격 관계대명사절이다.

7행 Specially **designed** software monitors players' brainwaves, ... to determine [*what* happens within the game].
▶ designed는 뒤의 명사 software를 수식하는 과거분사이다. what 이하는 determine의 목적어 역할을 하는 의문사절이다.

3 ⑤

해석 증거는 음악이 선사 시대 인류의 문화에서 중요한 역할을 했다는 것을 시사한다. 지금까지 발견된 가장 오래된 유물 중 몇몇은 약 40,000년 정도 된 것으로 추정되는 뼈로 만든 플루트와 같은 악기이다. 물론, 우리의 듣고 말하는 능력은 훨씬 더 멀리 거슬러 올라간다. 그러므로 Darwin과 Helmholtz가 그랬듯이 성악이 악기의 다양성을 앞선다고 추측하는 것은 타당하다. 이 성악은 부모에 의해 자식에게 불려지는 노래들을 포함한다. 그러한 노래들은 화석을 남기지 않는데 반하여 전 세계에 걸쳐 나타난다. 이 노래들이 정형화된 방식을 지니고 어디에나 있다는 것은 이것이 인류 보편적인 행동이라는 믿음을 뒷받침한다. 실제로, 성악을 인지하는 유아의 능력은 유전적으로 각인되어 있다고 여겨진다. 비록 인간이 모든 발달 단계에서 음악을 만들고 즐기기도 하지만, 음악 지각은 유아기에 가장 강하다.

어휘 **prehistoric** 선사 시대의 **artifact** 인공 유물 **uncover** 덮개를 열다; *(유적을) 발굴[발견]하다 **estimate** 추정하다 **approximately** 대략 **auditory** 청각의 **reasonable** 타당한, 사리에 맞는 **speculate** 추측하다 **precede** ~에 앞서다[선행하다] **offspring** 자식, 새끼 **fossil** 화석 **ubiquity** 도처에 있음 **stereotype** 정형화하다 **universal** 보편적인 **infant** 유아(**infancy** 유아기) **genetically** 유전적으로 **imprint** 각인시키다 **perception** 지각, 자각

정답해설

⑤ 부사절의 주어 humans에 대한 동사가 등위접속사 and에 의해 병렬 연결된 구조이므로, 앞의 동사 produce와 대등하도록 단수동사 enjoys를 복수동사 enjoy로 고쳐야 한다.

오답해설

① 「some of+복수명사」가 주어이므로 복수동사 are는 어법상 바르다.
② '훨씬'의 의미로 비교급(further)을 수식하는 부사 even은 어법상 바르다.
③ 앞의 명사 songs를 수식하는 분사로, 부모에 의해 노래가 '불려지는'으로 수동의 의미가 적절하므로 과거분사 sung은 어법상 바르다.
④ which는 these songs를 선행사로 하는 계속적 용법의 주격 관계대명사로 어법상 바르다.

구문해설

4행 ..., **it** is reasonable [**to speculate** that vocal music preceded the instrumental variety], as Darwin and Helmholtz *did*.
▶ it은 가주어, to speculate 이하가 진주어이다. did는 앞의 일반동사 speculate를 받는 대동사로, 과거의 일을 나타내므로 과거형으로 쓰였다.

6행 **While** such songs do not leave behind fossils, they *do* appear all across the globe.
▶ While은 '~하는 반면'이라는 의미의 접속사이다. do는 동사 appear를 강조하는 조동사이다.

8행 ..., supports the belief [**that** this is universal human behavior].
▶ that 이하는 the belief와 동격을 이루는 명사절이다.

4 ③

해석 창의적인 환경을 조성하려고 노력할 때, 기업들은 흔히 직원들을 더 행복하게 만드는 것에 중점을 둔다. 그러나 미국의 심리학자 Mark Davis는 이것이 더 나은 창의력에 이르는 가장 효율적인 길은 아닐지도 모른다고 생각한다. 그 주제에 대한 연구를 검토한 뒤에, 그는 긍정적인 기분이 브레인스토밍과 정보 처리, 아이디어를 생각해내기인 창의력의 초기 단계에서는 정말 사람들을 돕지만 두 번째 단계에서는 그렇지 않다는 결론에 도달했는데, 그 단계는 주로 문제를 극복하는 데 중점을 둔다. 대부분의 과학자는 이 다음 단계가 긍정성보다는 문제해결 능력에 더 의존한다는 데 동의한다. 그리고 문제를 해결하는 것은 비평하기, 실험하기 그리고 실패하기와 같이 일반적으로 기분 좋지 않은 것들을 포함하는 과정이다. 문제들로 인한 불쾌한 스트레스는 우리가 과업을 완수하도록 동기를 부여할 수 있기 때문에, 이러한 부정적인

감정들은 실제로 긍정적인 것들보다 우리를 더 창의적이게 만든다.

어휘 **foster** 조성하다, 발전시키다 **put an emphasis on** ~을 강조하다, ~에 중점을 두다 **path** 길 **come to a conclusion** 결론에 도달하다 **initial** 최초의, 초기의 **come up with** ~을 생각하다 **rely on** ~에 의존하다 **critique** 비평하다 **experiment** 실험하다

정답해설

(A) 주어인 Mark Davis에 대한 동사가 필요하므로 believes가 와야 한다. this 이하는 동사 believes의 목적어 역할을 하는 명사절이다.

(B) 주어로 쓰인 동명사구(solving problems)는 단수 취급하므로 단수동사 is가 오는 것이 알맞다.

(C) 동사 motivate는 목적격보어로 to부정사를 취하므로 to complete이 오는 것이 알맞다.

구문해설

1행 [**When trying** to foster a creative environment], companies often put an emphasis on [*making* their employees happier].

▶ When trying 이하는 접속사가 남아있는 분사구문이다. making 이하는 전치사 on의 목적어로 쓰인 동명사구이다. 「make+목적어+형용사」는 '~을 …하게 만들다'의 뜻이다.

4행 ..., he came to the conclusion [**that** a positive mood *does* help people with the initial stage of creativity — ... — but not with the second stage, **which** mainly focuses on overcoming challenges].

▶ that 이하는 the conclusion과 동격을 이루는 명사절이다. does는 동사 help를 강조하는 조동사이다. with가 이끄는 전치사구가 등위접속사 but으로 병렬 연결되었다. which는 the second stage를 선행사로 하는 계속적 용법의 주격 관계대명사이다.

10행 These negative feelings actually make us more creative than positive **ones**, *as* the unpleasant stress [caused by problems] ....

▶ ones는 앞의 feelings를 대신하는 부정대명사이다. as는 '~ 때문에'의 의미로 쓰인 접속사이다. caused by problems는 the unpleasant stress를 수식하는 과거분사구이다.

Actual TEST 04

pp.132-133

1 ② 2 ③ 3 ③ 4 ②

1 ②

해석 말에는 힘이 있다. 그것들은 우리의 관점을 만들어내고, 그렇게 함으로써, 우리의 태도를 바꿀 수 있다. 암을 예로 들어보자. 그것은 지독하고, 보통 치명적인 질병으로, 사람들 대부분이 이야기하고 싶어하지 않는 것이다. 암의 치유법이 찾기 어려운 상태로 남아있기 때문에, 초점은 치료에 있어왔다. 흥미롭게도, 그 병을 묘사하는 데 사용되는 언어가 그것이 치료되는 방식에 영향을 미칠 수 있다. 당신은 일부 폭력적인 단어와 군사 용어가 암에 대해 논의하는 데 때때로 사용된다는 것을 알아챘을지도 모른다. 암을 진단받은 사람들은 목숨을 위한 '전투' 혹은 '싸움'을 하고 있는 것으로 묘사된다. 그러한 언어가 사용되면, 의사들에게 더 공격적인 치료법을 쓰는 것을 고려하게 할 가능성이 있다. 반면에, 사람들이 그것이 긴 여행이라는 은유를 사용하는 것과 같이, 암에 대해 더 평화로운 방식으로 이야기하는 것을 들으면, 의사들이 공격적인 접근법을 취할 가능성이 더 적을 것이다.

어휘 **frame** 틀을 잡다, 만들어내다 **perspective** 관점, 시각 **vicious** 부도덕한; *지독한, 격심한 **fatal** 치명적인 **elusively** 찾기 힘들게 **treatment** 치료, 처치 **diagnose** 진단하다 **aggressive** 공격적인 **metaphor** 은유 **approach** 접근법

정답해설

② 주어를 설명하는 주격보어 자리이므로, 부사 elusively를 형용사 elusive로 고쳐야 한다. 동사 remain은 주격보어를 취하는 불완전자동사이다.

오답해설

① one은 앞에 나온 명사 disease를 대신하는 부정대명사로 어법상 바르다.

③ that은 동사 may have noticed의 목적어 역할을 하는 명사절을 이끄는 접속사로 어법상 바르다.

④ 앞의 consider는 동명사를 목적어로 취하는 동사이므로 동명사 using은 어법상 바르다.

⑤ 접속사(when)가 남아있는 분사구문으로, 생략된 주어는 주절의 주어(doctors)와 같다. 의사가 사람들이 이야기하는 것을 '듣는'이라는 능동의 의미가 적절하므로 현재분사 hearing은 어법상 바르다.

구문해설

4행 Interestingly, the language [**used** to describe the disease] can affect the way [*it is treated*].

▶ used 이하는 앞의 the language를 수식하는 과거분사구이다. it is treated는 앞의 the way를 선행사로 하는 관계부사절로, 관계부사 how와 선행사 the way는 함께 쓸 수 없어 how가 생략되었다.

7행 People [**who** are diagnosed with it] are described as being in a "battle" or "fighting" for their lives.

▶ who는 People을 선행사로 하는 주격 관계대명사이다.

9행 On the other hand, when **hearing** people **speak** about cancer in a more peaceful way, such as using the metaphor [*that* it is a long journey], ...

▶ 「hear(지각동사)+목적어+동사원형(목적격보어)」는 '~가 …하는 것을 듣다'라는 의미이다. that 이하는 the metaphor와 동격을 이

루는 명사절이다.

2 ③

해석 '배양육'이라는 용어는 조직 공학 기술을 이용하여 세포 배양으로 재배되는 고기를 일컫는다. 이 방식으로 고기를 생산하는 것은 환경적인 이익을 포함해 몇 가지 이점을 제공한다. 가축을 사육하는 것은 많은 양의 에너지를 소모하고 환경에 부정적으로 영향을 미친다. 그러나 배양육을 생산하는 것은 에너지 소비를 45%만큼 줄일 수 있으며 육류 산업이 현재 필요로 하는 땅의 2%만 필요로 해서, 이것을 우리의 인구 과잉 세계를 위한 합리적인 대안으로 만든다. 게다가, 배양육은 그것이 엄격히 통제된 환경에서 재배되고 살충제, 오염 물질, 또는 질병에의 노출을 거의 또는 전혀 겪지 않는다는 사실 때문에, 전통적인 고기보다 잠재적으로 더 건강하다. 마지막으로, 배양육은 마치 농장 가축으로부터 얻은 일반적인 고기 같은 맛이 난다고 한다. 비록 상업적 생산은 아직 진행되지 않고 있지만, 배양육은 10년 안에 슈퍼마켓 진열대에 오를 것으로 예상된다.

어휘 **culture** 배양하다; 배양 **cell** 세포 **tissue** 조직 **engineering** 공학 **fashion** 방법, 방식 **livestock** 가축 **consume** 소모하다(**consumption** 소비) **adversely** 불리하게 **impact** 충돌시키다; *~에 영향을 주다 **sensible** 합리적인 **alternative** 대안 **overpopulated** 인구 과잉인 **potentially** 잠재적으로 **strictly** 엄격히 **exposure** 노출 **pesticide** 살충제 **pollutant** 오염 물질 **commercial** 상업용의, 상업적인 **decade** 10년

정답해설

(A) 동명사구 주어 Raising livestock에 대한 동사가 등위접속사 and로 병렬 연결되어 있는 구조이므로, 앞의 동사 consumes와 대등한 단수동사 impacts가 오는 것이 알맞다.
(B) 뒤에 명사(the fact)가 이어지므로 전치사 because of가 오는 것이 알맞다. 접속사 because 뒤에는 절이 이어진다.
(C) 주절과 같은 시점의 일을 가정하고 있으므로 as if 가정법 과거인 「as if+주어+동사의 과거형」을 써야 한다. 따라서 동사의 과거형 were가 와야 한다.

구문해설

5행 ... and requires only 2% of the land [**that** the meat industry currently *does*], [making it a sensible alternative for our overpopulated world].
▸ that 이하는 the land를 선행사로 하는 목적격 관계대명사절이다. does는 앞의 일반동사 requires를 대신하는 대동사이다. making 이하는 결과를 나타내는 분사구문이다.

8행 ... than traditional meat because of the fact [**that** it is grown in a strictly controlled setting ...].
▸ that 이하는 앞의 the fact와 동격을 이루는 명사절이다.

3 ③

해석 2013년, 세계는 미국에 위치한 정보기관인 NSA(국가안보국)가 수백만 명의 사람들을 감시해왔던 것을 알게 되었다. 전 NSA 직원인 Edward Snowden이 기밀문서를 공개할 때까지는 이 감시 프로그램들에 대해 알려진 정보가 거의 없었다. 폭로된 것으로 판단하자면, 이 감시 프로그램들은 전화 도청, 이메일 계정 해킹, 그리고 인터넷 활동 추적으로 사람들의 개인 정보에 접근했던 것으로 보인다. 당연히 이 방법들은 많은 시민에게 비윤리적이고 비민주적인 것으로 보인다. 훨씬 더 심각한 것은, 미국 정보기관이 국제 정상 회담 동안 동맹국들을 감시했던 것도 폭로되었다는 것이다. 이 폭로는 전 세계에 상당한 파장을 일으켰다. 어느 정도는, 그 소란은 단순히 국가들 사이에 진행 중이던 경쟁에서 외교적인 영향력을 얻으려는 시도였다. 그러나 그 상황은 또한 미국과 다른 국가들 사이의 심각한 긴장 고조로 이어졌다.

어휘 **intelligence agency** 정보기관 **spy on** ~을 몰래 감시하다 **surveillance** 감시 **former** 예전의, 이전의 **release** 공개하다, 발표하다 **classified** 기밀의 **disclose** 폭로하다 **tap** 도청하다 **account** 계좌; *이용 계정 **understandably** 당연히 **unethical** 비윤리적인 **undemocratic** 비민주적인 **reveal** 드러내다, 폭로하다(**revelation** 폭로) **allied** 동맹한, 연합한 **summit** 정상; *정상 회담 **stir** 동요, 충격 **uproar** 대소동, 소란 **diplomatic** 외교의 **ongoing** 계속 진행 중인 **heighten** 고조되다

정답해설

③ 전치사 by의 목적어로 쓰인 동명사가 등위접속사 and로 병렬 연결되어 있는 구조이므로, 앞의 tapping, breaking과 대등하도록 동사원형 track을 동명사 tracking으로 고쳐야 한다.

오답해설

① 앞의 an intelligence agency를 수식하는 분사로, 정보 기관이 미국에 '위치되는' 것이므로 수동의 의미를 나타내는 과거분사 located는 어법상 바르다.
② 문맥상 '폭로된' 것이라는 수동의 의미가 적절하므로 수동태 was disclosed는 어법상 바르다.
④ 주격보어 자리이므로 형용사 unethical은 어법상 바르다. 동사 appear는 주격보어를 취하는 불완전자동사이다.
⑤ 뒤에 복수명사 countries가 이어지고 있으므로 부정형용사 other는 어법상 바르다.

구문해설

1행 In 2013, the world became aware [**that** the NSA, an intelligence agency located in the United States, *had been spying* on millions of people].
▸ that 이하는 became aware의 목적어로 쓰인 명사절이다. 「had been v-ing」는 과거 이전의 일이 과거 기준 시점까지 계속 진행되고 있었음을 나타내는 과거완료 진행형이다.

4행 **Judging from** [*what* was disclosed], these surveillance programs ....

▶ 「Judging from ~」은 '~으로 판단하건대'라는 의미의 비인칭 독립 분사구문이다. what은 선행사를 포함하는 관계대명사로 what이 이끄는 명사절이 전치사 from의 목적어로 쓰였다.

8행 ..., **it** was revealed [**that** U.S. intelligence agencies also spied on allied countries during international summits].

▶ it이 가주어, that 이하가 진주어이다.

4 ②

해석 '백지장도 맞들면 낫다'라는 옛 속담이 있다. 그것은 거의 모든 상황에서 맞지만, 학생들에게 특히 맞다. 협력 학습만큼 학생들에게 유익한 학습 전략은 거의 없는데, 그것이 의사소통, 팀워크, 협동과 같이 실생활에 필요한 기술을 가르치기 때문이다. 협력 학습은 학생들이 모둠을 만들어서 개인으로서보다는 팀으로서 문제를 해결할 필요가 있을 때 발생한다. 교사가 팀워크를 필요로 하는 복잡한 모둠 과제를 내주면, 서로 다른 강점들을 지닌 학생들은 그 과제를 완수하기 위해 서로 다른 역할들을 수행해야 한다. 그 과제는 한 명의 학생이 혼자서 해결하는 것이 불가능하도록 설계되어 있다. 실용적이고 잘 설계된 협력 학습 과제를 통해, 학생들은 또래 친구들의 기여에 감사할 수 있다. 이러한 경험에서 그들이 배우는 것은 남은 학교 생활과 그 이후에 걸쳐 그들에게 유익할 것이다.

어휘 **strategy** 전략 **beneficial** 유익한, 이로운 **collaborative** 협력적인 **cooperation** 협동 **assign** 부과하다 **complicated** 복잡한 **strength** 강점 **appreciate** 진가를 알아보다, 인정하다; *감사하다 **contribution** 기여, 공헌

정답해설

(A) 뒤에 셀 수 있는 명사의 복수형 learning strategies가 이어지고 있으므로 수량형용사 Few가 오는 것이 알맞다. little은 셀 수 없는 명사와 쓰인다.

(B) When이 이끄는 부사절의 주어 the teacher에 대한 동사가 필요하므로 assigns가 오는 것이 알맞다.

(C) 앞에 선행사가 없고, 뒤에 목적어가 빠진 불완전한 절이 이어지고 있으므로, 선행사를 포함하는 관계대명사 What이 오는 것이 알맞다.

구문해설

2행 Few learning strategies are **as** beneficial to students **as** collaborative learning, ...

▶ 「as+원급+as」는 '~만큼 …한'의 의미이다.

5행 ... when students **form** groups and **need** to solve problems *as a team rather than as individuals*.

▶ 동사 form과 need가 등위접속사 and에 의해 병렬 연결되어 있다. 「A rather than B」는 'B라기보다는 차라리 A'라는 의미로, 비교대상인 전치사구 as a team과 as individuals가 병렬구조를 이루고 있다.

Actual TEST 05

pp.134-135

1 ④ 2 ③ 3 ⑤ 4 ④

1 ④

해석 미래를 예측하는 유용한 방법 하나는 과거를 돌이켜보는 것이다. 근대 이전의 유럽에서 라틴어가 그랬던 것처럼, 영어는 현재 국제어의 지위를 누리고 있다. 라틴어는 원래 고대 로마인들의 언어였다. 로마 제국의 확장으로 퍼져나가, 라틴어는 제국의 공통 언어가 되었다. 제국이 몰락하고 오랜 뒤에 고전 라틴어는 작문의 수단으로 계속 번성했다. 반면에 통속 라틴어는 구어로 쓰였고, 여러 지역에서 점차 새로운 방언으로 변형되었다. 그 방언들이 프랑스어, 스페인어, 포르투갈어, 이탈리아어를 비롯한 근대 로망스어의 발생을 야기했다. 비슷한 발전이 오늘날 영어가 제2언어로 기능하는 몇몇 나라에서 관찰되어 왔다. 이는 이 언어의 가능한 미래, 즉 '중간 언어'의 출현을 시사하는데, 그 중간 언어에서는 영어의 요소가 현지 언어의 그것들과 병합되어 왔다.

어휘 **status** (사회적) 지위 **pre-modern** 근대 이전의 **originally** 원래, 본래 **spread** 퍼뜨리다, 확산시키다 **expansion** 확대, 확장 **empire** 제국 **thrive** 번창하다 **medium** 수단 **transform** 변형시키다 **dialect** 방언, 사투리 **region** 지방, 지역 **bring about** ~을 야기하다, 초래하다 **rise** 상승; *발생, 등장 **evolution** 진화; *발전 **indicate** 나타내다 **emergence** 출현 **merge** 결합하다, 융합되다

정답해설

④ 뒤에 완전한 절이 이어지고 있고, 선행사가 장소를 나타내는 some countries이므로, 관계대명사 which를 관계부사 where로 고쳐야 한다.

오답해설

① 주어가 전치사구(of predicting the future)의 수식을 받는 단수명사 One practical way이므로 단수동사 is는 어법상 바르다.

② 분사구문의 생략된 주어는 주절의 주어인 Latin과 같다. 라틴어가 '퍼져나간'이라는 수동의 의미이고, 주절의 과거 시점(became)보다 먼저 일어난 일을 나타내므로 완료 수동형 분사구문 Having been spread는 어법상 바르다.

③ 제국이 몰락한 것이 고전 라틴어가 계속 번성했던 과거 시점(continued)보다 먼저 일어난 일이므로 대과거 「had p.p.」는 어법상 바르다.

⑤ those는 앞에 나온 복수명사 elements를 지칭하는 대명사로 어법상 바르다.

구문해설

1행 One practical way of predicting the future is [**to look** backward to the past].

▶ to look 이하는 주격보어 역할을 하는 명사적 용법의 to부정사구이다.

1행 English currently enjoys the status of lingua franca, as Latin **did** in pre-modern Europe.

▶ did는 앞의 동사 enjoys를 받는 대동사로, 과거의 일(in pre-modern Europe)을 나타내고 있으므로 과거형으로 쓰였다.

6행 On the other hand, Vulgar Latin, [**which** was used in speech], was gradually transformed ....

▶ which 이하는 Vulgar Latin을 선행사로 하는 주격 관계대명사절이다.

10행 ... the emergence of "interlanguages," **in which** elements of English have merged ....

▶ which는 앞의 interlanguages를 선행사로 하며, 관계대명사절 안에서 전치사 in의 목적어 역할을 하는 목적격 관계대명사이다.

2 ③

해석 현대 문화에서, 성공 추구는 일종의 종교가 되었다. 그것은 지적인 수준과 정서적인 수준 모두에서 의미를 만들어내고, 우리가 하는 결정에 영향을 미치며, 그것 자체의 도덕성을 갖는다. 게다가, 그것은 자신들이 완전히 이해하지 못하는 이데올로기를 공유하는 사람들의 집단에 의해 행해진다. 이 종교에서, 성공은 자기 만족에 의해 측정되지 않는다. 대신에, 그것은 우리가 속한 집단의 사회적 계급 내에서 우리의 지위에 의해 결정된다. 성공의 종교는 위험하며, 심지어 우리 중에 우리가 삶을 그것의 재단 위에 올려두고 있다는 것을 알아차리는 사람은 거의 없다. 그것은 우리 삶의 너무나 필수적인 부분이 되어서 그것이 끊임없이 만들어내는 불안감을 알아채기 위해서는 우리는 멈춰서 자세히 들을 필요가 있다. 그러나 일단 우리가 그것을 인식한다면, 우리는 건강하지 못한 문화적 강박 관념보다는 개인의 지혜를 바탕으로 의사결정을 시작할 능력을 가지고 있는 것이다.

어휘 **pursuit** 추구 **religion** 종교 **contain** 함유하다, 포함하다 **morality** 도덕성 **practice** 연습하다; *행하다, 실천하다 **ideology** 이데올로기, 이념 **measure** 측정하다 **hierarchy** 계급, 계층 **belong to** ~에 속하다 **altar** 재단 **integral** 필수적인 **anxiety** 불안감 **constantly** 끊임없이 **obsession** 집착; *강박 관념

정답해설

(A) 문장의 동사가 「A, B, and C」의 구조로 병렬 연결되어 있으므로, 앞의 동사 creates, influences와 대등한 contains가 오는 것이 알맞다.

(B) 문맥상 '~을 두다, 놓다'의 의미가 자연스럽고, 뒤에 목적어(our lives)가 오고 있으므로 타동사 lay의 현재분사 형태인 laying이 오는 것이 알맞다. lie는 자동사로 '놓여 있다'의 의미이다.

(C) 문맥상 '주의하여, 열심히'라는 의미로 앞의 동사 listen을 수식하는 부사 closely가 와야 한다. close는 '가까운; 가까이'라는 의미이다.

구문해설

3행 Furthermore, it is practiced by groups of people [**who** share ideologies {(*which*[*that*]) they don't fully understand}].

▶ who 이하는 앞의 people을 선행사로 하는 주격 관계대명사절이다. they 앞에 ideologies를 선행사로 하는 목적격 관계대명사 which 혹은 that이 생략되어 있다.

7행 It has become **such** an integral part of our lives **that** we need to stop and listen closely [*to notice* the anxiety ...].

▶ 「such+a[an]+형용사+명사+that ~」은 '너무 …해서 ~하다'라는 의미이다. to notice 이하는 목적을 나타내는 부사적 용법의 to부정사구이다.

3 ⑤

해석 Arthur Miller의 희곡 「세일즈맨의 죽음」은 1949년 초연되었다. Miller의 불안정하고 낮은 실적의 세일즈맨인 주인공 Willy에 대한 성격 묘사는 평범한 인간이 여느 셰익스피어의 왕이 그런 것만큼 비극적인 인물이라는 Miller의 주장을 보여준다. Willy는 '아메리칸드림'을 진심으로 믿으며, 제2차 세계대전 이후 소비 호황기 동안 세일즈맨인 것을 고귀하게 생각하는 반면에, 결코 세일즈맨으로 성공해본 적이 없다. Willy는 그의 장남 Biff를 압박하기 시작한다. 그는 Biff가 사업가가 되기를 바라며 Biff의 성공이 그 자신의 실패를 보상해줄 것을 바란다. 그러나 이는 비현실적인 기대들이며, Biff는 그것들에 부응해 살고 싶지 않다. 슬프게도, Willy는 스스로를 이해하는 데 실패하고 자신과 아들이 그저 평범한 사람들이라는 것을 받아들이기를 거부한다. Willy가 간절히 실현시키고 싶어하는 그 가망 없는 꿈이 그를 비극적이고 공감할 수 있는 인물로 만든다.

어휘 **premiere** (연극 등이) 초연되다 **characterization** (등장인물의) 성격 묘사 **unstable** 불안정한 **underperform** 실적을 못 내다 **tragic** 비극적인 **figure** 인물 **Shakespearean** 셰익스피어의 **noble** 고귀한 **consumerism** 소비 **boom** 붐, 호황 **make up for** ~에 대해 보상하다 **live up to** ~에 부응하다 **unwilling** 꺼리는, 싫어하는 **desperate** 간절히 원하는 **relatable** 관련시킬 수 있는

정답해설

⑤ 앞의 복수명사 expectations를 가리키므로 복수형 대명사가 와야 한다. 따라서 it을 them으로 고쳐야 한다.

오답해설

① 앞에 as much a tragic figure가 쓰인 것으로 보아 「as+원급+as」 비교 구문이므로 as는 어법상 바르다.

② 「동사+가목적어(it)+목적격보어+진목적어(to-v)」 구문으로, 동사 considers의 목적격보어 역할을 하는 형용사 noble은 어법상 바르다.

③ start는 목적어로 동명사 또는 to부정사를 취하므로 동명사 pressuring은 어법상 바르다.

④ 문장의 동사가 등위접속사 and로 병렬 연결된 구조이므로, 앞의 단

수동사 wants와 대등한 hopes는 어법상 바르다.

구문해설

3행 ..., demonstrates Miller's argument [**that** the ordinary man is as much a tragic figure as any Shakespearean king is].

▶ that 이하는 Miller's argument와 동격을 이루는 명사절이다.

10행 The hopeless dreams [**that** Willy is desperate to fulfill] make him a character [*that* is both tragic and relatable].

▶ 앞의 that은 The hopeless dreams를 선행사로 하는 목적격 관계대명사이고, 뒤의 that은 a character를 선행사로 하는 주격 관계대명사이다.

4 ④

해석 작은 무인 항공기 드론이 일반 대중에게 처음 이용 가능하게 된 이후로, 그것의 용도는 소매업 부문으로 확대되어왔다. 다양한 기업들이 현재 드론으로 소포를 배달하는 전략을 탐색하고 있다. 한 실험에서, 드론은 온라인으로 구입한 물건을 한 거주지로 15분 이내에 운반했다. 그리고 이것은 아마 기술에 의해 주도되는 소비자 경험 변화의 시작에 불과할지도 모른다. 드론은 소포를 빠르고 정확하게 배달하면서, 교통체증과 노조 파업의 영향을 받지 않는다는 분명한 장점이 있다. 기업들이 당면한 주요 걸림돌은 안전상의 우려로 인한 영공의 사적인 이용에 대한 정부의 규제이다. 드론이 도시 지역의 현재 대기 오염과 소음 공해 수준에 원치 않는 기여를 할 수 있다는 것뿐만 아니라 드론에게 일자리를 뺏길 수 있는 배달 산업 종사자 수에 대한 우려도 제기되어 왔다.

어휘 **unmanned** (기계 등이) 무인의 **aircraft** 항공기 **expand** 확장되다 **retail** 소매 **sector** 부문, 분야 **multiple** 다수의, 다양한 **via** ~을 통하여 **trial** 시험, 실험 **purchase** 구매; *구입한 것 **residence** 거주지 **transformation** 변화, 탈바꿈 **distinct** 분명한, 뚜렷한 **labor strike** 노조 파업 **accuracy** 정확도 **restriction** 규제 **airspace** 영공 **apprehension** 우려, 불안 **contribution** 기여, 공헌

정답해설

(A) since가 이끄는 부사절이 쓰여 과거에 시작된 일이 현재까지 계속되고 있음을 나타내고 있으므로 현재완료 시제인 has expanded가 오는 것이 알맞다.

(B) Drones가 주어이고 the distinct advantage가 목적어로, 문장의 동사가 없다. 따라서 동사 have가 오는 것이 알맞다.

(C) 우려가 '제기되어 왔다'라는 수동의 의미가 적절하므로 수동태 been raised가 오는 것이 알맞다.

구문해설

6행 ... being unaffected by traffic and labor strikes [**while delivering** packages with speed and accuracy].

▶ while delivering 이하는 접속사를 생략하지 않는 분사구문이다.

7행 The main obstacle [(**which**[**that**]) businesses face] is government restrictions ....

▶ businesses 앞에 The main obstacle을 선행사로 하는 목적격 관계대명사 which 혹은 that이 생략되었다.

9행 ... the number of humans in the delivery industry [**that** could lose their job to drones], *as well as* the unwanted contribution ....

▶ that은 앞의 humans를 선행사로 하는 주격 관계대명사이다. 「B as well as A」는 'A뿐만 아니라 B도'라는 의미이다.

MEMO

올클 ALL CLEAR
수능 어법 완성